# The
# Thinker's
# Toolkit

# The
# Thinker's
# Toolkit

## Fourteen Skills
## for Making
## Smarter Decisions
## in Business
## and in Life

## Morgan D. Jones

**TIMES
BUSINESS**

RANDOM HOUSE

*Grateful acknowledgment is made to the following for permission to reprint previously
published material:*

*The Washington Post*: "Bike Trail Turns Into Mean Street" by Steve Bates (May 15,
1994), "U.S. Contractors in Dogfight over MiG Modernization" by John Mintz (June
14, 1994), and "Groping Toward a Way to Share the Reins: A Major Survey Finds
That Most Employees Want Cooperation and a Voice, if Not a Union, on the Job" by
Frank Swoboda (December 11, 1994). Copyright © 1994 by The Washington Post.
Reprinted by permission.

*Steve Sternberg*: Excerpt from "Tracking a Mysterious Killer Virus in the Southwest"
by Steve Sternberg (*The Washington Post*, June 14, 1994). Copyright © 1994 by Steve
Sternberg. Reprinted by permission of Steve Sternberg, a Washington-based feelance
writer and media fellow at the Kaiser Family Foundation in Menlo Park, California.

*Firehouse Magazine*: Excerpt from "Juvenile Firesetters: Part II: Effective Intervention"
by Jessica Gaynor, Ph.D. and Daniel Stern, Ph.D. (October 1993). Reprinted by
permission of *Firehouse Magazine*.

*Simon and Schuster, Inc.*: Excerpt from *Thinking in Time: The Uses of History for
Decision-Makers* by Richard E. Neustadt and Ernest R. May. Copyright © 1986 by
Richard E. Neustadt and Ernest R. May. Adapted with permission of The Free Press, a
division of Simon and Schuster, Inc.

Library of Congress Cataloging-in-Publication Data

Jones, Morgan D.
    The thinker's toolkit : fourteen skills for making smarter
decisions in business and in life / Morgan D. Jones.
        p.    cm.
    Includes bibliographical references and index.
    ISBN 0-8129-2601-3 (cloth)
    1. Decision-making—Problems, exercises, etc.   I. Title.
HD30.23.J66    1995
153.4'3—dc20                                95-19164

Design by Leon Bolognese

Manufactured in the United States of America on acid-free paper

98765432

FIRST EDITION

Dedicated to my beloved wife,
Rita, whose deep affection and
devoted care liberate whatever
creativity God gave me

# Acknowledgments

To John B. Chomeau, for brilliantly leading the way seventeen years ago in the search for practical innovative techniques that empower objective analysis.

To Noel E. Firth, for inviting me to develop and help teach his splendid course on *Analysis for International Security* at Georgetown University, for his imaginative ideas for devising improvements in the analytic structuring techniques we taught, and for his insightful, creative suggestions concerning the manuscript for this book.

To Lt. Col. Thomas H. Murray (USA Ret.), for letting me tap his abundant intellect as I probed the method and madness of different analytic techniques, for demonstrating in the classroom how to teach them, and in particular for independently collaborating with Richards J. Heuer, Jr., in conceiving the hypothesis-testing matrix that is described herein.

To Karl Weber, managing director of Times Business Books, for granting me this opportunity, for skillfully, patiently, and with keen professionalism guiding me through the intricacies of publishing, and most of all for his unwavering faith in the merit of my work.

To Nancy Inglis and Eleanor Wickland of Times Business Books for their unstinting help along the way, and to Lynn Anderson for her skillful editing.

# Introduction

All of us regularly make mistakes of judgment based on faulty analysis—mistakes as minor as buying the wrong brand of cereal at the grocery and as major as investing a million dollars in a losing enterprise. While some of these errors can be blamed on a lack of information or education, most occur because of the way our minds work. Our minds frequently mislead us, giving us a false understanding of events and circumstances and causing our analysis of events and circumstances to be flawed. In some cases, the consequences can be costly, even deadly.

But we don't have to passively accept the analytic batting average that nature has given us. By learning about the mental barriers and pitfalls that impede effective analysis and acquiring the skills and techniques to overcome them, our batting average can be improved, and significantly so. That improvement might be the determining factor in a decision that is crucial to personal happiness, professional success, or even life itself. The skills and techniques I speak of are what this book is about: ways of *organizing*, or *structuring*, our analysis of problems.

The book explains what it means to *structure* analysis; identifies and describes the mental traits that tend to lead us astray; explains how structuring our analysis of problems defeats the ill effects of these traits; describes fourteen easily understood structuring techniques; and provides exercises through which the reader can begin to master them.

Exactly what does *structuring one's analysis* mean? The word *analysis* means separating a problem into its constituent elements. Doing so reduces complex issues to their simplest terms.

One can find countless informative descriptions of this approach in any library. One I find especially appealing is that of the English philosopher Bertrand Russell, who in 1901 wrote in his classic *Princi-*

*ples of Mathematics* that, with regard to interpreting the language of philosophic theories, the solution is *the analytic method*—the breaking down of language until a theory shows itself to be either a set of sensible substatements or just nonsense. In this way, he said, many philosophic "problems" just disappear. Russell's book changed the way English philosophy was conducted by establishing the "analytic approach" as the only reputable method of studying philosophical questions.

To *structure* one's analysis means separating the constituent elements of a problem *in an organized way*. An example of structuring is the diagram we were taught in elementary school for doing division: $\overline{)\phantom{xx}}$ . Most of us visualize this diagram when we do division in our heads. Another familiar structuring device is the fearsome IRS Form 1040, which breaks down the process of computing one's taxes into a manageable, though complex, series of steps. Indeed, we use such devices all the time.

Our normal approaches to analyzing problems are usually adequate for dealing with 90 percent of our problems. It's the other 10 percent—the big problems, the ones that matter most—where these normal approaches are unlikely to give us the best solution. All of us want to make sound, effective decisions in our professional and private lives, but that's not easy when the problems we face are complex and manifold. And in the pell-mell pace of modern living, we usually don't have the time or patience to seek the *best* solution. The crushing necessity to make the problem "go away now" makes us receptive to *any* solution that will provide even temporary relief from an oppressive situation. In this pressure-cooker atmosphere it is difficult to fully resolve, much less fully understand, the problems that confront us. We therefore tend to make do with partial solutions that we justify, not altogether incorrectly, as the best we could do *under the circumstances*.

We settle for partial solutions because our minds simply can't digest or cope with all of the intricacies of complex problems. We thus tend to oversimplify, hopping from one problem to another like jittery butterflies, alighting briefly and only on those elements we can comprehend and articulate and to which we can confidently assign values and probabilities. Having done so, we are then satisfied to downplay and disregard those elements we do *not* comprehend and to which we *cannot* confidently assign values or probabilities.

If we are to solve problems, from those confined to a single individual to those afflicting whole nations, we must learn how to identify and
break out of restrictive mind-sets and give full, serious consideration to
alternative solutions. We must learn how to deal with the compulsions
of the human mind that, by defeating objective analysis, close the mind
to alternatives. Failure to consider alternatives fully is the most common cause of flawed analysis.

In other words, we must learn how to keep an open mind—one of
the most difficult things we human beings can do. So any technique we
can impose on the mind to force it open is helpful. It should come as
no surprise, then, that *all* of the techniques presented in this book have
the effect of opening the mind. The fact is, structuring one's analysis is
the quickest, surest path to opening the mind to alternatives.

Don't confuse *analysis* with *structuring*; they aren't the same thing.
Structuring is to analysis what a blueprint is to building a house. Would
you build a house without a blueprint? You could, of course, but there's
no telling what you'd end up with. Building a house, building anything,
without a plan is, to say the least, ill advised. And what structuring is to
a blueprint, the techniques of structuring are to a carpenter's tools—not
components of a single, unified system for analyzing problems but an
assortment ot techniques that can be used singly or in combination, as
a problem requires. And different problems usually require different
analytic tools.

But other than showing, as Bertrand Russell said, whether the elements of a problem are sensible or nonsensical, what does structuring—separating elements in an organized way—buy us? The answer is
a number of things, all of which are necessary for effective problem
solving.

First, structuring helps the mind make sense out of complex problems. Most problems, even the ones we regard as fairly simple, are
much too complex and ambiguous to analyze without some kind of
structuring. I use structuring when I work a jigsaw puzzle. I group
pieces of the same or similar color or texture together—the all-blue sky
pieces, for example. I then arrange these pieces in subgroups according
to their shape. This approach allows my mind to focus on the subgroup
of pieces that will most likely fit, eliminating hundreds of alternatives
from consideration. Were I not to group the pieces, I would be forced

to continually scan the entire field of unused pieces to find the few that are likely candidates. Yet this is exactly how most of us work a problem. We take in the entire problem (the entire puzzle) with all its complex dimensions (all of its pieces) in one gulp and try to digest it. Structuring frees us from this trap.

Second, structuring allows us to compare and weigh one element against another. Instead of looking at a whole bowl of vegetable soup, we look at the soup's ingredients, one ingredient at a time. This identifies which factors and relationships are critical not only to our analysis but also to the concerns of those who will make use of our findings.

Third, structuring helps us focus our analysis. The mind instinctively *focuses*. That's how the mind works, so it's going to focus whether we want it to or not. Therefore, we're better off to work *with* the mind than *against* it and, in doing so, control what it focuses on. If we don't, it will do its own focusing, and its shortcuts can lead us down the wrong path.

Fourth, structuring focuses on one element at a time, which, compared to our instinctive scattershot approach of tackling all elements simultaneously, is more systematic, more thorough, and more productive of relevant ideas.

Fifth, by establishing rational, systematic frameworks within which to analyze problems, analytic structuring techniques enable us to *impose our analytic will* on our subconscious mind, preventing it from following the instinctive mental traits that lead to faulty analysis.

Finally, all of the structuring methods presented in this book are visual processes that involve writing or depicting elements of a problem on paper or on a display board or computer screen, where we can *see* them. Why is *seeing* them important? By enabling the brain actually to *see* the words or numbers or depictions of the problem, we engage more brainpower in analyzing and solving the problem and so gain added insights. Indeed, when elements of a problem are seen visually, we often discover correlations we missed when we simply *thought* about them. The old adage—"A picture is worth a thousand words"— speaks to the power of engaging the brain's visual capabilities.

While structuring one's analysis is always helpful and sometimes indispensable, effective problem solving depends, in the end, not on how we structure our analysis but on the soundness of our thinking, and for that we have to use our mind. But structuring makes that a whole lot easier. Structuring is no substitute for thinking. It is rather a means of facilitating and empowering thinking. Used properly and creatively, structuring techniques will significantly enhance our ability to analyze, understand, and solve problems, lead to more effective analysis and sounder decisions, and make us feel better about those decisions.

Nowhere else are the methods that are presented in this book taught from such a practical do-it-yourself perspective. What you're going to learn from reading this book is not theory. These techniques really work. I think you'll be amazed at their immense potential to open a problem to analysis, and you will wonder, as I did when I first encountered them at the age of forty-nine, why no one told you about them long ago, when you could have applied them to tough problems. I am confident that, if you complete this book, do the exercises, and practice the techniques, you not only will acquire an array of valuable analytic tools but, what I believe is of greater value, you will gain a totally new and enlightened perspective on problem solving.

# Contents

Part **Three**
# Where Do We Go from Here?

Part **One**

# Why We
# Go Astray

# 1
# Thinking About Thinking

 "The next item on the agenda," said Tom Darfield, president of Family Frozen Foods, "is adding a fifth truck to our fleet." The three senior company officers seated at the conference table gave him their full attention. "When Marty made this proposal a few months ago, we dismissed it. But I think it's time to discuss it again in view of our increased sales and signs that this growth will continue."

All eyes shifted to Martin Bloomfield, who was in charge of sales and deliveries of the company's varied lines of frozen meat and prepared foods. "I know," he said, clearing his throat and nodding. "You're tired of hearing this proposal, but you've got to admit we have more business than four trucks can handle. The last time we talked about this, our fleet was already straining to meet deliveries. You all decided it was premature to add another truck; better to wait and see how business went. Well, business is booming."

"I agree," said Darfield, asserting his dual role as presiding officer and final decision maker. "It's time to reconsider Marty's proposal."

"The issue isn't simply the amount of business," interjected Dorothy Pellman, the company's chief administrative officer, who handled budgeting, finance, and personnel matters. She fixed her eyes on

3

Darfield. "Marty wants to buy a sixteen-wheeler. Ben and I feel a standard delivery van would be more than adequate."

Ben Augmeyer, who managed the processing and packaging of the company's products, leaned forward and looked at Bloomfield. "Are you still set on a semi?"

"It would be shortsighted not to be," he replied. "Given the favorable outlook for sales, in twelve months we'll be glad we bought the larger vehicle."

"Which outlook are you talking about?" asked Ben.

"Last month's forecast."

"That forecast was flawed. As we agreed last week, those sales estimates don't take account of seasonal variations," said Augmeyer.

"They sure as hell do," countered Bloomfield. "Dotty said so herself yesterday."

Augmeyer's expression soured as he turned to Pellman. "Since when?"

"He's right, Ben," she said with a rueful shrug, reluctant to lend any support to Bloomfield's proposal. "I recomputed the data using the most recent market analysis. The trends clearly point to a regional upturn in consumer interest in our line of products. Even without increasing our advertising, the growth in sales should continue."

"Do you believe that, Tom?"

"Sure, Ben. The trades say the same thing."

"Then why not buy the larger truck?" declared Bloomfield.

Pellman shook her head. "Hiring a reliable, qualified driver will be a lot easier with a smaller vehicle."

"That's true," added Darfield, inclining his head toward Bloomfield.

"Remember the trouble we had three years ago," said Augmeyer, "trying to keep drivers for that huge used semi we bought? They hated it because it drove like a Sherman tank."

"They quit because we didn't pay them enough, not because of the truck," argued Bloomfield. "Now we can offer competitive pay. And for what it's worth, the new semis are easy to drive."

"No sixteen-wheeler is *easy* to drive, Marty!" exclaimed Pellman.

"How would you know?" he challenged. "You've never driven one."

"The main issue," said Augmeyer, changing the subject, "is load capacity. How many times will a semi be filled to capacity or even half capacity? Dotty and I believe that a van will be adequate for most deliveries, and in those few instances when it isn't, we can make up the shortfall with overtime."

"And a van gets better mileage," said Pellman, "and is easier to maintain, which means it'll be more reliable."

"That's true, Marty," said Darfield.

Marty felt beleaguered. "But you aren't taking into consideration economies of size. One semi can do the work of three or four vans. And what about the company's public image? Small vans connote small business; a semi with our company logo splashed across its sides says 'big business.' It would enhance our reputation and increase sales."

"Maybe so," argued Pellman, "but have you looked at what a semi costs? Three times the price of a van."

"She has a point, Marty," said Darfield.

"Exactly," affirmed Augmeyer. "The bottom line is dollars. And how have our two major competitors enlarged their delivery fleets? With vans, that's how!"

"Is that right?" stated Darfield, more as a fact than a question.

"But their situations are different," argued Bloomfield.

"We're all in the same business, Marty," said Darfield. "Dotty and Ben make a strong case, and we've got to move on to other pressing matters. I think we should go with a van."

So they did. Six months later, sales had grown to the point where the company's fleet of trucks again could not keep up with deliveries, and they were forced to purchase another delivery vehicle. Bloomfield had been right; they should have bought the semi.

Why did they make the wrong decision? Where did their discussion of the proposal—of the problem—go astray? What could they have done differently? What should they have done?

The above dialogue is typical of business and professional meetings. Discussion—analysis of a problem—jumps haphazardly from one aspect to another as the conferees make points supporting their views and attacking those of others. Of course, a host of other factors also come into play to cloud the issues and defeat objective analysis, such as the differing but unstated assumptions on which the participants base their proposals to solve the problem, conflicting analytic approaches, personality differences, emotions, debating skills, the hierarchical status of the conferees within the organization, the compulsion of some members to seek to dominate and control the meeting, and so on. The cumulative result all too often is confusion, acrimony, wasted time, and ultimately flawed analysis, leading to unsatisfactory decisions.

While training people how to run a meeting and how to interact effectively in group decision making will help, the best remedy for the ineffectiveness of the meeting of the managers of Family Frozen Foods—and every other similarly afflicted meeting—is *structure*. By structure I mean a logical framework in which to focus discussion on key points and keep it focused, ensuring that each element, each factor, of a problem is analyzed separately, systematically, and sufficiently.

Why is imposing a structure on deliberations like those of Family Frozen Foods so important? The answer lies in the uncomfortable fact that, when it comes to problem solving, we humans tend to be poor analysts. We analyze whatever facts we have, make suppositions about those aspects for which we have no facts, conceive of a solution, and (like the managers of Family Frozen Foods) *hope* it solves the problem. If it doesn't, we repeat the process until we either solve the problem or resolve to live with it. It's the familiar *trial-and-error* technique. We humans therefore tend to muddle through in problem solving, enjoying moderate success, living with our failures, and trusting in better luck next time.

Wouldn't you think, with all the breathtaking advances modern humans have made in every field of endeavor in the past couple of centuries, that we would have achieved some breakthroughs in how to analyze problems? Don't we have marvelous new insights from cognitive science into the workings of the brain? Haven't we created and made available to everyone computers of prodigious capability that enable us to gather, store, and manipulate information on a scale and at a speed unheard of even ten years ago? And, as a world, don't we know more about everything than humankind has ever known before? So what's the problem? How come we haven't broken new ground in the way we analyze problems? How come we haven't developed new, innovative analytic techniques? How come we haven't adopted more effective analytic approaches? How come?

The fact is that new ground *has been broken,* innovative techniques *have been developed,* more effective approaches *have been devised.* Powerful, practical, proven techniques for analyzing problems of every type *do exist.* The problem is that they are one of the world's best-kept secrets. Even though these techniques are used with excellent effect in certain specialized professional disciplines, they have not found wide application elsewhere.

Ah, you ask, but if these techniques are so powerful, practical, and proven, why aren't they used more widely?

There are two reasons: one is excusable, the other is not. Let me explain the inexcusable first.

## Schools Don't Teach Analytic Techniques

That's not exactly true. Educational institutions do teach these analytic techniques, but only to a chosen few. Universities and colleges (high schools, too) treat these techniques as esoteric methods relevant only to special fields of study, not as standard analytic approaches in mainstream curricula. Thus, comparatively few college graduates (and only a handful of high school graduates) are aware of these techniques and their immense potential as aids to problem solving.

I base this statement not on any statistical survey but on my personal experience. For example, only two of the forty-eight graduate students to whom a colleague, with my assistance, taught these techniques for four semesters in Georgetown University's School of Foreign Service in Washington, D.C., had ever before been exposed to them—and neither had been exposed to *all* of the techniques. In my daily contacts, I often ask people if they are familiar with this or that technique; rare is the person who knows what I'm talking about. If you doubt the validity of this statistic, do a little data gathering yourself: ask a friend, your spouse, or a casual acquaintance if, in high school or college, he or she was ever taught any of the analytic techniques you'll learn in this book. And don't bother telling me their answers; I know what they'll say.

So why do schools restrict the teaching of this knowledge? Why don't they incorporate these analytic techniques into mainstream curricula? Why don't they teach all students, regardless of their academic focus, how to apply these techniques to problem solving? The answer is the second—the excusable—reason why these techniques are not widely employed.

## Human Beings Tend to Avoid Analytic Structure

Sometimes, when I offer to show people how to structure their analysis of problems, they say, "Sorry, but I'm awfully busy." "No, thank you. We don't use things like that here." "Very interesting, but it sounds a bit arcane." "I wouldn't think of using such Byzantine methods."

The rejection is so spontaneous and emphatic that it could be only a mental knee-jerk reflex, not a reasoned response. What could be causing this unreasoning reflex? Because they have not learned and understood the techniques, they could not have performed any cost-benefit analysis on them. They therefore have not assimilated any data on which to base a reasoned judgment. The only conclusion one can draw is that their reactions are purely intuitive, meaning they come from the subconscious mind. And why would the subconscious mind reject these techniques out of hand? *Because structuring one's analysis is fundamentally at odds with the way the human mind is accustomed to work.*

## Homo Sapiens—The Problem Solver

Human beings are problem solvers by nature. When our species arrived on the scene, every kind of human-eating predator could outrun us over a short distance—and a short distance was all a predator needed. Yet we managed to survive, not because of our physical attributes but because of our newborn intellect. Brain power had conveniently shifted the odds in *Homo sapiens*' favor. But it wasn't the size or weight of our brain that tilted the scales; it was the way we humans used our brains to

solve problems, first and foremost being how to stay alive. Human problem-solving prowess not only ensured survival of our species but led
ultimately to our dominion over the planet. Our present society, with its
tiered self-government, legal institutions, medical practitioners, public
services, educational institutions, modern conveniences, and sophisti-
cated technology, bears unmistakable witness to our impressive capability to solve problems.

Most of us are quite comfortable with, if not proud of, our ability
to analyze and solve problems, and we generally do moderately well
at it—at least, we like to think we do. The fact is, however, that we
mess up in our efforts to analyze problems much more often than we
recognize or are willing to admit. Indeed, the road to humankind's
impressive achievements has invariably been paved with failures,
many of which have set back our accomplishments by decades and
longer. For every forward stride there have been telling missteps,
because the problem-solving approach that has proven most practical
and effective for the human species is the *trial-and-error* method. For
every invention that finds its way to the marketplace, others end up in
junkyards. For every new business that succeeds, others fail. For every
business decision that earns big bucks, others lose money. In all
human affairs, from marriage to marketing to management, success is
generally built upon failure. And while some failures are justly attrib-
utable to bad luck, *most result from faulty decisions based on mistaken
analysis.*

## The Fallibility of Human Reasoning

The unwelcome fact is that, when it comes to problem solving, our
mind is not necessarily our best friend. The problem lies in the way the
mind is designed to operate.

I believe that psychologist Morton Hunt said it best in *The Universe
Within,* his book about "the dazzling mystery of the human mind,"
when he described our approach to problem solving as "mental messing around." Naturally, if we *structure* our analysis, the mind can't be
totally free to mess around. That's why the subconscious rebels when

it's asked to structure its thinking. Housemaids don't do windows; the untrained human mind doesn't do structuring.

Even so, structuring one's analysis is intuitively a sound idea, so why do people reject it out of hand? Are they being irrational or paranoid? Neither. According to Professor Thomas Gilovich in his wonderful book, *How We Know What Isn't So*, they are simply victims of "flawed rationality" caused by certain instinctive, unconscious tendencies of the human mind.

Over the past several decades cognitive science has discovered that we humans are unknowingly victimized by instinctive mental traits that defeat creative, objective, comprehensive, and accurate analysis. As a result, we unwittingly, repeatedly, habitually commit a variety of analytic sins. For example:

☐ We commonly *begin* our analysis of a problem by formulating our *conclusions*; we thus *start* at what should be the *end* of the analytic process. (That is precisely what happened at the meeting of Family Frozen Foods managers. Darfield began the discussion with the decision—a conclusion—that the solution to the backlog in deliveries was to expand the fleet of delivery trucks.)

☐ Our analysis usually focuses on the solution we intuitively favor; we therefore give inadequate attention to alternative solutions. (Alternative solutions to Family Frozen Foods' problem were never discussed. Moreover, the debate over which kind of truck to purchase was, at the very outset, restricted to two choices. Again, alternatives were never discussed.)

☐ We tend to confuse "discussing/thinking hard" about a problem with "analyzing" it, when in fact the two activities are not at all the same. Discussing and thinking hard can be like pedaling an exercise bike: they expend lots of energy and sweat but go nowhere.

☐ Like the traveler who is so distracted by the surroundings that he loses his way, we focus on the *substance* (evidence, arguments, and conclusions) and not on the *process* of our analysis. We aren't interested in the process and don't really understand it.

☐ Most people are functionally illiterate when it comes to structuring their analysis. When asked how they structured their analysis of a particular problem, most haven't the vaguest notion what the questioner is talking about. The word "structuring" is simply not a part of their analytic vocabulary.

What are the troublesome mental traits that produce all these analytic missteps?

# Problematic Proclivities

There are too many of these traits to treat all of them here, so I'll focus on the six (covered in detail in the Hunt and Gilovich books and in other cognitive scientific literature) that I believe have the greatest adverse effects on our ability to analyze and solve problems:

### 1. Subconscious mental activity continuously influences our analysis and even determines our conclusions.

We humans tend to believe that, by consciously focusing our mind on a problem, we are controlling our mental faculties and are fully aware of what's going on in our gray matter. Unfortunately, that simply isn't true. Most of what goes on in the mind involves "mental shortcuts" that occur without our knowledge and beyond our conscious control. These subroutines—which are comparable to computer "subroutines"—whir away constantly every second we are awake and, for all anyone knows, while we're asleep. We normally aren't aware they exist until we think about the lengthy, elaborate sequence of mental steps involved in an unconscious act such as catching a lightbulb someone playfully tosses at us. "Here, catch!" the tosser says, and without thinking we spontaneously dive to catch the bulb. Psychologists refer to this as a *reflex action*. It is also a mental shortcut—a subroutine.

Imagine the lengthy, intricate sequence of perception, association, recognition, coordination, and reaction the mind must go through to activate the muscles that move the arm, hand, and fingers to a position that will precisely intersect the lightbulb at a predicted point in its downward trajectory to catch the bulb and close the fingers gently around it. In a fraction of a second, the mind issues all of these complex motor commands and, what is more important, in the correct sequence, without our precognition or conscious participation. The mind accomplishes this remarkable feat by recalling from memory the commands, made familiar by lifelong practice, for catching an object with our favored hand. Obviously, the brain does not make a decision on each individual step of the entire sequence before sending the commands to the muscles. If it did, the bulb would smash on the floor long before the sequence was completed. Instead, the mind retrieves from memory the entire ready-made sequence and executes it.

The identical mental process occurs when we analyze a problem. The intricately interwoven neural networks of our brain react in concert to everything the brain senses: every sight, every sound, every bit of information. As Lawrence Shainberg wrote in *Memories of Amnesia*, "The name rang a bell. And once the bell was rung, others rang as well. That's the miracle of the brain. No bell rings alone." Each perception triggers hidden reactions whose silent tolling secretly influences our thoughts. For example, we hear someone say he or she is on a diet. We instantly stereotype that person according to our views concerning dieting. This stereotyping is an unconscious reaction of the mind. We do not consciously decide to stereotype; the mind does it for us automatically without our asking. It is a connection—a mental shortcut—that the mind instantly makes through its neural networks and that influences our perception of that person.

Mental shortcuts express themselves in a variety of other forms with which we are all familiar: personal bias, prejudice, jumping to a conclusion, a hunch, an intuition. Two examples:

> Your spouse—or a great and good friend who will accompany you—asks where the two of you should go on your next vacation. You think about it for a moment (the subroutines are whirring) and decide you'd like to go hiking in Vermont. Your spouse or friend suggests two alternatives, but they don't appeal to you (whir, whir) as much as your idea does. And the more you think about your idea (whir, whir), the more appeal it has and the more reasons (whir, whir) you can think of why it's a good idea. And in two minutes you're in a heated argument.

> You are briefed by a subordinate on a problem in your office. You immediately recognize (whir, whir) what the problem is, the source of the problem (whir, whir), and how to resolve it (whir, whir). You confidently instruct the subordinate what corrective action to take. Ten days later the corrective action has failed to be corrective, the problem has worsened, your subordinate mistrusts your judgment, you look bad, and so on.

We cannot "teach" the mind how to work; it works as it works, and taking shortcuts is one of its ways. These shortcuts are beyond our conscious control. We cannot stop the mind from taking shortcuts any more than we can will our stomachs to stop digesting the food we eat. And where those shortcuts lead our thinking is anyone's guess.

## 2.  We are driven to view the world around us in terms of patterns (especially cause and effect).

The human mind instinctively views the world in terms of patterns, which it recognizes based on memories of past experiences. We see a face (a pattern). Our mind searches its memory (the bells are ringing), finds a matching face (pattern), and delivers to our consciousness the name and other information stored with that pattern. *This is not a conscious process.* We don't *decide* to remember the name associated with the face. The name just pops into our head. The unconscious mind, unbidden, does it for us.

We see patterns in *situations*. Let's say the lights go out. We are not flustered or frightened. We light a candle or turn on a flashlight and wait for the electric company to restore power. How do we know power will be restored? Because such outages have occurred before; we know the pattern. Or let's say we are watching a football game and see a referee give a hand signal. We know what the signal means; we've seen it before.

We see patterns in *sequences of events*. We know when to put mail into the mailbox because the postman arrives at the same time each day. We encounter a traffic jam, watch a police car and ambulance pass ahead of us with sirens wailing, and deduce that a traffic accident is blocking the road. It's a familiar pattern. When we arrive home from work, our spouse does not greet us with a kiss and a smile; something has happened to upset the pattern. Because our brain is so thoroughly optimized as a pattern-recognition mechanism, we need only a fragment of a pattern to retrieve the whole from memory. And that retrieval is unconscious.

While this impressive capability is beneficial to our ability to function effectively, our compulsion to see patterns can easily mislead us when we analyze problems.

In the first place, patterns can be captivating. Consider, for example, the following numerical sequence: 40–50–60–__. Can you feel your mind pushing you to see 70 as the next number? If the mind were totally objective, it would evince no preference concerning the next number. But the mind is *not* objective; it perceives a pattern, is captured by it, and, having been captured, is disinclined to consider alternatives. Even though we may force the mind to consider other numbers, 70 will remain its preferred choice.

Unfortunately, the mind also can easily misconstrue random events as nonrandom, perceiving a pattern where, in fact, none exists. What do you see in Figure 1-1? An irregular hexagon? A circle? Actually, it is nothing more than six disconnected, randomly placed dots, but that's not what our mind sees. It sees the dots as a pattern—related elements of a whole. It instinctively, compulsively fills in the spaces between them and imprints the resulting image in our functional memory. It can't help itself. It's the way it works.

A striking example of mistaken patterning was the initial reaction to the attack on Nancy Kerrigan prior to the U.S. National Figure Skating Championships in January 1994. Several newspaper columnists rashly cited the incident as further evidence of the rising risk to professional athletes of wanton violence *by deranged fans*. In short order, however, it became clear that the attacker was neither deranged nor a fan but a hit man hired by the ex-husband of Kerrigan's chief competitor. The columnists had jumped to the wrong conclusion; they had mistaken the pattern.

But, what is worse, when we *want* to see a particular pattern or *expect* to see it, or have *become accustomed* to seeing it, not only do we

**FIGURE 1-1**

fill in missing information but our brain *edits out* features that don't fit
the desired or familiar pattern.

> We hear that a trusted colleague with whom we have worked for years
> is accused of sexually molesting children. We can't believe it. We *won't*
> believe it. It must be a mistake.

The book *Day of Infamy*, a historical account of the Japanese attack
on Pearl Harbor, cites a perfect example:

> People all over Oahu couldn't believe that what they were seeing
> was an enemy attack: unidentified planes, falling bombs, rising
> smoke. It was just the Army fooling around, it was just this, it was
> just that. Anything but the unbelievable truth.

The ease with which the human mind can misidentify a pattern is
one of the things that makes us laugh at jokes. Take this story:

> A man, walking down the street, passes a house and notices a child
> trying to reach a doorbell. No matter how much the little guy
> stretches, he can't reach it. The man calls out, "Let me get that for
> you," and he bounds onto the porch and rings the bell. "Thanks,
> mister," says the kid. "Now let's run."

What makes the anecdote funny is that our mind has quickly con-
jured an image—a pattern—of a nice man helping a sweet little child,

when suddenly we discover we are fooled. It's a prank. We misidentified the pattern.

*Stereotyping* is a form of patterning: perceiving a similarity between two events or things because of superficial features and then, based on that perceived similarity, *unconsciously* ascribing to one of the events additional attributes of the other. We live by stereotyping; it underlies a great deal of our everyday behavior; it is a principal mechanism of the mind.

Stereotyping, of course, governs racial, ethnic, and every other type of bigotry. Let's say that I don't like a particular law firm in my city. I meet someone and ask where he or she works. The person says he or she works for that firm. Instantly, in a thousandth of a second, before I can reason my thinking, my prejudice against the law firm dominates my reasoning and I get a negative impression of this person. The insidious part is that I have to struggle against this impression to see this person as he or she really is; *I have to struggle against my own mind.* As I said, the mind is not always our best friend.

ABC-TV's *Prime Time Live* conducted a fascinating experiment that demonstrated the hidden power of stereotyping. The results, presented on the program on June 9, 1994, revealed blatant age discrimination in hiring by a number of different companies. In the experiment the interviewee (an actor) played the role of two men (one in his twenties, the other disguised to appear in his fifties). In a number of interviews, despite the fact that the older man had more relevant job experience, the younger man received the job offers; the older man received none. Even when two of the job interviewers were told of the double role playing, they insisted their decision to hire the younger man had not been influenced by age bias. However, the hidden video-audio tapes of the interviews showed, without any question, that the interviewers were *instantly* put off by the older man's age.

The ABC segment demonstrated two powerful features of the mind's instinct to pattern: the patterning is instantaneous, and the mind's owner is unconscious of it. The two interviewers' denial that they had been biased shows that people don't want to admit there are things going on in our minds that we aren't aware of and that we have no control over. We like to think we are in control of our minds, but the ABC experiment clearly showed we are not.

Another kind of patterning is the tendency of the human mind to look for cause-and-effect relationships. Regarding this tendency, Morton Hunt said in *The Universe Within* that attributing causality to an event which is regularly followed by another is so much a part of our everyday thinking that we take it for granted and see nothing extraordinary about it. We seem to view the world in terms of cause and effect, and we somehow instinctively know the difference between the two concepts. This has been demonstrated unequivocally in experiments, even with infants. So we by nature strive to know why something has happened, is happening, or will happen and what the result was, is, or will be. Anthropologist Stephen Jay Gould said of patterning: "Humans are pattern-seeking animals. We must find cause and meaning in all events . . . everything must fit, must have a purpose and, in the strongest version, must be for the best."

This compulsion, while obviously helpful in dealing with the world around us, can deceive us when we analyze problems, because we often perceive cause and effect when no such relationship exists.

A man awoke one morning to find a puddle of water in the middle of his king-size water bed. To fix the puncture, he rolled the mattress outdoors and filled it with more water so he could locate the leak more easily. But the enormous mattress, bloated with water and impossible to control on his steeply inclined lawn, rolled downhill, smashing into a clump of thorny bushes that poked holes in the mattress's rubbery fabric. Disgusted, he disposed of the mattress and its frame and moved a standard bed into his room. The next morning he awoke to find a puddle of water in the middle of the new bed. The upstairs bathroom had a leaky drain. Mistaken cause and effect. It happens all the time.

It is the false perception of a cause-and-effect relationship that enables magicians to trick us—or more correctly, to trick our minds—so easily with illusions. False perceptions also enable con artists to fleece people out of huge sums of money on pretexts that, in the clear light of retrospect, are flatly implausible and make the victims wonder how they were so easily fooled.

Another example. Retail sales drop during a period of heavy snowstorms. A sales manager has observed this pattern before and figures sales will rebound when the weather clears. Perhaps they will, but he should consider alternative interpretations in case he has misread the cause-and-effect relationship. But will he consider alternatives? Probably not. His subconscious mind is captivated by the presumed connection (the cause-and-effect pattern) between the weather and the loss of sales.

### 3. We instinctively rely on, and are susceptible to, biases and assumptions.

Bias—an *unconscious belief* that conditions, governs, and compels our behavior—is not a new concept. Eighteenth-century philosopher Immanuel Kant theorized that the mind is not designed to give us uninterpreted knowledge of the world but must always approach it from a special point of view . . . with a certain bias.

Almost everything we do is driven by biases. For instance, when we walk into a dark room (and recognize the dark room "pattern"), we instinctively reach for the light switch on the wall. What prompts this action is the unconscious belief (the bias) that flipping the switch will bring light to the room. We know this because we have experienced the "flip-the-switch-make-the-light-go-on" cause-and-effect pattern before. The depth of our bias becomes apparent whenever we flip the switch and the light *doesn't* come on. We're surprised; our belief has been invalidated; suddenly we are *conscious* of the bias. We get the same reaction when we turn the spigot on a faucet and no water comes out—something we have always assumed was true (a cause-and-effect pattern) turns out to be false. I will keep reaching for the wall switch until I determine through experience that doing so won't produce light. Then I'll have a *new* bias: the bulb has burned out, and switching it on won't bring light. I'll then operate on the basis of the new bias until the bulb is replaced, at which point I'll revert to the original bias.

The shortcut mechanism of bias is, like the other mental traits, instinctive and outside our control. Acquiring a bias is not a conscious mental process; we really don't have a role in it. The mind does it for us without our knowledge or conscious input. So we are stuck with biases whether we want them or not, and they influence everything we think about and do. It's the way the mind works.

Although customarily viewed as a pejorative term, bias is generally a good thing. As with our other human mental traits, we would be dysfunctional without it. It is bias that enables us to repeat an action we have taken before without going through all of the mental steps that led to the original act. In this sense, bias is a preconditioned response. Thus, I am inclined (biased) to hold a golf club in a certain way because I have held it that way before. I shave my face every day as I have shaved it before. I brew coffee today as I did yesterday.

For the most part our biases, and the assumptions they both breed and feed upon,* are highly accurate and become more so as we grow older. This phenomenon is evidenced, for example, by the fact that older drivers have fewer accidents than younger drivers, despite the younger set's quicker, sharper reflexes. Older drivers have experienced more dangerous situations (patterns), have seen what happens when certain actions are taken in those (cause-and-effect) situations, and have developed self-protective biases that avoid accidents. In short, much more often than not, our biases lead us to correct conclusions and reactions, and they do it exceedingly fast. They *are* what make us humans smart. Without them, we would be unintelligent.

While biases enable us to process new information extremely rapidly by taking mental shortcuts, the rapidity of this process and the fact that it is unconscious—and thus uncontrolled—have the unfortunate effect of strengthening and validating our biases at the expense of truth. The reason, explained in Section 5 below, is that we tend to give high value to new information that is *consistent* with our biases, thus reinforcing them, while giving low value to, and even rejecting, new information that is *inconsistent*. New information that is *ambiguous* either is construed as consistent with our biases or is dismissed as irrelevant. In this respect, biases are, like deadly viruses, unseen killers of objective truth.

Hidden biases are the prime movers of the analytic process. They spring to life spontaneously whenever we confront a problem. They are imbedded like computer chips in our brain, ready to carry out their stealthy work at the drop of a problem. By "stealthy" I don't mean to

---

*Biases and assumptions enjoy a mutually dependent relationship: assumptions beget biases, biases beget assumptions. Although assumptions and biases are distinctly different in nature, their effects on our thinking are nearly identical. Therefore, my use of the term "bias" subsumes the concept of "assumptions."

indicate that all of our hidden biases are detrimental or sinister; as I said, they enable us to function effectively in the world. But biases, like those other instinctive human mental traits, can lead us astray. Because it is uncharacteristic of *Homo sapiens* to identify, much less evaluate or—heaven forbid, challenge—the hidden biases underlying one's perspective of a problem, we are unwitting slaves to them. What is more, because most biases are hidden from our consciousness, we aren't aware of their existence or of their effects, good or bad, on our analysis, conclusions, and recommendations.

It is only when the truth jolts our complacency, making us realize there is something wrong with our reasoning, that we are moved to identify and rethink our biases. Maybe all white southerners *aren't* racists. Maybe all Italians *aren't* members of the Mafia. Maybe violence on TV *does* have a harmful effect on our society.

The trouble with biases is that they impose artificial constraints and boundaries on what we think. The insidious part is that we aren't even aware that our thinking is restricted. We go about our daily problem solving believing we are exercising freedom of thought, when in fact our thinking is as tightly bound by our biases as an Egyptian mummy is by its wrappings.

A store manager discovers that money is missing from a cash box, but she dismisses the idea that Glenn, the cashier, stole the money. If he was responsible for the cash being missing, he made an honest mistake. Her instantaneous conclusion (it pops into her head before she can say Abraham Lincoln) is "Of course he didn't steal the money. He's as honest as the day is long." Then those other troublesome mental traits take over and finish what the unconscious shortcut began. Having rationalized away the possibility that he was a thief, she defends her instant conclusion from challenges from those who aren't acquainted with the cashier and who, like their Missouri relatives, need to be shown that the cashier is as Lincolnesque as she purports. She casts aside their doubts and dismisses their arguments, placing greater stock in her own assessment of his integrity. That assessment is based, of course, on the assumption (the bias) that the cashier is an honest person. If it turns out he is dishonest, her whole line of reasoning collapses like a windblown house of cards.

Another troublesome phenomenon, this one linked with Alexander Pope's enduring maxim "A little knowledge is a dangerous thing," is that the more we know about a subject, the more our biases affect our understanding of it, for better or worse. As you can well imagine, this phenomenon can play havoc with analysis of problems. That exact phenomenon is occurring at this very moment with regard to your knowledge of what it means to *structure analysis*. The more you learn about the subject, the clearer your perceptions about it become. But I use the word "clearer" advisedly, because your biases are hard at work and there's no telling how they may be distorting your understanding of what you're reading here.

Rank the risk of dying in the following seven circumstances—rank the most risky first, the least risky last:

### Risk of Dying

For women giving birth

For anyone thirty-five to forty-four years old

From asbestos in schools

For anyone for any reason

From lightning

For police on the job

From airplane crashes

The following table gives the actual rank order and odds of dying.

**Risk of Dying**

| | |
|---|---|
| For anyone for any reason | 1 in 118 |
| For anyone 35 to 44 years old | 1 in 437 |
| For police on the job | 1 in 4,500 |
| For women giving birth | 1 in 9,100 |
| From airplane crashes | 1 in 167,000 |
| From lightning | 1 in 2 million |
| From asbestos in schools | 1 in 11 million |

*Source:* Robert J. Samuelson, "The Triumph of the Psycho-Fact," *The Washington Post,* May 4, 1994, p. A25.

How accurate was your ranking? Did you greatly overrate the risk of one of the circumstances? If so, a likely reason is another factor related to bias that inhibits our ability to analyze problems objectively. It is called the *vividness effect*. Information is vivid because it was acquired either traumatically or recently and thus has made a strong impression on our memory. Information that is vivid is therefore more easily remembered than pallid, abstract information and, for that reason, has greater influence on our thinking. This influence can far exceed what the information really deserves.

A house burns down, and authorities suspect a child's playing with matches was the cause. If you set fire to your house as a child while playing with matches, the image of a child lighting matches would be vivid and personal. You would therefore be prone to put more credence in the authorities' suspicion than someone who had not had your experience, and your objectivity would be reduced accordingly.

The vividness effect is not something we elect to have. It's an inherent feature of the human mind—a package deal. It comes with the way our minds are programmed. It's the way the mind works.

### The Analog Mind

The reason biases can so easily lead us astray is that the mind doesn't rigorously test the logic of every new piece of information it receives. If it did, our mental processes would grind to a halt, and the mind—and we—would be dysfunctional. Instead, the mind takes a shortcut by patterning: treating the new information as it did the old, drawing the same conclusions, experiencing the same feelings, taking the same actions. Thus, the mind operates *analogically*, not logically.

In *The Universe Within*, in a section entitled "A Flunking Grade in Logic for the World's Only Logical Animal," Morton Hunt writes:

> Most human beings earn a failing grade in elementary logic. . . .
> We're not just frequently incompetent [in thinking logically], we're
> also willfully and skillfully illogical. When a piece of deductive
> reasoning leads to a conclusion we don't like, we often rebut it
> with irrelevancies and sophistries of which, instead of being
> ashamed, we act proud.

(This brings to mind the emphatic denial by the two interviewers in ABC's experiment that they had been guilty of age discrimination.)

Jeremy Campbell, an Oxford-educated Washington correspondent of the *London Standard* newspaper, in his book about the human mind, *The Improbable Machine,* agrees with Hunt's observation:

> Compelling research in cognitive psychology has shown that we are logical only in a superficial sense; at a deeper level we are systematically illogical and biased. . . . Highly intelligent people, asked to solve a simple problem calling for the use of elementary logic, are likely to behave like dunderheads. . . . If we want to get to know the mind, logic is the wrong place to start. There is no innate device in the head for doing logic.

A prime illustration of how innately illogical most of us are is how people rush to buy tickets in a multimillion-dollar lottery in the days preceding the drawing, knowing their chances of winning are less than their chance of being struck twice by lightning in bed on the same night. They justify their illogical behavior with a variety of silly statements such as "Someone is going to win, and it might as well be me" and that all-time winner "I have as good a chance as anyone."

As Hunt says, "Despite the uncertainties [of our analogical approach to problem solving], it seems over the millennia to have been fixed in us . . . by success; the errors we make are small in comparison to our gain in coping with the world." People who place great stock in logical thinking may look down upon human analogical reasoning, but, as Hunt observes, we humans could not survive without it.

Recall my example of entering a darkened room. I didn't have to go step by step through a logical sequence of thoughts to decide to reach out and flip the light switch. My mind, comparing this situation with others I had encountered and finding a matching pattern, retrieved from memory what action I had taken previously. My mind thus leapfrogged (took a shortcut) over an otherwise complex logical sequence and directed me to flip the switch. This is the principal way in which we interpret and deal with the physical world around us: we interpret new experiences in light of old ones and make inferences based on similarities.

One of the inferences we routinely and unconsciously make is detecting when something is "illogical." What if someone asks, "How high can a giraffe fly?" Instantly our mind tells us the question is "illogical." We don't have to think about it; we instantly *know*. Yet *how* do we know? An educated guess is that the mind compares the new information about the giraffe with the old information the mind has stored away about the animal. Not only does the new information not match the old, it clashes violently, and the mind tells us it doesn't match, meaning it doesn't make sense. This is a far cry from *reasoning* or *rational thinking*, and it's certainly light-years away from formal logic. Formal logic would address the question in something like the following chain of syllogisms:

A giraffe is an animal.

Only animals that have wings can fly.

A giraffe does not have wings.

A giraffe cannot fly.

It goes without saying that the human mind does not think by means of syllogisms. We all know this because we know how we think. Thinking via syllogisms, as anyone who has ever had the misfortune to study formal logic will agree, is as unnatural as a three-legged chicken wearing combat boots. Thinking in terms of syllogisms is awkward, difficult, and frustrating and strains the intellect of even the most intelligent members of our species.

It stands to reason that, given early humans' acquisition of a giant brain of immense intellectual potential, some members of the species may have experimented with logical thinking. I can visualize Rodin's statue of *The Thinker* as an early human sitting naked on a boulder outside his cave, head down, chin in hand, formulating syllogisms to explain the nature of existence. (Don't laugh!) If logical thinking was ever seriously toyed with by early humans, it was quickly extinguished as an evolving human trait, for not only did it offer no redeeming advantage, it was downright dangerous.

Imagine two early humans—A and B—walking together across the ancient savanna. It is the close of the day, and the sun is low on the horizon. A gentle breeze is cooling the hot, dry air. Suddenly, the pair catch sight of a shadow moving nearby in the tall grass. Early Human A stops to ponder logically what the shadow might be. A gazelle? A water buffalo? A chimpanzee? Perhaps a wild boar? Perhaps a lion? Meanwhile, Early Human B has run off to find safe refuge in a tall tree or a cave. Those early humans represented by A, who analyzed the situation logically to determine what steps to take, were, as modern-day Darwinian personnel managers would say, "selected out," while early humans of the B type, who instead applied what cognitive scientists call "plausible reasoning," survived to plausibly reason another day.

What is *plausible reasoning*? "Plausible" means "seemingly true at first glance." Plausible reasoning (also referred to as "natural" reasoning) is our practice of leaping to a conclusion that is *probably* correct based on the recognition of similarities between the situation confronting us at the moment and one that confronted us in the past. This is analogical thinking—patterning. We infer from the similarities that the two situations are probably alike. In the case of Early Human B spotting a shadow in the grass and recalling an earlier occasion when the shadow was a lion, B could plausibly conclude that it would be in his or her best interest in the present situation to get the hell out of there.

As Morton Hunt put it, "Natural [plausible] reasoning often succeeds even when it violates laws of logic. What laws then does natural reasoning obey?" He cited two: *plausibility* and *probability*. "In contrast to logical reasoning," said Hunt, "natural reasoning proceeds by steps that are *credible* [plausible] but not rigorous and arrives at conclusions that are *likely* [probable] but not certain."

Because logic, to be effective, requires total consistency and total certainty, logical thinking is unsuited for dealing with the real world in which the only certainty (other than taxes and TV commercials) is ultimate death. But plausible reasoning requires neither consistency nor certainty. If we had to be wholly consistent and certain, we could hardly think at all, for most of our thinking, as Hunt astutely observed, is as imperfect as it is functional.

Thus, when early *Homo sapiens* was confronted with potential threats, plausible reasoning traded an uncertain probability of risk for the certainty of survival. If there were only a 1 percent chance that the shadow moving in the grass was a carnivore, then, on average, one out of every umpteen times a human stuck around to find out what the shadow was, the human would get eaten. But if the human ran away whenever a shadow moved in the grass, that human survived 100 percent of the time. It doesn't take a graduate degree in formal logic to figure out which course of action was more beneficial to survival of the human species. Plausible reasoning ensured survival; logical reasoning didn't. Logical reasoners were penalized (weeded out over time); plausible reasoners were rewarded (proliferated over time). We therefore can confidently conclude, without need of extensive confirmatory studies through congressionally funded federal grants, that *thinking logically* (*logical thinking*), was not only *not* a prerequisite for our survival as a species but was, in fact, a liability.


### *Mind-set*

The mother of all biases is the "mind-set." Each of us, over time, as we acquire more and more knowledge about a subject, develops a comprehensive, overall perspective on it, as in President Ronald Reagan's famous view of the Soviet Union as an "evil empire." We call such a perspective a mind-set, which refers to the distillation of our accumulated knowledge about a subject into a single, coherent framework or lens through which we view it. A mind-set is therefore the summation or consolidation of all of our biases about a particular subject.

A mind-set thus exerts a powerful influence, usually for the best, on how we interpret new information by spontaneously placing that information in a preformed, ready-made context. For example, when we learn that a close relative has died, we instantaneously experience various sentiments generated by our mind-set concerning that relative. We don't first systematically recall and reexamine all of our interactions with that person, gauge our reactions to each one, and then decide to feel remorse about the person's death. The feelings come upon us in a flash; we don't think about them before we sense them. Such is the power of mind-set.

Upon learning from a radio sports program that our favorite team has won a particular game, our mind-set on that team makes us pleased. But we are ambivalent about the results of other games because we have not developed mind-sets on the teams involved. When we read a novel, the personality of a particular character evolves from page to page as the author furnishes us bits of information about the character's life, desires, fears, and such. At some point, our absorption and interpretation of these small details solidifies into a particular mind-set. If the author is skilled, this mind-set is precisely the one he or she intended us to acquire. We perceive the character as good or evil, happy or sad, ambitious or content and interpret the character's thoughts, statements, and actions within the framework of this manufactured mind-set.

Mind-sets enable us to interpret events around us quickly and to function effectively in the world. We unconsciously acquire mind-sets about everything—friends, relatives, neighbors, countries, religions, TV programs, authors, political parties, businesses, law firms, government agencies, whatever. These mind-sets enable us to put events and information immediately into context without having to reconstruct from memory everything of relevance that previously happened. If I ask you, "What do you think of the collapse of health care reform?" you know instantly what I'm talking about. I don't have to explain the question. Mind-sets therefore provide us instant insight into complex problems, enabling us to make timely, coherent, and accurate judgments about events. Without mind-sets, the complexity and ambiguity of these problems would be unmanageable, if not paralyzing.

Being an aggregate of countless biases and beliefs, a mind-set represents a *giant shortcut* of the mind, dwarfing all others the mind secretly takes to facilitate thinking and decision making. The influence a mind-set has on our thinking is thus magnified by many orders of magnitude over that of a simple bias, such as the way I shave in the morning. For that reason, mind-sets are immensely powerful mechanisms and should be regarded both with awe for the wonderful ease with which they facilitate our functioning effectively as humans and with wariness for their extraordinary potential to distort our perception of reality.

Consider, for example, the observation of newspaper columnist William Raspberry concerning the pretrial hearing of O. J. Simpson for the murder of his former wife and her friend.

Sixty percent of black Americans believe O. J. Simpson is innocent of the murder charges against him; 68 percent of white Americans believe him guilty. How can two groups of people, watching the same televised proceedings, reading the same newspapers, hearing the same tentative evidence, reach such diametrically opposed conclusions?

The answer, of course, is—*mind-sets.*

Donna Britt, a *Washington Post* newspaper columnist, writing about racism's influence on the public's pretrial attitudes concerning Simpson's culpability, said that some blacks believe that no black person can be guilty of wrongdoing, no matter what the accusation or evidence. She said these blacks have an ingrained cultural memory of their men being dragged away into the night, never to be seen again; they have grappled with racism, have found it staring at them, taunting them, affecting them so often that sometimes they see it even when it isn't there: "It can obscure people's vision so completely that they can't see past it. . . . Some stuff goes so deep, we may never get past it."

The case of the mysterious explosion on the battleship U.S.S. *Iowa,* which serves as the subject of one of the exercises in Chapter 11, presents another example of a mind-set. An article in *U.S. News & World Report* described how different people interpreted the personal belongings in the bedroom of Seaman Clayton Hartwig, whom the Navy suspected of intentionally causing the explosion: "Indeed, the lines of dispute are so markedly drawn that Hartwig's bedroom seems emblematic of the whole case. Some see only a benign collection of military books and memorabilia. Others see criminal psychosis in the very same scene."

Once a mind-set has taken root, it is extremely difficult to dislodge because it is beyond the reach of our conscious mind. And unless we carefully analyze our thinking, we probably won't be aware that we have a particular mind-set. The question then is, if we aren't aware of our biases and mind-sets, how can we protect ourselves against their pernicious negative effects? It seems to be a Catch-22.

There is only one way to change undesirable biases and mind-sets, and that is by exposing ourselves (our minds) to new information and letting the mind do the rest. Fortunately, the mind is, to a large degree, a self-changing system: give it new information, and it will change the bias. We sample a food we've always avoided, only to discover it tastes good. We read a book by an author we have always detested, only to find we enjoy her writing. We are forced by circumstances to collaborate on a project with someone we have always disliked, and we end up liking that person.

Most biases and mind-sets, however, are highly resistant to alteration and are changed only gradually, eroded away by repeated exposure to new information. An example was white America's awakening bit by bit through the 1950s and '60s to the reality and evils of racial discrimination. Some biases and mind-sets are so deeply rooted that they can be corrected only by truth shock treatment. After the capitulation of the Nazi regime in World War II, many German citizens who for years had stubbornly denied reports of Nazi atrocities were forced to tour "death camps." The horrors they saw there instantly and permanently expunged their disbelief. Similar shock treatment sometimes occurs in marriage counseling and drug addiction therapy when people are confronted with the stark reality of their aberrant or harmful behavior.

### 4. We feel the need to find explanations for *everything*, regardless of whether the explanations are accurate.

It isn't that we humans *like* to have explanations for things; we *must* have explanations. *We are an explaining species.* Explanations, by making sense of an uncertain world, apparently render the circumstances of life more predictable and thus diminish our anxieties about what the future may hold. Although these explanations have not always been valid, they have enabled us through the millennia to cope with a dangerous world and to survive as a species.

The compulsion to explain everything drives our curiosity and thirst for knowledge of the world. As far as I know, *Homo sapiens* is the only species that seeks knowledge or evinces any awareness of the concept. Knowing—finding an explanation for an event—is one of the most satisfying of human experiences. There is great comfort in recognizing and making sense out of the world. Doing so creates order and coherence, and, where there is order, there is safety and contentment.

We are instantly aware of the loss of this inner feeling of safety and contentment the moment we don't recognize a pattern in a situation that confronts us.

Finding explanations goes along with our compulsion to see cause-and-effect relationships and other patterns. Once we identify a pattern, we generally have little trouble explaining or having someone else explain for us how it came to be and what it means. It's an automatic, uncontrollable response that we experience constantly. We *explain* our actions to others and listen attentively while others *explain* their actions to us. We say to a friend, "Mary's late for work today." And the friend immediately *explains*, "Oh, she's probably . . ." And we acknowledge the explanation: "Yeah, maybe you're right." News media *explain* current events while we assimilate the explanations like students in a classroom. Sports commentators "calling" a game *explain* the meaning of the plays and the teams' competing strategies while we happily process their comments. A young man *explains* to his father how the family car became dented while the father eagerly but skeptically awaits a full explanation. We are an explaining species; we could justifiably have been labeled *"Homo explainicus."* As Gilovich says: "To live, it seems, is to explain, to justify, and to find coherence among diverse [things. It would seem the brain contains a special module]—an explanation module that can quickly and easily make sense of even the most bizarre patterns of information."

Read the following paragraph; it's a puzzle:

> I walked to the bank. No one was there. It was Tuesday. A woman spoke to me in a foreign language. I dropped a camera and, when I stooped to pick it up, the music began. It had been a long war. But my children were safe.

Do you feel your mind struggling to make sense of these seemingly disconnected bits of information? Do you experience a subtle but nonetheless tangible frustration and discomfort as you grope to shape these bits into a recognizable pattern? But you can't. The information is too jumbled, truncated, and disconnected. Still, something inside us tries to make sense of it, to sort it out—if you'll pardon the expression—

*logically.* We unconsciously grapple with the sentences looking for a connection, some common thread that will bind the information together as a whole.

If we can't immediately perceive a connecting pattern, the mind manufactures one, either by filling in "missing" information, as happened with the six randomly placed dots, or by eliminating "unrelated" or "irrelevant" information. In something akin to desperation, we force-fit a pattern to relieve our discomfort. Edmund Bolles, in his fascinating book about human perception, *A Second Way of Knowing,* says, "We expect *everything* we perceive to mean something. When presented with an image that has no larger meaning, we find one anyway."

Of course, the whole process of force-fitting a pattern occurs so quickly that we usually are not conscious of any discomfort. But make no mistake about it, the discomfort is there, in our mind. And if our mind is unable to come up with a satisfactory pattern after only a few seconds, the discomfort will become palpable.

This is the same discomfort we feel when we hear a dissonant chord in music. We don't need to be told or taught that the chord is dissonant; we instinctively know it, just as we instinctively feel a combined sense of relief and pleasure when the chord resolves into a harmonious mode. That's what the word *harmony* means in music: an agreeable, pleasing combination of two or more tones in a chord. Harmony (knowing) is pleasing; dissonance or disharmony (not knowing) is displeasing.

But, you don't need to manufacture a pattern for the seemingly unrelated sentences in the puzzle paragraph above. I'm furnishing you the solution or, as Paul Harvey puts it, "the rest of the story":

> The end of World War II had just been declared. I was in a little French town on my way to a bank. That Tuesday happened to be a French national holiday, so the bank was closed. A French woman, celebrating the armistice, handed me her camera and asked me to take a photograph of her and her husband. I accidentally dropped the camera, at which point the French *Marseillaise* began playing from a loudspeaker in the center of the town. I was touched with emotion. My two sons had fought with American forces. It had been a long war, but they were safe.

Don't you now experience a certain mixed feeling of satisfaction, relief, and contentment in seeing how the sentences relate to one another?

Humans have to know things. Knowing is satisfying and comforting; not knowing is unsettling. Wanting to know, needing to know, is a fundamental human trait. We giggle at the reader who skips to the last pages of a mystery story to learn whodunit, but that reader, who unconsciously responded to a deep-seated instinct ingrained in our species over the millennia and whose curiosity has been sated, cares not what we think. On a grander, nobler scale, historians spend years doing in-depth research to understand—find explanations for—the course of human events. And here, in this book, I the author and you the reader are likewise looking for explanations. It is what we humans do. It is, like all those other traits, what makes us human.

Unfortunately, our compulsion to explain things can, like those other traits, get us in trouble. When presented with an event that has no particular meaning, we find one anyway, and we subconsciously don't care whether the explanation is valid.

Likewise, when analyzing problems, we sometimes come up with explanations that don't represent the evidence very well, but we use them anyway and feel comfortable doing it. Again, we subconsciously don't care whether the explanation is valid. Its validity is simply not a factor. It's those pesky biases and mind-sets at work again.

Our indifference to the validity of our explanations is stunningly profound! It speaks volumes about the human mental process, for the astonishing, sobering, worrisome fact is that the explanations we give for things *don't have to be true to satisfy our compulsion to explain things.*

Let's pause a moment and reflect on this observation, which, in my humble opinion, presents an awesome insight into the workings of the human mind and into human behavior. Think about it. There's an autonomous, unconscious mechanism in your mind and mine that switches to "satisfied" when we've finished formulating an explanation for something.

**We are awakened late at night in our upstairs bedroom by a noise downstairs. We tell ourselves it's the cat. And we roll over and go back to sleep.**

And, being satisfied, we are then blithely content to move on to something else without seriously questioning our explanation. This is one of the reasons we humans don't give sufficient consideration to alternatives. And not considering alternatives is, as I pointed out at the beginning of this book, the principal cause of faulty analysis.

5.  **Humans have a penchant to seek out and put store in evidence that supports their beliefs and judgments while eschewing and devaluing evidence that does not.**

Please do a quick experiment with me. Stop reading this page and direct your attention for a few seconds to the wall nearest you.

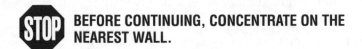 **BEFORE CONTINUING, CONCENTRATE ON THE NEAREST WALL.**

If you did as I requested, you immediately asked yourself, "What about the wall? What am I supposed to be looking for?" And you were right to ask that question, because I didn't tell you what to *focus* on. You see, our eyes are almost always focused, always riveted on some object. But our eyes are merely an appendage, an extension of the mind. They do the mind's bidding, and that constant bidding is to focus. When we don't let the mind focus, it goes into a quasi state of shock, sort of a miniparalysis, which we sense through mild mixed feelings of disorientation, anxiety, and frustration. Imagine being told to look at that wall near you for thirty minutes without knowing what you're supposed to be looking at. The very thought of it makes me shudder. In such a situation, the mind becomes discomforted and communicates that discomfort by making us nervous and impatient. We thus are prompted to think or even say aloud "What am I supposed to be looking at? What's the point?" In other words, *what's the focus?*

### Focusing

We humans are focusers by nature. It is a trait deeply imbedded in our mental makeup, one we share with every other warm-blooded creature on this planet. (In fact, all living organisms are prone to focus "mentally," but we'll save that discussion for another day.) Consider, for example, the playful, skittish squirrel. While scampering about the ground, foraging for food, the squirrel suddenly freezes in an upright posture. Some movement or sound has caught its attention. The animal holds perfectly still, watching, waiting, ready to dash up a tree to safety at the first sign of danger. While the animal remains in this stock-still position, its "mind" and all of its senses are totally focused on the potential threat. All other interests of the squirrel are in abeyance. Focusing is, indeed, not a uniquely human trait.

In *A Second Way of Knowing*, Edmund Bolles says the following about "attention" (a synonym for "focus"):

> We shift attention from sensation to sensation, watching only part of the visual field, listening to only some sounds around us, savoring certain flavors amid many. Our capacity to select and "impart intensity"* to sensations prevents us from being slaves to the physical world around us.
>
> Reality is a jumble of sensations and details. Attention enables us to combine separate sensations into unified objects and lets us examine objects closely to be sure of their identity.

While all of our mental proclivities have contributed to our survival as a species, none has played a greater role than our instinctive ability to focus our thoughts. Our species could not have survived very long if our distant ancestors had been a bunch of congenital airheads, incapable of focusing their thoughts, wandering aimlessly in the savanna, easy prey for any predator. Today, as eons ago, this instinct enables us to carry on a conversation over dinner in a noisy restaurant. Through neural processes that cognitive science does not yet fully understand, our brain filters out all of the background noise of clattering dishes, loud music, and chattering people, permitting us to hear and comprehend what our dinner partners are saying. Focusing

---

*A quotation from German psychologist Johannes Müller's two-volume *Handbook of Human Psychology*, published in the 1830s.

enables us to communicate, to drive a car, to eat, to read this book, to do everything.

## EXERCISE 1   The Riddle

Who is the person in the following riddle?

> The new chief executive, one of the youngest in his nation's history, is being sworn into office on a bleak, cold, cloudy day in January. Standing beside him is his predecessor, a military leader who had led the nation through a world war. The new chief executive was raised as a Catholic and rose to his new position in part because of his vibrant charisma. He is revered by the people and will play a crucial role in a military crisis that will face his nation. His name will become legendary.

Nearly every American who reads this riddle thinks it refers to John F. Kennedy, but they are mistaken. While the description fits him very well, the person I really have in mind is Adolf Hitler, standing beside President Paul von Hindenburg, who led Germany through World War I.

People misinterpret the riddle because the phrase "one of the youngest in his nation's history" instantly brings Kennedy to mind. It's the *vividness bias* at work. Their memories of Kennedy are more vivid than of Hitler, thus more retrievable and more of a force in their minds.

Once the idea of Kennedy has been planted, we instinctively *focus* on it and look for supporting evidence, which we readily find:

Predecessor was military leader—Eisenhower
Catholic—yep
Charismatic—yep
Revered—by most people
Crucial role in a military crisis—the Cuban missile crisis
Legendary—certainly

As the evidence confirming Kennedy mounts, we are certain we have the answer. (It's the *explaining compulsion* at work.) Because we feel comfortable and confident in our judgment that it was Kennedy, we are disinclined to consider other alternatives.

Likewise, the manager I mentioned earlier who rejected out of hand the possibility that her cashier had stolen the missing money did so because she *focused* on the explanation that someone else was guilty. Someone else *had* to be guilty. Her mind-set regarding the cashier's honesty would not permit her to entertain the alternative—that he was dishonest.

The riddle about Hitler and the example of the missing money demonstrate that, for all its merits, focusing has an immense downside when we analyze problems. It tends to make us view problems one-dimensionally, meaning we tend to focus on (glom on to) the first solution that makes sense—that offers an explanation—as we interpret reality through the lens of our biases.

Having focused on a solution, we are captivated by it and thus become uninterested in alternative solutions. Our fixation on our chosen solution therefore causes us to value evidence that supports that solution and to devalue, disbelieve, discredit, and discard evidence that does not. We therefore tend to accept at face value information that is consistent with our beliefs and to critically scrutinize and discount information that contradicts them. One can see, then, how the mind's tendency to focus can warp the objectivity of our analysis.

> We're looking for a night job. We hear of one with really good pay, but it's located in a high-crime area. We need the money, so we downplay the risk. We do the opposite when the case is reversed. Let's say we *don't* want a night job but are being urged to find one. We're told of a really well-paying job in a high-crime area. Now we cite the high crime as the reason *not* to apply for the job.

We tend to see in a body of evidence what, according to our mind-set, we expect and want to see and tend *not* to see, again according to our mind-set, what we *don't* expect or *don't* want to see. The mind subtly, unconsciously reconfigures the evidence to make it consistent with our expectation.

If you doubt that this tendency exists or that its effects are significantly detrimental to problem solving, try the following experiment on a friend. Ask your friend to identify an issue about which he or she has strong feelings. Ask your friend to state his or her position on the issue and to defend that position with argumentation. When your friend has finished *making a case,* quietly and calmly ask him or her to make the opposite case. If your friend was *for* something, ask him or her to make a case *against* it. If your friend was *against* something, ask him or her to make a case *for* it. Chances are your friend will be struck dumb for a moment, unable to respond. (I suspect it's the subconscious going into shock.) When your friend does speak, the answer will be something like "Make a case *against* it? I just told you I'm *in favor* of it!" Then say, "I realize that. You said such and such should happen. Now explain to me why it *shouldn't* happen!" Most people can't do it effectively; some can't do it at all and become quite upset when asked to. They are so focused on their interpretation of the issue that they cannot adequately articulate the other side (or sides).

### Advocacy

The hallmark of focusing is the revered human institution of *advocacy*—taking a position on an issue, marshaling supporting evidence, and defending that position against the arguments of those holding (focusing on) opposing views. We are a society of advocators. The most ignorant, uneducated person and the most intelligent, lettered scholar both instinctively take an advocatory, self-oriented approach to life. Advocacy is the traditional scholarly approach and one regularly used on radio and television talk shows and by newspaper columnists, scientists, researchers, and others to debate issues. It is, moreover, the way most of us—wives and husbands, children and parents, friends and relatives, supervisors and subordinates, labor and management—deliberate problems and seek solutions . . . through advocacy.

I hold our educational institutions largely responsible for this excess of advocacy. And it is excessive. From kindergarten to postgraduate school, through the mechanisms of classroom discussions, book reports, term papers, final examinations, dissertations, and debates in which advocacy is venerated and rewarded, these institutions teach us, the students, the art and skill not of objective analysis but of subjective argumentation. Select a thesis and defend it; take a position and defend it; make an argument and defend it; take a stand and defend it. In short, be an advocate! (I'm doing that very thing in this paragraph.) Educators did not, of course, invent advocacy; they have merely gone along with the way the human mind is genetically programmed. It's the way the mind works. The question is whether it works to our advantage when analyzing problems.

There's no question that advocacy works. It is, after all, the foundation of our judicial system, in which the prosecution prosecutes, the defense defends, and neither side does both. Advocacy is also the foundation of our political system; indeed, the foundation of our democracy, which guarantees to every citizen the right to advocate his or her interests. So advocacy does work, *when someone other than the advocator makes the decision*—such as a judge or a jury, the electorate, the board of directors, or the boss, whoever that might be.

But when the advocator is also the decision maker, advocacy can be destructive of sound, effective, and profitable solutions because advocacy feeds and perpetuates our mind-sets, biases, beliefs, and prejudices. It thus nurtures our tendency to focus and, in doing so, defeats objectivity. When we defeat objectivity, we limit, even prevent, our full understanding of problems.

### 6. We tend to cling to untrue beliefs in the face of contradictory evidence.

It turns out that a great many of our most cherished individual beliefs, upon careful examination, are simply untrue. Gilovich explains that we don't hold questionable beliefs because we have not been exposed to the truth. On the contrary, we tend to hold fast to these beliefs in the very face of incontrovertible contradictory evidence. How? We simply rationalize away the disparity. As Sir Francis Bacon observed long ago, we prefer to believe what we prefer to be true. A battered housewife believes her husband won't beat her again because he loves her. An emaciated anorectic looks in the mirror and believes she is fat. The owner of a miserably failing business looks over his books and believes he is doing all right.

Why do we cling so tenaciously to our beliefs? The answer is, of course, as complicated as any other question about human behavior, but psychologist Robert Abelson offers compelling insight. He contends that we humans treat beliefs like material possessions. We acquire and retain material possessions because of the functions they serve and the value they offer. What it comes down to is that our possessions make us feel good, and for that reason we cherish and protect them. Abelson asserts that the same can be said of beliefs, and he notes that the similarity between beliefs and possessions is revealed in our language. We *have* beliefs. We *adopt, inherit, acquire, hold,* and *cling* to them. If we reject a belief, we say we *don't buy it.* When we give up a belief, we *lose, abandon,* and *disown* it.

Whatever the reason may be for why we persist in holding untrue beliefs, the compulsion to do so can have disastrous impact on our ability to analyze and resolve problems.

# The Bottom Line

The formidable power of these six mental traits is illuminated by a quotation from a biography of the artist Georgia O'Keeffe. The quotation appears in Bolles's book *A Second Way of Knowing:* "Georgia was suddenly struck by the realization that her feelings governed the way she saw the scene. It was a moment of transformation: the entire visual world, she realized, was dependent on the emotional world." Said Bolles:

> That day she learned the artist's secret; what you perceive depends on who you are. Analytical thinkers have generally assumed that we perceive reality as it is; they then use a process of abstract reasoning to interpret that perception. O'Keeffe realized that the perception *is* the interpretation. It rests on an internal reality that governs the meaning we find in our sensations.

The *internal reality* Bolles speaks of is, in fact, controlled by the mental traits I've been talking about. Thus, it is those hidden traits that determine the meaning we find in the information our senses pick up and transmit to the brain. This is an alarming phenomenon because we have no direct awareness of, or conscious control over, these traits.

When we consider these traits acting in combination, is it any wonder that we humans, as Alexander Pope observed over two centuries ago, are prone to err? We view the world through a dense veil of burdensome, thought-warping biases and mind-sets. Through this veil we sometimes perceive cause and effect and other "patterns" where there are none. We are prone to grace these nonexistent patterns with self-satisfying explanations with whose validity we are instinctively unconcerned. Finally, we convert these explanations into rock-hard beliefs that we defend in the face of incontrovertible contradictory evidence. Ladies and gentlemen, I give you . . . *Homo sapiens!*

# 2
# Insights into Problem Solving

 Before addressing the core topic of this book—analytic structuring techniques—allow me to offer five important insights into effective problem solving.

## Major Factors, Major Issues

First, nearly all situations, even the more complex and dynamic, are driven by only a few *major factors*. *Factors* are things, circumstances, or conditions that cause something to happen. Factors, in turn, beget *issues*, which are points or questions to be disputed or decided.

Consider an accident involving two cars. The *major factors* (the circumstances that caused the accident) are such things as reckless driving, driving under the influence of alcohol or drugs, failure to yield the right-of-way, excessive speed, mechanical failure, and so on. The *major issues* (the points to be disputed or decided) are derived from such factors as: Who was driving each car? How fast were they driving? Had they been drinking alcoholic beverages? Did they violate any laws? And so on. Factors beget issues; issues stem from factors.

Major factors and major issues are the navigational aids of analysis; they tell us where our analysis should be headed. And they will normally change as we become aware of new information and gain a deeper understanding of the problem. If we lose sight of them, we lose our way in the analytic process.

We should concentrate our analytic efforts on the major factors and issues. Studying subtleties (lesser factors and issues), incorporating them into our analysis, and weighing their impact on the situation and its possible outcomes are usually a waste of time because subtleties never play a significant role. We should analyze subtleties only to the point where we recognize them for what they are. "But subtleties," you say, "can be important." I disagree. If a subtlety is important, it is, by definition, no longer a subtlety; it's a major factor or issue and should be treated as such.

The first insight, therefore, is to create at the outset and maintain throughout the problem-solving process a list of major factors and issues, adding and deleting items as necessary.

## Convergence and Divergence

The second insight relates to the two fundamental modes of analysis. At any point in the analytic process, from the very beginning to the very end, we are in one of two modes: convergent or divergent.

*Convergence* means bringing together and moving toward one point. Whenever we take a narrower view of a problem, focusing our mind on a single aspect of the puzzle or eliminating alternative solutions, we are in a convergent mode. Convergence is the opposite of *divergence*, which means to branch out, to go in different directions, from a single point. Whenever we take a broader view of a problem, whether by examining evidence more thoroughly, gathering new evidence, or entertaining alternative solutions, we are in a divergent mode.

While divergent thinking opens the mind to new ideas and thoughts, convergent thinking closes the mind by viewing a problem ever more narrowly until it focuses on—and produces—a single solution. An apt simile is a camera lens that can be adjusted to broaden the field of view around a subject (divergence) or to zoom in till the subject fills the aperture (convergence).

Both divergence and convergence are necessary for effective problem solving. Divergence opens the mind to creative alternatives; convergence winnows out the weak alternatives and focuses on, and chooses among, the strong. Without *divergence*, we could not analyze a problem creatively or objectively; without *convergence*, we would just keep on analyzing, never coming to closure. It is therefore vital to effective problem solving that the analyst be prepared and able to shift back and forth between divergent and convergent approaches easily and at will, using each mode to its best effect as the problem-solving process dictates.

What is more, our conscious awareness of (1) the diametrically opposite roles of convergence and divergence and (2) which mode we are in at any given moment in the analytic process will, by itself, greatly enhance our ability to solve problems.

Unfortunately, it is extremely difficult for humans to shift back and forth between these two ever-opposite, ever-warring approaches. Most of us are not inherently good divergers; divergence is not one of our instinctive processes. Indeed, most of us habitually resist divergence — sometimes passionately, even angrily.

One unambiguous symptom of our convergent tendency is the difficulty most humans have in trying to brainstorm. Most people use the word "brainstorm" to mean *sharing ideas* about something, as in "Let's get together tomorrow morning and brainstorm your proposal for the new project." "Brainstorm" has thus come to mean "discuss" and usually amounts to nothing more than each of the participants presenting and arguing over his or her individual views. That is *not* what I mean when I say "brainstorm." By brainstorm, I mean the freewheeling process of generating ideas randomly and spontaneously without worrying about their practicality. It's usually done in a group of people. The fact that most people are resistant to brainstorming (in my experience, resistance appears to rise with one's level of education) tells us how deeply rooted and dominant the convergent tendency is in our mental machinery and, by the same token, how damaging it can be to effective problem solving.

Have you ever read a book or article or paper on how to converge? Have you ever seen a TV program on "New Horizons in Mental Convergence"? How many courses have you heard of that teach convergent techniques, what we might call "ways of getting to the point"? None, of course. Humans don't need to be taught how to converge. It comes naturally. But, there are literally hundreds of books, articles, videotapes, lectures, and courses on how to diverge, how to open the mind, how to brainstorm, how to generate creative alternatives. What does that tell us? That divergence doesn't come naturally; we have to be *taught* how to do it. It tells us that, when it comes to diverging, humans are in trouble and need help.

# Analytic Confidence

While problems come in all varieties, shapes, and sizes, each can be categorized in terms of the roles that *fact* and *judgment* play in analysis of the problem. This categorization, represented in Figure 2-1, is called the "Taxonomy of Problem Types."

Please don't be overwhelmed by the seeming complexity of this diagram; it's really quite simple. What it shows is that, in analyzing a problem, there is an inverse relationship between the number of facts and the amount of judgment required to solve a problem. Moving to the right on the diagram, the fewer facts we have, the more judgment is required. Moving to the left, the more facts—the less judgment. From this relationship we can define four basic types of problems:

**Simplistic**
☐   There is only one answer, no more.
  Examples: Who is buried in Grant's tomb?
        Who is the governor of New York?

**Deterministic**
☐   Again there is only one answer, but it is determined by a formula. To get the answer, we must have all of the data as well as the correct formula. If either is lacking, we can't solve the problem.
  Examples: What is the area of a square whose side is 20 feet?
        If the circumference of a tire is 50 inches, how many revolutions must the tire make to travel one mile?

**FIGURE 2-1**

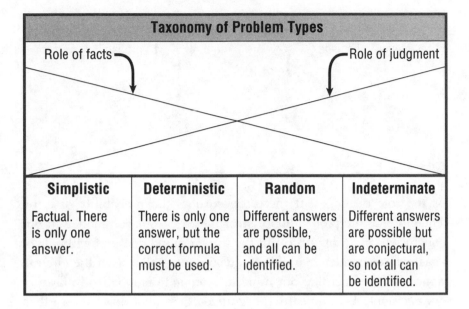

| Simplistic | Deterministic | Random | Indeterminate |
|---|---|---|---|
| Factual. There is only one answer. | There is only one answer, but the correct formula must be used. | Different answers are possible, and all can be identified. | Different answers are possible but are conjectural, so not all can be identified. |

### Random
☐ Different answers are possible, and *all* can be identified.
  Examples: Which of the candidates will win the election?
        Which of the builders who submitted a bid will get the contract?

### Indeterminate
☐ Different answers are possible, but, because all or some are conjectural, not all possible answers can be identified.
  Examples: How will permitting gays to serve in the military affect the next presidential election?
        What are the prospects for U.S.-Russian relations?

The Taxonomy of Problem Types provides our third insight into problem solving. As Figure 2-2 shows, and as common sense would tell us, there is a direct correlation between the role of facts and the confidence we have in our findings. The greater the role of facts in analyzing a problem, the greater our confidence in the findings of that analysis; the fewer facts, the less confidence. Likewise, and more important, there is a direct correlation between *judgment* and *probability of error,*

**FIGURE 2-2**

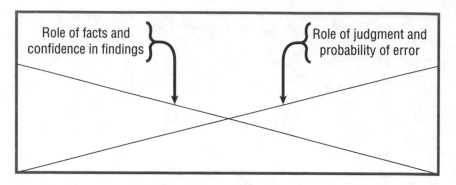

As the role of judgment increases, so does the probability of error. Therefore, as the probability of error increases, our confidence in our conclusions *must diminish*. But the human mind does not willingly or usually lose confidence in its conclusions, no matter what the circumstances. Remember that our minds are prone to rationalize in favor of our decisions. As I said earlier, cognitive experiments have shown that, even when the explanation we come up with doesn't represent the evidence very well, we use that explanation anyway and feel comfortable doing so. What's more, we defend that explanation in the face of strong contrary evidence, which we rebut with irrelevancies and sophistries. That's just how the human mind works.

The insight, then, is to be wary of conclusions that are based largely on judgment, not facts. And if you are the author of those conclusions, take pains to couch them in language that accurately conveys the degree of your confidence in them. To do otherwise is, frankly, dishonest both to ourselves and to those who base decisions on our analysis.

# Sanity Testing

The fourth insight is a basic rule that, when we have finished using any analytic structuring technique, we always do a "sanity check" by asking ourselves, "Does this make sense?" If the analytic result is reasonable, we're probably okay. But if our intuition tells us something doesn't seem right, we should go back and reexamine or completely redo our analysis.

# The Analytic Power of a Group

Finally, experiments in group process have shown that, in most circumstances, the analytic power of a *group* of analysts is greater than that of any of its single members. For that reason, the group's consensus judgments are likely to be more accurate than the judgments of any individual member. Yet when a group of people sits around a table and analyzes a problem, rare is the group member who believes that the other members *collectively* know more about the problem, understand it better, and can come up with a better solution than that member can, particularly when that member's opinion is at odds with the group's. Structuring group analysis of problems facilitates the exchange of ideas and the examination of alternatives that are necessary for building a consensus.

The varied and subtle ways in which humans interact to render groups of two or more dysfunctional spawned, years ago, an entire field of psychology that seeks to understand and explain group behavior and to find systematic ways of making human interactions more productive and effective. That research has made significant progress in unearthing the causes of group dysfunction and prescribing remedies. I strongly urge anyone who has occasion to work as a member of a problem-solving group to attend training courses in group process. The insights gained will be of utmost help in making the member's contribution more meaningful and making the group as a whole more effective.

A host of things—such as individual mind-sets, conflicts over who is in authority, domination by a clique, lack of group focus—can decimate the effectiveness of a group as, of course, can all of the mental traits described in Chapter 1. These interactions within the group tend to divide and confuse its members and to defeat their common purpose. This is where structuring analysis can help.

By organizing in a sensible, informative way the problem being analyzed, structuring greatly facilitates a group's work. Because group analysis tends to jump erratically from one topic to another as members press for acceptance of competing ideas, a principal beneficial effect of structuring is to help the group perceive the problem's full dimensions, to focus its attention on individual aspects of the problem, and to keep track of where the group is in the analytic process.

Training each member of the group in the analytic techniques presented in this book will bring great benefits. The analytic empowerment that structuring affords the individual members is multiplied many times by the collective empowerment of the group, which is transformed into a powerfully creative and effective problem solver.

Part **Two**

# The Fourteen Tools

# 3
# Problem Restatement

 Remember the anecdote about the guy who thought his water bed was leaking? He defined the problem as "How can I fix the leak?" His analysis was guided by that definition—by that *statement*—of the problem. As it turned out, he had defined the problem incorrectly. He should have asked, "What is the source of the water on my blanket?" Had he done so, his analysis would probably have considered alternative sources and revealed the source to be not the water bed but a leaky drain in an upstairs bathroom. How we define a problem usually determines how we analyze it. And how we analyze a problem *absolutely* determines whether we find a solution and what the quality of that solution is.

We frequently discover, based on information and perceptions gained midway through the analysis, that the initial problem statement was far off the mark. We can find examples all around us of people whose narrow definition of a problem caused their analysis to be short-sighted, overlooking alternative and possibly more beneficial solutions. Take the case of two parents concerned about their teenage son's poor grades in high school.

FATHER: "He just doesn't apply himself."
MOTHER: "I know. He really isn't interested. His mind wanders."

FATHER:       "I'm tired of harping about it all the time."
MOTHER:       "Me, too. It doesn't seem to have any effect."
FATHER:       "Maybe he needs tutoring in how to study."
MOTHER:       "Lord knows it wouldn't hurt. He has terrible study habits."
FATHER:       "I'll call the school tomorrow and arrange something."
MOTHER:       "Good. I'm sure it will help him."

The parents are pleased. They have defined the problem, arrived at a solution, and are taking corrective action. But are "lack of interest" and a "wandering mind" really the core problem? Will tutoring the son in how to study resolve it? Perhaps. But the parents may be addressing only symptoms of a deeper problem. Chances are the son himself doesn't know what the problem is. He knows only that he isn't motivated to study. But why isn't he? *What is the real problem?*

Here's another example:

The parking lot outside an office building is jammed with workers' cars. Management decide to tackle the problem, so they convene a working group and charge it with devising different ways to redesign the parking lot to hold more cars. The working group does its job, coming up with half a dozen different ways to increase the lot's capacity.

In this case, management defined the problem as *how to increase the lot's capacity,* and the solutions they sought were accordingly restricted to that statement of the problem. Nothing wrong with that, is there? After all, the lot *is* jammed. Obviously, more parking space is needed.

But there are other ways to view (state) the problem, such as how to *reduce the number of cars* in the parking lot. (Options for doing that might be carpooling, moving elements of the company to other locations, and eliminating jobs to reduce the number of employees.)

Let's do an exercise.

## EXERCISE 2    Algona Pollution I

The Environmental Protection Agency (EPA) has discovered volatile organic compounds in effluents from a processing plant of the Algona Fertilizer Company in Algona, Iowa. These toxic waste products bypass the city of Algona but are carried into the East Fork Des Moines River, a tributary that feeds into Saylorville Lake, the principal source of water for Des Moines, a city of more than 300,000 people. The Des Moines city council, through news media and political channels, is putting enormous public pressure on state and federal environmental agencies to shut down the Algona plant. Environmental action groups, with full media coverage, demonstrated yesterday in front of the Iowa governor's mansion demanding immediate closure of the plant. Local TV news and talk shows are beginning to focus on the issue. The company's executive board has convened an emergency working group to consider what the company should do.

Take a moment and write down on a sheet of paper what you think "the problem" is. *AND DON'T CHEAT BY NOT WRITING.* You'll miss the full benefit of this book if you don't do all the exercises. So ponder the question for a minute or two and then write down what you think "the problem" is.

**STOP** **BEFORE CONTINUING, WRITE DOWN WHAT THE PROBLEM IS.**

As you may have discovered, there's more than just one problem here, because the problem changes depending on whose perspective or self-interest we consider. Here's a sampling of perspectives on the Algona pollution problem:

Company management
Company employees
Company union management
Company union members
Residents of Algona
Residents of Des Moines
News media of Des Moines
National news media
The Des Moines city council
The governor of Iowa

The opposing political groups

The Iowa state legislature

People who make recreational use of the affected waterways

Farmers who irrigate from the affected waterways

Federal environmental authorities

State environmental authorities

Environmental action groups

Other fertilizer companies in the Des Moines area

Other fertilizer companies in Iowa

Other fertilizer companies in the United States

Every problem, from major ones, such as abortion and national health care, to mundane ones, such as an overdrawn checking account, can be viewed from multiple conflicting perspectives. And what drives these differing perspectives? Biases, those unseen killers of objective truth, determine our perspective of any problem. That perspective in turn drives our analysis, our conclusions, and ultimately our recommendations.

Given the tremendous influence of biases on our thinking, it makes good sense at the outset of the problem-solving process (before we begin seriously analyzing the problem) to deliberately strive to identify and examine our biases as they relate to the problem at hand. What we learn may surprise us and put us on the track to solutions.

Although identifying and examining biases is the rational, commonsense thing to do and will obviously greatly benefit our analysis and lead to better solutions, I know from personal experience and from observing others that attempting to make ourselves aware of our biases is extremely difficult, if not impossible. Let's face it, the human mind by design works to conceal the biases that drive our thinking. Circumventing that design is a formidable task.

So if identifying our biases through introspection is impracticable, what are we to do? How are we to circumvent our biases when analyzing a problem?

I recommend an indirect approach, which is to *restate (redefine) the problem in as many different ways as we can think of.* We simply shift our mental gears into a divergent mode (more easily said than done, I realize) and start pumping out restatements without evaluating them. The key here, as in all divergent thinking (discussed in Chapter 5), is letting the ideas flow freely, without attempting to justify them.

Sometimes restating the problem is difficult because the original statement was poorly articulated. All the more reason, then, to more clearly define it.

One can generally gain most of the benefits of restating a problem in five or ten minutes. However, those minutes are *quality time* where analysis is concerned. A problem restatement session will rather quickly, almost magically, focus on the crux of a problem—the core issues—and reveal what the problem is really all about, leaving our biases in the dust, so to speak. Identifying the crux of a problem saves immense time, effort, and money in the analytic phase. Sometimes restating a problem even points to a solution.

If, as is often the case, we are analyzing a problem for someone else's benefit, it is best to generate the problem restatements *in that person's presence*. Doing so in an open discussion will reveal our consumer's prime concerns and what he or she considers to be the key issues. This will facilitate reaching agreement at the start concerning what the problem is and what our analysis will aim to find out.

### The Technique

The aim of problem restatement is to broaden our perspective of a problem, helping us to identify the central issues and alternative solutions and increasing the chance that the outcome our analysis produces will fully, not partially, resolve the problem.

There are countless ways of restating a problem. Here are two basic approaches applied to the parking lot example:

*Paraphrase:* **Reword the problem without shifting its primary focus.**

How to increase the number of parking spaces near the office.

How to increase the number of cars that park in the lot without
    increasing the number of parking spaces.

*Make a 180-Degree Turn:* **Shift the problem's focus by viewing it from the opposite direction.**

How to reduce the number of cars that park in the lot.

How to transport people to work without using automobiles.

Most important of all, restatements should, whenever possible, be put into writing so we—and our consumer, if the problem is owned by someone else—can study them. A record copy of the agreed-upon problem statement should be retained for reference as our analysis proceeds. Retaining it not only enables us to check from time to time to see if our analysis is *on target,* it also offers us protection in case our consumer complains afterward that we addressed the wrong problem. Keep in mind, however, that the goal of problem restatement is to expand our thinking about the problem, not to solve it.

Let's do another problem restatement exercise.

## EXERCISE 3    Gays in the Military

Consider this question: *Should gays be permitted to serve in the military?* Does this question accurately address "the problem"? What *is* the problem? Rephrase the question in at least a *dozen* different ways and see how doing so affects your perception of the problem and how you might analyze it.

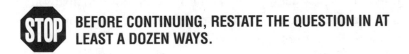 **BEFORE CONTINUING, RESTATE THE QUESTION IN AT LEAST A DOZEN WAYS.**

### *The Importance of Grammar*

A valuable tip when restating problems is to make them *simple, positive,* and in *active voice.* The mind works more easily and quickly with simple, positive, active-voice sentences than with complex, negative, passive-voice sentences. Let me demonstrate with examples.

### Simplicity Pays Off

How many variable health insurance programs have been adopted by privately owned companies in the metropolitan Washington, D.C., area, including the more densely populated municipalities and counties of northern Virginia, with from 50 to 1,000 employees with profits greater than $1 million but not less than $500,000 during FY92 compared with health insurance programs adopted by larger companies in the Baltimore area with profits less than $500,000?

It's a struggle to wade through this statement, however accurate and comprehensive it may be. The information it contains may well be precisely what the "owner" of the problem believes he or she wants to know, but surely there's a simpler way to express it.

### Positive Is Preferable

In *The Universe Within*, Morton Hunt describes an experiment conducted at Stanford University by Herbert Clark and a colleague that demonstrates that we humans take longer to process a negative thought than a positive one. The subjects of the experiment were shown cards like those in Figure 3-1 and were asked to say as quickly as they could whether the statement on each card was true or false. Try it yourself. It took them two-tenths of a second longer to reply to the false statement than to the true one. The explanation offered by Clark and his colleague was that, when we seek to verify a statement, we instinctively assume it is true and try to match it against the facts. If they match, we do no further mental work. If they don't, we take the extra step of revising our assumption, thus answering a trifle more slowly. It thus takes half a second or more longer to verify denials than affirmations. We seem programmed to think more readily about what *is* rather than what is *not*.

This phenomenon is easily demonstrated. Read the following sentences, pausing briefly between them.

Is the ball in the bottle red?

Is the ball not in the bottle red?

**FIGURE 3-1**

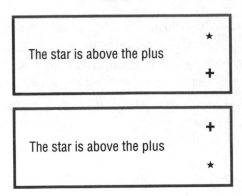

Did you feel your mind scramble for a fleeting moment at the end of the second sentence to make sense of it? Negatives can do that to our minds so easily.

If negatives give us pause, look what a double negative can do:

Is the ball that is not in the bottle not red?

Huh?

### Active Voice Facilitates

Just as a simple, positive statement is easier to deal with mentally than a complex, negative one, so a statement in *passive voice* takes longer to process than one in *active voice*. That's because the mind's basic linguistic programming interprets and forms sentences in terms of *actor-action-object*, not *object-action-actor*. When children first begin speaking, they say, "Tom throws the ball," not "The ball is thrown by Tom." Of course, children quickly learn to make sense of passive voice, but, to do so, they first have to mentally rearrange the sentence to identify the *actor*, the *action*, and the *object*. By the time we're adults, our minds have become adept at forming and interpreting complicated statements in passive voice. Nevertheless, our mental linguistic machinery, which is hardwired into the brain, doesn't change. When the *object* in a statement comes first, the mind must still set the *object* aside until the *actor* and *action* become known. See if this isn't the case as you read the following sentence:

The fan was waved by Mary.

The mind instinctively assumes that the first object in the sentence (the fan) is the subject, the *actor,* but the verb instantly reveals that the fan is the *object* instead. Can you sense your mind rearranging the parts of the sentence? Read the sentence again:

The fan was waved by Mary.

Note how much easier it is to interpret the active-voice version:

Mary waved the fan.

The reason is that no rearranging is necessary; the mind immediately goes about the business of interpretation.

The slight difficulty we have with passive voice probably stems from the mind's built-in propensity to view the world in terms of cause-and-effect relationships. Thus, the mind is programmed (hardwired) to see cause first and effect second. But passive voice puts effect ahead of cause, so the mind has to reverse their order to interpret the statement.

Worrying about the phraseology of a problem statement may seem trivial, but I assure you it isn't. As I said at the beginning of this section, how we define a problem determines how we analyze it. The wording of that definition is therefore crucial, and anything we can do to clarify and simplify it is significant.

Jerome Robbins, in his script for Leonard Bernstein's musical *West Side Story,* captured the essence of problem restatement in the scene where gang members are bemoaning their lot as social misfits. Pointing to one of their members, they restate his *problem* several ways to reflect how various misguided social workers had defined it:

*The trouble is he's lazy.*
*The trouble is he drinks.*
*The trouble is he's crazy.*
*The trouble is he stinks.*
*The trouble is he's growing.*
*THE TROUBLE IS HE'S GROWING!*

So *that's* the problem! He's growing!

# 4
# PROs-CONs-
# and-FIXes

For some reason humans are compulsively negative. This instinctive trait is inimical to effective problem solving because, by seriously biasing our analysis, negative thoughts defeat creative objective thinking. At the drop of a hat, we can think of twenty reasons why an idea, suggestion, proposal, or you-name-it is no good. Being negative and contrary is such a universal human trait that it's downright extraordinary when a new idea meets with instant approval. Negative thoughts and reactions—reasons we don't like something—come to mind one after another almost magically. We don't consciously orchestrate their generation. They just happen spontaneously. Many books, articles, and papers have been written on how to overcome negative thinking—like how to sell a new idea—but you won't find much literature on how to criticize a new idea. Criticizing comes to us naturally.

Because our compulsion to be critical is so strong, we tend, when we evaluate the merits of something, especially when the something is new or unconventional and we are discussing it with others, to focus on the negative aspects to the virtual exclusion of the positive. Negative thoughts can quickly overwhelm and preempt positive considerations.

A powerful but simple technique for dealing with this problem is called PROs-CONs-and-FIXes. This rigorous technique compensates for negative thinking by forcing us to identify the positives *first*. Only then are we allowed to indulge joyously in negatives. But the technique goes a step further by examining the negatives and trying to think of actions that could be taken to "fix" them, either converting them into positives or, if that isn't feasible, eliminating them altogether. Those negatives (cons) that can't be "fixed" represent the price one must pay, the burden one must bear, if the thing being evaluated is to be adopted or accepted.

## The Five Steps of PROs-CONs-and-FIXes

The procedure involves five fairly simple steps. I will demonstrate them as a means of evaluating Marty Bloomfield's proposal (see the opening of Chapter 1, in which the Family Frozen Foods company decides to expand its fleet of delivery trucks) to purchase a semi tractor-trailer instead of a standard delivery van. To give balance to the analysis, I am including a third option—not purchasing an additional delivery vehi-cle—which I dub the "status quo."

### *Semi Step 1:* List all the PROs.

We first make a list of all the "PROs"—the positives, benefits, merits, and advantages—of buying a semi; the reasons why we believe a semi is better than a van for delivering Family Frozen Foods. We think hard and try to be creative. We are in a divergent mode.

#### *Semi PROs (why a semi is* better *than a van)*

Has three to four times as much load capacity as a van.

Can handle the expected growth in the company's sales.

Advertising on a semi will be more effective than on a van.

### *Semi Step 2:* List all the CONs.

Next, we make a list of all the negatives—reasons why a semi is worse than a van. We don't have to think hard; the negatives come easily. Again, we're in a divergent mode.

### Semi CONs (why a semi is worse than a van)

Gets less mileage per gallon of fuel.

Fuel costs are greater.

Maintenance and repair are more costly.

Purchase price is three times greater.

Is wasteful (trailer will not always be filled to capacity).

Is more difficult to drive.

Thus: More accidents and more damage to the vehicle.
More difficult to find and keep qualified drivers.

Liability is greater.

Insurance is more costly.

State and local taxes are greater.

Competitors are expanding their delivery fleets with vans.

## Semi Step 3: Review and consolidate the CONs, merging and eliminating.

In the third step, we consolidate the CONs, merging those that are similar and eliminating those that are redundant. Now we are in a convergent mode.

### Semi CONs (why a semi is worse than a van)

Purchase price is three times greater.

Gets less mileage per gallon of fuel.

~~Fuel costs are greater.~~ [Delete: redundant to mileage.]

Maintenance and repair are more costly.

Is wasteful (trailer will not always be filled to capacity).

Is more difficult to drive.

Thus: More accidents and more damage to the vehicle.
More difficult to find and keep qualified drivers.

~~Liability is greater.~~ [Merge with "Insurance is more costly."]

~~Insurance premium is more costly.~~ [Merge with "Liability is greater."]

Liability is greater, insurance premium is higher.

~~Competitors are expanding their delivery fleets with vans.~~ [Delete: irrelevant.]

## Semi Step 4: Neutralize as many CONs as possible.

In the fourth step, we think of what can be done, what measures can be taken, either to convert each CON into a PRO or to neutralize it. We write each measure next to the affected CON, being as imaginative as we can. We are in a divergent mode again.

| *Semi CONs* | *Semi FIXes* |
| --- | --- |
| Purchase price is three times greater. | Semi has greater capacity; is more efficient and profitable. |
| Gets less mileage per gallon of fuel than a van. | Design delivery routes that are more cost-effective. |
| Maintenance and repair are more costly. | Design delivery routes that are more cost-effective. |
| Is more difficult to drive than a van. | (No FIX) |
| More accidents, more damage to vehicle. | Pay incentives for safe driving. |
| Harder to find and keep qualified drivers. | Pay competitive wages. |
| Insurance premium is higher. | (No FIX) |

Our analysis indicates that we can eliminate or mitigate all but two CONs: more difficult to drive and higher insurance premium. These two negatives are the price—the burden—the company must accept if it purchases the semi.

We now do Steps 1 through 4 with the other two options: the van and the status quo.

## Van Step 1: List all the PROs.

In this particular example the PROs for a van are the exact opposite of the CONs for the semi.

### Van PROs

Purchase price is one-third as much.

Gets more mileage per gallon of fuel.

Maintenance and repair are less costly.

Is less difficult to drive.

Fewer accidents, less damage to vehicle.

Easier to find and keep qualified drivers.

Insurance premium is lower.

## Van Step 2: List all the CONs.

Again, the van's CONs are the opposite of the semi's PROs.

### Van CONs

Has only one-fourth to one-third the load capacity of a semi.

Cannot handle the expected growth in the company's sales.

Advertising on a van will be less effective than on a semi.

## Van Step 3: Review and consolidate the CONs, merging and eliminating.

There is nothing to merge or eliminate.

## Van Step 4: Neutralize as many CONS as possible.

| Van CONs | Van FIXes |
| --- | --- |
| Has only one-fourth to one-third the load capacity. | (No FIX) |
| Cannot handle expected sales growth. | (No FIX) |
| Advertising on a semi is more effective. | (No FIX) |

Now we evaluate the PROs and CONs of the third option: the status quo.

### *Status Quo Step 1:* List all the PROs.

#### *Status Quo PROs*

No outlay of funds for purchase.

No additional tax payments.

No additional maintenance and repair costs.

No hiring of an additional driver; no increase in personal services costs.

### *Status Quo Step 2:* List all the CONs.

#### *Status Quo CONs*

Deliveries are falling ever farther behind sales.

### *Status Quo Step 3:* Review and consolidate the CONs, merging and eliminating.

There is nothing to merge or eliminate.

### *Status Quo Step 4:* Neutralize as many CONs as possible.

| *Status Quo CONs* | *Status Quo FIXes* |
|---|---|
| Deliveries falling behind sales. | (No FIX) |

### *Step 5:* Compare the PROs and unalterable CONs for all options.

Here's where straightforward, old-fashioned, meat-and-potatoes *analysis* comes to the fore. As I said in the Introduction, structuring is not a substitute for analysis (thinking). Effective problem solving depends, in the end, on sound analysis. Whether, based upon your analysis of the pros and cons of Family Frozen Foods' three options, you decide to buy the semi or the van or to remain with the status quo is immaterial as far as the efficacy of the structuring technique is concerned. The PROs-

CONs-and-FIXes technique has fulfilled its role by organizing the elements of the problem in a logical way so that each element can be analyzed separately, systematically, and sufficiently.

As preparation for the exercise that follows, let's review the five steps in PROs-CONs-and-FIXes:

(Perform Steps 1 through 4 for each option.)

*Step 1*: List all the PROs.

*Step 2*: List all the CONs.

*Step 3*: Review and consolidate the CONs, merging and eliminating.

*Step 4*: Neutralize as many CONs as possible.

*Step 5*: Compare the PROs and unalterable CONs for all options.

### EXERCISE 4    Part-Time/Full-Time Employees

Apply the PROs-CONs-and-FIXes technique to the question of whether the workforce in a new small business should consist entirely of part-time or full-time employees. Use either an imaginary business or one with which you are familiar. Limit your analysis to these two options. Perform the five steps and make a recommendation as to which option the business should adopt. Don't be concerned that you need more facts or that you may lack the knowledge or experience to render a sound professional judgment on an issue of this type. The purpose of the exercise is simply to teach you the technique, so follow the steps and apply whatever knowledge and experience you have. You may, if you wish, contrive "facts" to facilitate the exercise. There is no *right* answer here.

**BEFORE CONTINUING, APPLY THE PROs-CONs-and-FIXes TECHNIQUE TO THE TWO WORKFORCE OPTIONS AND MAKE A RECOMMENDATION.**

### EXERCISE 5    Business Location

A fast-food chain restaurant is going to be built in your vicinity. Identify three disparate sites for the restaurant, analyze the three options using the PROs-CONs-and-FIXes technique, and decide which site would be the most lucrative for the restaurant's corporation. Again, this is purely an exercise, so use whatever knowledge and experience you have, contriving "facts" where necessary. Remember, there is no *right* answer. The purpose is to teach you the technique.

 **BEFORE CONTINUING, APPLY THE PROs-CONs-and-FIXes TECHNIQUE TO ANALYZE WHICH OF THE THREE SITES WOULD BE MOST LUCRATIVE.**

The PROs-CONs-and-FIXes technique can be applied to any problem and at any point in the analytic process. Practice the technique on really simple problems at first, to get the hang of it and gain confidence in using it. For instance, the next time you are choosing among restaurants, do a quick PROs-CONs-and-FIXes on each one, compare the results, and make a selection. It's fun, fast, and, most important of all, effective. Try it—you'll like it!

# 5
# Divergent Thinking

There are numerous techniques that innovative people have conceived to facilitate divergent thinking. As I have pointed out, we humans are not very good at diverging. Most of us were not endowed with an inherent ability to think divergently. For that reason, when we are compelled by circumstances, such as participating in a brainstorming session, to think divergently, it can be stressful, even painful—but also amusing. I always shake my head in wonderment at why people can't just open up and let ideas come forth. Why is opening up such a struggle? Most people tend to guard divergent thoughts as if letting them out would infect others with some dread contagious disease. And when they do offer a novel idea, they are careful to word it in inoffensive language to forestall or at least mute the criticism or ridicule that they seem sure it will provoke. Fear of criticism and ridicule is, of course, not unreasonable. As I noted earlier, we humans are the fastest criticizers and ridiculers in the galaxy. We can think of ten reasons why someone's idea is stupid before he or she even finishes explaining it. Negative thoughts flood our minds and overwhelm those tiny rivulets of positive notions. The foremost challenge in analyzing problems is to think divergently, not just at crucial points in our analysis but at *every stage* of the process.

I have had formal training in brainstorming techniques and have led and taken part in many such sessions. And I use brainstorming in my professional work with good effect. However, I regard as unnecessary overkill the wild, frenzied brainstorming methods that some people advocate, such as playing childish (childlike) games, drawing stream-of-consciousness pictures, and taking "excursions" into other topics and then returning to the primary subject. Such methods are what I call blitzkrieg tactics. Clearly, we need to stretch our minds, to let go of our self-imposed restraints on ideation, and to blow holes through fixed, narrow thinking, but I've found that most people can do that quite effectively without resorting to blitzkrieg methods. Nevertheless, if blitzkrieg methods suit your purpose, use them. And if you have never had training in brainstorming, get some. It's loads of fun and will greatly empower your analysis.

The purpose of brainstorming or any other divergent technique is to generate creative ideas about a topic (the more the better) and to allow ideas of every kind to flower, flourish, and multiply in order to enrich the thinking process and the inventiveness of solutions. But brainstorming is more than just about quantity; it is also about receptivity.

It does little good to formulate a hundred new ideas if minds are closed to them. I have witnessed many a brainstorming session in which intelligent people go through the motions of generating ideas but treat the entire process as a kind of game. When it's over, they depart, leaving the ideas behind like chips and playing cards on a table after a poker game. To analyze a problem effectively, we need to be open to ideas, at any time and from any source, from the very outset to the very end of the analytic process.

# The Four Commandments of Divergent Thinking

The First Commandment: *The more ideas, the better.*

This commandment is obvious and never causes anyone a problem. It means quantity is more important than quality, so keep the ideas coming, one after another. The more the merrier. Who can argue with that?

The Second Commandment: *Build one idea upon another.*

The power of brainstorming lies in the freedom and spontaneity of the process: one idea spawns another and another and another in rapid succession. Participants are encouraged to say aloud that the idea one is suggesting "builds on" someone else's idea. This statement, which rewards and flatters that someone else and reaffirms the connectivity of ideas, adds momentum to the process.

The Third Commandment: *Wacky ideas are okay.*

Wild and wacky ideas help us break out of conventional thinking and open the way to new, practical ideas. Wacky ideas also incite humor, which relaxes our paranoid grip on the mind's generative capabilities and liberates more ideas. This commandment, however, bothers most people. Conventional wisdom dictates that "new" ideas must be *sensible, reasonable, constructive, practical* . . . you know, not silly or foolish. But "silly" and "foolish" are subjective modifiers that people tend to apply to any idea that does not conform to what they define narrowly as a *risk-free* standard of "sensible, reasonable, constructive, practical." What troubles people is not that an idea is silly or foolish but that they will *feel and look* silly and foolish suggesting it. For that reason they fear criticism and ridicule.

The Fourth Commandment—The Golden Rule: *Don't evaluate ideas.*

Neither yours nor especially someone else's. This rule liberates people from their self-imposed restraints in generating ideas. Prohibiting the "evaluation" of ideas precludes criticism and ridicule, which in turn eliminates people's fears, which in turn frees their minds. In brainstorming, the practicality of ideas is irrelevant.

Let's do an exercise and see how well you can apply the Four Commandments of divergent thinking.

## EXERCISE 6    Bike Trail

Read the following article:

BIKE TRAIL TURNS INTO MEAN STREET

# Tipper Gore Among Many Victims of Rising Tensions and Tacks

### by Steve Bates
WASHINGTON POST STAFF WRITER

Riders on a busy Northern Virginia bicycle path faced a tack attack yesterday morning that punctured dozens of tires, delaying biking commuters and recreational cyclists, including the vice president's wife.

It was not a happy trail. It also was not the first time.

In the last two weeks, someone has repeatedly spread tiny carpet tacks on the Mount Vernon Bike Trail, causing what one bicycle shop estimated have been 300 to 500 flat tires. Authorities believe that someone may have a grudge against cyclists.

The crowded trail, which runs 19 miles along the Potomac River . . . , has been the scene of countless run-ins this spring between cyclists, joggers, walkers and Rollerbladers as they compete for space on the narrow ribbon of asphalt.

Among yesterday's victims was Tipper Gore, who was riding in northern Old Town Alexandria, accompanied by a Secret Service agent, when one of her tires was punctured. "This is very dangerous, particularly for children," the vice president's wife said after the incident.

Many regular users of the path say that even without the tacks, at times the bike trail is hell on wheels.

"There is an incredible amount of tension," among the competing groups on the path, said [one rider] who commutes by bike daily between his

[Virginia] home and his . . . Washington office.

[He] said he has seen collisions, heated arguments and even an occasional fight along the trail. "A lot of people don't know the rules of the road," [he] said. "There needs to be better enforcement."

In the spring, the trail is crowded with weekday commuters and with evening and weekend recreational riders. On a sunny weekend day, at least 2,500 people use it, the National Park Service says.

Many bicyclists feel that the narrow path is theirs; after all, it's called the Mount Vernon *Bike* Trail. Runners and walkers say they have just as much right to use it and shouldn't have to worry about being run down by 18-speed bikes. And Rollerblade cruisers have added to the dangerous mix in recent years.

[A woman] who runs on the path regularly said an inexperienced Rollerblader, swinging from side to side, can take up most of both sides of the trail. Cyclists and runners can be dangerous, too, she said. "Last summer I got knocked on the ground" by a group of runners."

Some trail users say commuting and racing bicyclists are the most dangerous. "Coming downhill, they must go 25 or 30 miles per hour," said [a man]. "An old person can hardly walk."

Trail users and U.S. Park Police speculate that the tacks are being spread by someone angry at bicyclists. "It could be somebody who really got ticked off and said, 'I'm going to get those bikers,' " suggested [a man], a bicycle commuter, who said he has had six flat tires in the last two weeks.

"There seems to be more during weekdays, aimed at commuters," said [a Park Police sergeant], who said the Park Service has cleanup crews standing by to clean up the tiny black tacks when they are discovered.

Most of the flat tires have occurred near the Daingerfield Island sailing marina, between National Airport and Old Town [Alexandria], but some have been reported as far south as Mount Vernon.

"There have easily been 300 to 500 flats in the last couple of weeks," said the owner of the 'Round the Town shop in Alexandria. The owner, who rents bikes and Rollerblades and considers himself a "Rollerblade missionary," said he encourages users of the in-line roller skates to head for a nice, big parking lot to enjoy their sport.

"There have been some gruesome accidents on the trail," said the executive director of the Road Runners Club of America, a jogging group. "Common courtesy isn't being obeyed."

Except at one Alexandria bike shop, that is. The manager of Big Wheel Bikes said he didn't charge Tipper Gore for fixing yesterday's flat. He said he's had plenty of business in the past two weeks, and "I considered it a public service."

Apply the divergent thinking technique to the situation described in the article. The technique has three steps. First, brainstorm (observing the Four Commandments) on a sheet of paper as many different ideas as you can think of to remedy the problems that users of the bike trail are experiencing.

 **BEFORE CONTINUING, WRITE ON A PIECE OF PAPER AS MANY REMEDIES AS YOU CAN THINK OF.**

Compare your ideas with those I generated (see Part 1 of the Solution to Exercise 6).

When we've finished diverging (exhausted our reservoir of ideas), the next step is to *focus* by winnowing out the impractical stuff and clustering ideas that are similar. We are now in a convergent mode.

 **BEFORE CONTINUING, WINNOW AND CLUSTER YOUR IDEAS.**

Part 2 of the solution to Exercise 6 shows how I winnowed and clustered my ideas. As I read through the list, I determined that they fell into six general categories: making and enforcing rules and regulations, punishing offenders, physical construction, enforcement, cleaning up the tacks, and promoting courtesy and safety. A seventh "category" included those ideas that were impractical and to be winnowed out.

In the third step, we select those ideas that are intuitively practical and promising.

 **BEFORE CONTINUING, SELECT PRACTICAL, PROMISING IDEAS.**

I selected an assortment of ideas (Part 3 of the solution to Exercise 6) that together could make up a realistic program over the short term for redressing the situation through public appeals, imposition of lawful rules governing and restricting use of the trail, and modest penalties for violations. I also selected a single longer-range solution: widening of the trail to allow for separate lanes for each group's exclusive use. At the same time I also revised (further developed) several of the ideas. These revisions are products of continued divergent thinking. As I said, we should be prepared to diverge — to engage in creative thinking — throughout the analytic process, even at the very end.

Although the selection of practical, promising ideas concludes the divergent-thinking technique, a further useful step one can take is to perform PROs-CONs-and-FIXes on each of the selected ideas to identify their strengths and weaknesses and to evaluate their feasibility. This step also provides an opportunity to revise the ideas, enhancing and fine-tuning them.

## EXERCISE 7    Copier Cheaters

People in another division of the company by which you are employed make regular — but unauthorized — use of your division's copying machine. As a consequence, the machine is often tied up. What is more annoying, the interlopers from the other division frequently fail to refill the paper dispenser, replace the ink cartridge, remove jammed paper that renders the machine inoperable, or report mechanical problems. The workers in the other division have their own photocopier, but it is located on the next floor up. Thus, they find it more convenient to use your division's machine. Using the divergent-thinking technique, generate some practical, promising measures to stop this infringement. The three steps again are:

*Step* 1: Brainstorm.
*Step* 2: Winnow and cluster.
*Step* 3: Select practical, promising ideas.

 **BEFORE CONTINUING, APPLY DIVERGENT THINKING TO GENERATE PRACTICAL, PROMISING CORRECTIVE MEASURES.**

In summary, let me repeat what I said about the divergent mind-set. We should train ourselves to be ready at any moment, when we are analyzing a problem, to shift from our normal convergent mode to a divergent mode and back again, taking from the divergency new ideas. Sometimes divergent thinking will yield only a single new idea, but that idea may be very helpful, even crucial, to the analysis of a problem and to its solution. Frequently, when I'm discussing a problem with someone, I'll switch to a divergent mode. But I know that if I don't tell the person I'm switching, he or she will get upset, thinking I'm either off on some wild tangent or that I'm really serious about some idea I've raised for discussion when, in fact, I'm only testing the analytic waters. So I always tell people when I'm brainstorming, and I recommend you do the same.

# 6
# Sorting, Chronologies, and Time Lines

 Sorting—what I do in grouping jigsaw puzzle pieces—is the most basic structuring technique. For that reason, one would think we could give it short shrift here and move on to techniques less well known. Unfortunately, sorting is both underused and misused. Some of us never sort problems into their component parts. (Remember, we are instinctively disinclined to use any structuring technique.) Others of us sort, but we do it incoherently or according to misleading assumptions about the nature and similarity of the parts. All of us tend to believe that only complex problems require sorting. The fact is, analysis of even the *simplest* problems benefits from *simple* sorting.

For example: In preparing a grocery list, it facilitates shopping to group items on the list according to their location in the store. Otherwise, one's eyes are constantly scanning the whole list to ensure that items have not been missed as one moves from one aisle to another.

Of course, as the complexity and ambiguity of a problem increase (as it moves from facts to judgment, from simplistic to indeterminate), sorting and the nature of the sorting become critical to effective analysis.

## EXERCISE 8   Biographics

On a sheet of paper, sort the following information in whatever way you wish:

### Biographic Information

Mary is 35 years old, married, with three children. She works part time as a waitress. A Catholic, she was born in Boston, and votes Republican.

John, a bus driver, is a Presbyterian, single, and a rabid Democrat. He is 50 years old and was born in Philadelphia.

Sue was born in Pittsburgh and is a dentist's receptionist. She is 25, a Catholic, single, a Democrat.

Gloria, a Methodist, is a full-time computer programmer. Born in Lancaster, Pennsylvania, she is 37, a Democrat, married, and has two children.

Bob is 26, born in York, Pennsylvania, a Baptist, married without children, a marketing specialist, and a Republican.

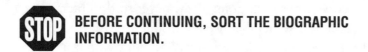 **BEFORE CONTINUING, SORT THE BIOGRAPHIC INFORMATION.**

There are numerous ways, all of them perfectly satisfactory, to sort this information. By sorting it, we are in a position to answer any of a wide range of questions about these people. What is their average age? How many are Catholic? Which persons were born in Pennsylvania? The principle involved is the same one I use to assemble jigsaw puzzles: putting similar pieces together in groups. What could be simpler? What could be more helpful in analyzing a problem?

# Chronologies and Time Lines

Another highly useful but elementary technique for organizing information is a *chronology*, or what Harvard professors Richard Neustadt and Ernest May call a *time line* in their thoroughly engaging, highly informative book *Thinking in Time*. (I would do their exceptional book injustice by trying to summarize its compelling contents. I therefore urge the reader to read *Thinking in Time*. Its method supplements very well the analytic structuring techniques I present here.)

We humans instinctively think chronologically. Read the following sentence: *John and Mary had their first child in 1985, met on a blind date in 1979, moved to Texas in 1981, and were married in 1980.* Did your mind register a silent but nonetheless perceptible protest when you discovered that the dates were out of chronological order? Mine did. It said, "Huh?" It does that every time I stumble over information that I expect to be chronological that isn't. At the same time I can feel my mind trying to rearrange the statements to put them in chronological order. Did yours do that? It's an irresistible compulsion.

This compulsion to view events chronologically is related to our instinct to view the world in terms of cause-and-effect relationships. As I said earlier, the mind is programmed to see *cause* first and *effect* second. Event A causes (leads to) Event B. Naturally, then, A should precede B. If we read something that upsets the chronology, describing Event B first and Event A second, the mind, in order to interpret the report, silently reverses the events, just as it reverses the order of *object* and *actor* in passive voice.

Reports written by journalists, historians, researchers, scientists, and members of other analytic professions customarily present their findings chronologically as a means of facilitating understanding, both for the author and for the reader. Novelists and historians occasionally employ *flashbacks* and other nonchronological approaches as a presentational device that serves some special purpose in the author's work. But anything that disrupts the chronology of events can, and often does, confuse the reader—as well as the author—because thinking chronologically is how our minds prefer to work.

Consider the following newspaper article in *The Washington Post* of June 14, 1994:

A Navajo was the first to die. Autopsies showed that both had essentially drowned, their lungs soaked with serum from their own blood.

But, on May 14, 1993, her fiancé, Navajo runner Merrill Bahe, 20, died too. After all, Florena Woody did have a history of asthma. Then he collapsed. His horrified sister-in-law stopped at a general store and dialed 911. And no one knew why. One day Florena Woody, 21, was healthy; the next day she could no longer breathe. Bahe began gasping for air during the 55-mile drive across the state from the couple's trailer in Little Water, N.M., to Woody's funeral in Gallup. Although many grieved, her abrupt death on May 9 was not alarming. Bahe paced, agitated, his skin tinged with yellow, his lips and fingernails turning blue.

Did your mind say "Huh?" or even several mega-huhs as you read this paragraph? That's because I randomly rearranged the order of the sentences in the original article. Did you feel your mind trying to sort and rearrange the sentences to put them in chronological order as you read?

Here's what the article actually said:

A Navajo was the first to die. One day Florena Woody, 21, was healthy; the next day she could no longer breathe. Although many grieved, her abrupt death on May 9, 1993, was not alarming. After all, Florena Woody did have a history of asthma. But five days later her fiancé, Navajo runner Merrill Bahe, 20, died too. Bahe began gasping for air during the 55-mile drive across the state from the couple's trailer in Little Water, N.M., to Woody's funeral in Gallup. His horrified sister-in-law stopped at a general store and dialed 911. Bahe paced, agitated, his skin tinged with yellow, his lips and fingernails turning blue. Then he collapsed. Autopsies showed that both had essentially drowned, their lungs soaked with serum from their own blood. And no one knew why.

Clearly, chronological order is not merely important to understanding; it can be indispensable. A chronology (time line) allows us to understand and appreciate the context in which events occurred, are occurring, or will occur. We are then in a far better position to interpret the significance of each event with respect to the problem. Sometimes putting events in chronological order points to a solution. "A time-line," write Neustadt and May, "is simply a string of sequential dates. To see

### TABLE 6-1
### Neustadt and May Placement of Dean Rusk,
### Secretary of state under President John F. Kennedy

| "Events" Public History (general knowledge) | | "Details" Private History (recorded) |
|---|---|---|
| Date | Event | Dean Rusk |
| 1908 | Taft elected | Born, rural Georgia |
| 1917–18 | WWI (U.S.) | Hard up |
| 1931 | Manchuria | Rhodes scholar at Oxford |
| 1936–39 | Spain | Professor at Mills College |
| 1940 | Fall of France | Army service: with Stillwell in Burma and at Pentagon |
| 1947 | Truman Doctrine | Department of State (follows George Marshall) |
| 1948 | Berlin airlift | Assistant secretary, United Nations |
| 1953 | Eisenhower | President, Rockefeller Foundation |
| 1960–63 | JFK | Scarsdale, "Everybody's second choice" Secretary of state, 1961–69 |
| 1963 | Lyndon Johnson | |
| 1965–73 | Vietnam War (U.S.) | |
| 1969 | Richard Nixon | Professor, University of Georgia |

#### "Inferences"

Conventional

Dutiful

Loyal

Brainy

Nominal Democrat

Bipartisan establishment

Essentially diplomat

*Source:* Richard Neustadt and Ernest May, *Thinking in Time* (New York: The Free Press, 1986), pp. 168–169.

the story behind the issue [the problem], it can help merely to mark on a piece of paper the dates one first associates with [the problem's] history. Because busy people often balk at looking very far into the past, we stress the importance of beginning with the earliest date that seems at all significant." Neustadt and May urge decision makers of all shapes, interests, and venues to place greater reliance on history. "Implicitly: vicarious experience acquired from the past, even the remote past, gives such guidance to the present that [the history of the problem] becomes more than its own reward."

A special form of time line is what Neustadt and May call "placement," which means arraying chronologically the events in public history and details in private life that may affect the outlook of a decision maker whether the latter be a person or an organization. From this history and details we draw inferences about the decision maker's thinking—motives, prejudices, and so on8. An example of placement is that prepared by Neustadt and May of former Secretary of State Dean Rusk (see Table 6-1). Placement is treated again in Chapter 12 in the context of role-playing one's competitors in order to gain insights into their decision making.

# 7
# Causal Flow Diagramming

 Imagine a mechanic trying to repair a malfunctioning engine whose components and inner workings he doesn't understand. "Kick it!" urges a bystander. "That'll make it work!" And *kick it* is what so many people do in trying to solve a problem whose internals they do not fathom. Even when we fully understand what "the problem" is, we all too often have a poor comprehension of what is causing it; lacking that vital knowledge, we resort to that timeworn problem-solving method called *trial and error* with its focus glued to the first plausible corrective option we think of.

All events in life are the results, the outcomes, of previous events. Life itself is a collage of ecological cycles, all intertwining, mingling, overlapping, sharing, and competing, all linked together in countless ever-evolving chains of cause-and-effect relationships. Likewise, every problem we analyze is the product of a definable cause-and-effect system. It stands to reason, then, that identifying that system's components and how they interact to produce the problem is essential to effective problem solving. Moreover, illuminating these components and their interactions can validate or invalidate our initial assumptions about how the system works and uncover hidden biases and erroneous perceptions.

Therefore, when confronted with a problem, the first questions we should ask ourselves are: *What is causing this problem? How are the major dynamic factors interacting to produce this result?*

## The Five Steps of Causal Flow Diagramming

There are five steps for defining and analyzing a problem's cause-and-effect system:

Step 1: Identify major factors.

Step 2: Identify cause-and-effect relationships.

Step 3: Characterize the relationships as direct or inverse.

Step 4: Diagram the relationships.

Step 5: Analyze the behavior of the relationships as an integrated system.

Let's take the steps one at a time. First, we identify the key elements—the major factors—of the situation. (Note: We are concerned in causal flow diagramming only with *dynamic* factors, those that expand and contract, rise and fall, etc.) Let's consider five major factors in a typical large manufacturing business: sales, profits, research and development, marketing of new products, and competitors' marketing of comparable products. (This is, of course, an oversimplified representation. There are many other factors involved, but I am using these five simply to demonstrate the technique.)

The second step is to identify the cause-and-effect linkages among the factors. To do that we use a two-column "Cause-and-Effect Table" (Figure 7-1). In the left-hand column we list the causal factors, in the right-hand column the affected factors.

Sales affect profits. Profits affect R&D capability. R&D capability affects the marketing of new products. Marketing of new products affects competitors' marketing of comparable new products. The marketing of competitive new products affects sales.

The third step is to characterize these cause-and-effect relationships as *direct* or *inverse*. If the affected factor *increases* as the causal factor

FIGURE 7-1    Cause-and-Effect Table

| Causal Factor | Affected Factor |
|---|---|
| Sales | Profits |
| Profits | R&D capability |
| R&D capability | Marketing of new products |
| Marketing of new products | Competitors' marketing of new products |
| Competitors' marketing of new products | Sales |

*increases* and *decreases* as the causal factor *decreases*, we have a *direct relationship* (Figure 7-2).

If, in the opposite case, the affected factor *increases* as the causal factor *decreases* and *decreases* as the causal factor *increases*, we have an *inverse relationship* (Figure 7-3).

We indicate a direct relationship with a "D" and an inverse relationship with an "I" (Figure 7-4).

In the fourth step we portray these linkages in a *causal flow diagram* (Figure 7-5). I recommend drawing a circle around each of the factors to highlight them visually, accentuating their distinctiveness.

The most powerful driving force in any cause-and-effect scheme is the so-called *feedback loop* in which two or more factors are linked circularly in continuous interaction. The behavior of a feedback loop is significant and predictable. If, as in Figure 7-6, all of the linkages are direct relationships, or if there is an *even number* of inverse linkages, the loop is inherently unstable and will eventually spiral out of control—*in*

FIGURE 7-2    Direct Relationship

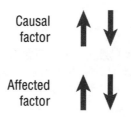

Causal
factor

Affected
factor

**FIGURE 7-3**   Inverse Relationship

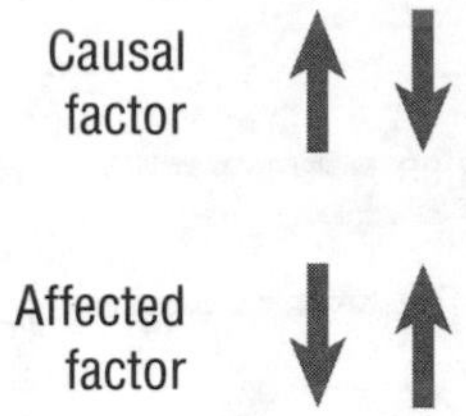

*either direction.* If sales increase, profits increase, R&D increases, marketing of new products increases, causing a further increase in sales, and so on. A "(U)" signifies an unstable feedback loop.

If there is an *odd number* of inverse linkages, as in Figure 7-7, the loop is inherently self-stabilizing and will achieve equilibrium at some point. If sales *increase*, profits *increase*, R&D *increases*, and marketing of new products *increases*; but competitors' marketing of new products also

**FIGURE 7-4**

| Causal Factor | Affected Factor |
| --- | --- |

Sales ▬▬ D ➤ Profits
*(Direct relationship: if sales increase, profits increase;*
*if sales decrease, profits decrease.)*

Profits ▬▬ D ➤ R&D capability
*(Direct relationship)*

R&D capability ▬▬ D ➤ Marketing of new products
*(Direct relationship)*

Marketing of new products ▬▬ D ➤ Competitors' marketing
of new products
*(Direct relationship)*

Competitors' marketing
of new products ▬▬ I ➤ Sales
*(Inverse relationship: if competitors increase marketing*
*of comparable new products, sales decrease; if competitors*
*decrease marketing of such products, sales increase.)*

**FIGURE 7-5** Causal Flow Diagram

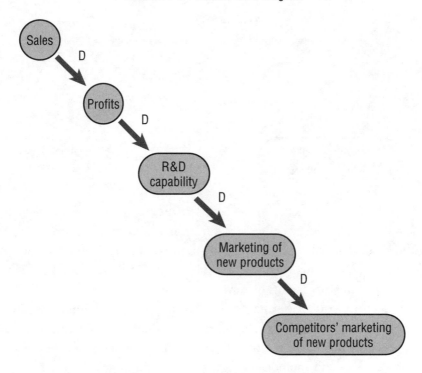

*increases* and sales *decrease*. When sales *decrease*, so do profits, R&D, marketing of new products, and competitors' marketing of new products, resulting in *increased* sales. And so the causal flow interactions increase and decrease cyclically. An "(SS)" signifies a self-stabilizing feedback loop.

**FIGURE 7-6**

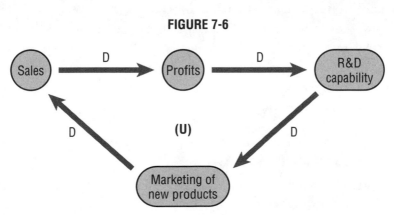

**FIGURE 7-7**   Self-Stabilizing Feedback Loop

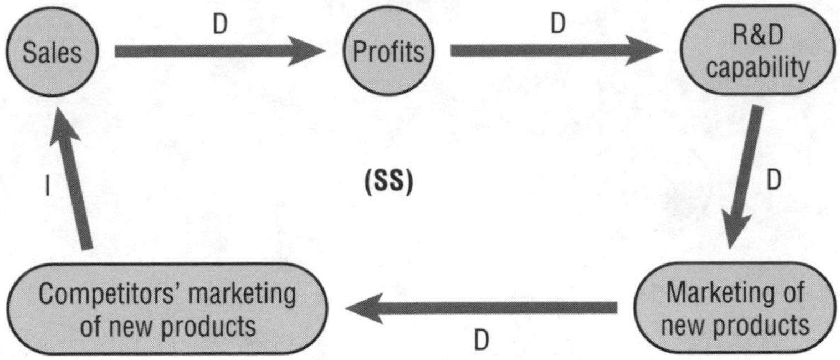

In the fifth and final step we analyze the behavior of the system as an integrated whole, seeking to determine which factors are the most influential. And when a problem occurs, we analyze which factor is creating the problem and how the problem might be resolved by modifying or eliminating factors or introducing new ones.

One way (sort of a sanity check) of validating whether we have accurately portrayed the cause-and-effect relationships is to add a value of +1 to any factor and see how this increment affects the system as a whole. Let's try this method on Figure 7-7, beginning with "sales."

If we increase the value of "sales" by 1, the value of "profits" increases by 1 because there is a direct relationship between the two factors (Figure 7-8). "R&D capability" then also increases by 1, as do "marketing of new products" and "competitors' marketing of new products." But then the value of "sales" decreases by 1 because of its inverse relationship with "competitors' marketing of new products." This decrease starts a new cycle, decreasing the value of each of the other factors by one, which causes the value of "sales" to increase by one, triggering yet another cycle. Figure 7-8 shows how the value of each factor alternates between positive and negative, reflecting the self-stabilizing nature of this feedback loop.

## EXERCISE 9   Parking Spaces

Construct a causal flow diagram for the following situation, indicating with "D" or "I" whether the cause-and-effect relationships are direct or

**FIGURE 7-8**

|  | First Cycle | Second Cycle | Third Cycle |
|---|---|---|---|
| Sales | +1 | −1 | +1 |
| Profits | +1 | −1 | +1 |
| R&D capability | +1 | −1 | +1 |
| Marketing of new products | +1 | −1 | +1 |
| Competitors' marketing of new products | +1 | −1 | +1 |

inverse and identifying any feedback loop(s) as unstable (U) or self-stabilizing (SS):

> With the expectation of increasing its clientele and thus its sales, a shopping mall in the suburb of a large city enlarged an area of the mall's parking lot located near a subway station used regularly by commuters to and from the city. Commuters who did not shop at the mall parked their cars in the new lot, greatly reducing the spaces available to shoppers. As a consequence, the slight increase in sales generated by the new parking spaces did not offset the cost of construction. So the mall constructed more parking areas, but again commuters used up most of the spaces.

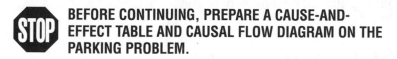 **BEFORE CONTINUING, PREPARE A CAUSE-AND-EFFECT TABLE AND CAUSAL FLOW DIAGRAM ON THE PARKING PROBLEM.**

The solution to Exercise 9 shows one representation of these cause-and-effect relationships. As space for public parking at the mall increases, nonshopping commuters make greater use of mall parking (direct relationship), parking spaces available to shoppers decrease (inverse relationship), sales by stores in the mall decrease (direct relationship), and construction of new public parking spaces increases (inverse relationship). This is an unstable feedback loop indicating that the problem will continue to worsen until it ultimately reaches a crisis stage.

### EXERCISE 10    Algona Pollution II

Portray in two stages the causal flow dynamics of the "Algona Pollution" problem (Exercise 2 on page 52). First, prepare a cause-and-effect table listing the major factors, showing how they interacted with one another, and indicating whether those relationships were of a direct or inverse nature. Second, construct a causal flow diagram illustrating these relationships.

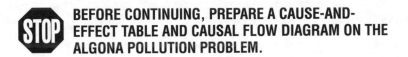 **BEFORE CONTINUING, PREPARE A CAUSE-AND-EFFECT TABLE AND CAUSAL FLOW DIAGRAM ON THE ALGONA POLLUTION PROBLEM.**

The solution to Exercise 10 presents my interpretations. Each major dynamic factor from "toxic effluents" through "corrective action by Algona management" interacts, one to the next, in a direct relationship. The link, however, between "corrective action by Algona management" and "toxic effluents" is an *inverse* relationship. Thus, we have a self-stabilizing feedback loop. The *more* pressure mounts on Algona management to take corrective action to clean up the effluents, the *more* corrective action it takes, and the *fewer* effluents there are. The *fewer* effluents, the *less* contamination, and so on.

### EXERCISE 11    Starvation in Somalia

Try your hand at diagramming the starvation scenario in Somalia in 1983–84. Consider four major factors: starvation, media coverage, foreign assistance, and local warlords profiteering from the foreign assistance. Link the four factors together in a feedback loop and annotate the linkages with a "D" or "I" to indicate direct or inverse relationships. Is this a stable or unstable loop?

### BEFORE CONTINUING, DRAW ON A PIECE OF PAPER A CAUSAL FLOW DIAGRAM LINKING THE FOUR FACTORS.

Part 1 of the solution to Exercise 11 shows what you should have drawn. As all of the linkages are direct relationships, the loop is unstable and, as history showed, spiraled out of control. The diagram shows that as starvation increased, media coverage increased, prompting increased foreign assistance and warlord profiteering, resulting in increased starvation, increased media coverage, and so on.

Now revise the diagram to include three additional factors:

The presence of aid workers

Violent attacks on aid workers by warlord forces

The presence of U.S. military forces

Identify as many feedback loops as you can, and indicate whether the linkages are direct or inverse relationships. What is the overall impact on the situation of the inclusion of these three factors?

### BEFORE CONTINUING, REVISE THE DIAGRAM.

There are countless different ways to diagram cause-and-effect relationships. Part 2 of the solution to Exercise 11 presents one rendition of the Somalia situation. The diagram identifies four feedback loops:

### Self-stabilizing

Starvation

    Media coverage

        Foreign assistance

           Starvation

Starvation
> Media coverage
>> Foreign assistance
>>> Aid workers present
>>>> Warlord attacks on aid workers
>>>> U.S. military presence
>>>>> Warlord profiteering
>>>>>> Starvation

Warlord attacks on aid workers
> U.S. military presence
>> Warlord attacks on aid workers

### *Unstable*

Starvation
> Media coverage
>> Foreign assistance
>>> Warlord profiteering
>>>> Starvation

Note that foreign assistance and U.S. military presence have opposite relationships with warlord profiteering. This had a stabilizing effect on warlord profiteering and on the situation as a whole. However, the deaths of a number of U.S. servicemen with the peacekeeping forces in Somalia ultimately led to the withdrawal of U.S. forces. How would you diagram the factor "U.S. military fatalities"?

 **BEFORE CONTINUING, REVISE THE DIAGRAM.**

Part 3 shows how I would diagram "U.S. military fatalities." As warlord attacks increased, U.S. military fatalities increased, causing a reduction in U.S. military presence. (The deaths led to strong U.S. public and congressional disenchantment with the U.S. administration's policy in Somalia and prompted the eventual withdrawal of U.S. forces.) This reduction emboldened the warlords, who increased their attacks on workers and U.S. military forces, causing further casualties. This was an unstable feedback loop.

In the larger picture, the reduction in U.S. military presence encouraged increased profiteering by the warlords, causing increased starvation, and so on. The feedback loop linking all eight factors was thus rendered unstable.

# Summary

Causal flow diagramming does for a problem-solving analyst what disassembling a wristwatch does for a watch repairman. The repairman lays out on his workbench all of the watch's components so he can (1) understand the internal mechanisms and how each piece interacts with the others, (2) determine what is causing the watch to malfunction, and (3) identify ways to repair it.

A causal flow diagram likewise establishes a visual framework—a structure—within which to analyze separately, systematically, and sufficiently the major factors—the engines—that drive a problem. The causal flow diagram:

☐ Identifies the major dynamic forces—the engines—that drive a situation, how they interact, and whether these interactions are direct or inverse relationships or form feedback loops.
☐ Enables us to view these cause-and-effect relationships as an integrated system and to discover linkages that were either dimly understood or obscured altogether.
☐ Facilitates our determining the source(s) of the problem.
☐ Enables us to conceive of alternative corrective measures and to estimate what their respective effects would be.

Causal flow diagrams can be particularly helpful in bringing to light how different analysts working on the same problem view it. If each analyst constructs a diagram representing the causal flow system and submits it to the others for study and comparison, the ensuing discussion will quickly and clearly reveal how and where their perceptions differ and what their underlying assumptions are. This knowledge will greatly enhance understanding of the problem and of possible solutions.

Causal flow diagramming is, of course, a form of modeling and can be as simplistic or complex as the analyst desires. I prefer to make such diagrams only as complicated as needed to understand the major forces at work. Going beyond that, albeit interesting and even entertaining, can be counterproductive, making the analyst aware of intricate causal relationships that, while perhaps accurate (but perhaps not), add only complexity and ambiguity to the overall picture.

Keep in mind that the principal purpose of diagramming is to establish a basic structure for analyzing the major driving factors, not to replicate in precise detail every dynamic of the problem situation. What we are seeking is insights into possible solutions. Once we acquire those insights, the diagram has served its purpose and may be set aside.

If, on the other hand, you have need of a diagram that portrays in detail the inner workings of the problem situation, indicating how the system as a whole reacts to changes in one factor or in a combination of factors, I recommend you look to literature and training courses in the field of operations research.

# 8
# The Matrix

Read the following problem and answer the questions.

## EXERCISE 12   The Bakery*

A few days before Thanksgiving—the busiest grocery shopping period of the year—a bakery that produces specially prepared bread with a unique blend of ingredients for several grocery chains is having serious problems. Scores of loaves are emerging from the ovens either burned or dark and crusty. In either case, the loaves are worthless.

This bread is produced by three crews of workers, all of whom work the late shift from 4:00 P.M. till midnight. Each crew is responsible for preparing its own dough and is equipped with its own set of five large gas ovens which are used in sequence as the dough is prepared. Each oven has a capacity of fifty loaves. Each crew produces ten batches of bread, fifty loaves in a batch. It takes five hours to produce a batch: four hours for mixing, kneading, and rising and one hour for baking. One batch is begun every hour for the first five hours of work. A crew on the midnight-to-8:00 A.M. shift packages the loaves for delivery.

---

*The bakery described in this problem is entirely fictitious. For illustrative purposes, liberties have been taken with bakery processes.

Ted Swanson, the bakery's production manager, became aware of the problem at 11:00 P.M., when he heard Fernando Rodriguez, the baker of Crew 1, shouting and cursing. Swanson rushed out of his office and found the baker and his seven-person crew frantically hauling bread pans out of an oven and emptying their blackened contents into several large garbage cans.

"What the hell's going on, Fernie?"

"Do you see this?" yelled the baker, his face red with anger. "They're all burned! Every damn one of them! All fifty loaves!"

"What happened?" asked Swanson.

"Damned if I know. The oven is set at three hundred fifty degrees, right on the button, and when we put the pans in an hour ago the dough looked fine."

Wanda Parnell, who ran the warehouse, had been attracted by the commotion and came out of her office to see what was going on. She literally smelled trouble and, being the bakery's union representative, liked to keep herself informed when problems arose.

"Maybe the thermostat is malfunctioning," said Swanson. "I'll call the service company and have them send someone over to check it out. Which oven is it, number three?"

"Yeah." Fernie continued working with his crew, pulling pans of blackened loaves from the oven and slamming them down noisily onto a wide stainless steel table. "This has never happened to me before. Never!"

Swanson patted him on the shoulder. "Don't worry about it. There's a first time for everything. Chalk it up to experience." Swanson turned to leave. "Let me know what the serviceman says. In the meantime, let's turn off that oven. If it's acting up, we'll need to fix it right away. We can't afford downtime during the Thanksgiving rush."

As Swanson entered his office, Henry Willis, the bakery manager, hailed him from the adjoining room. "Hey, Ted! What's all the ruckus about?"

"Oh, nothing. Fernie's crew burned a batch of bread."

"That's not like them," said the manager, frowning. "What happened?"

"Don't know. I'm having the oven's thermostat checked. I'll let you know what they find."

"Did you shut the oven down?"

"Yep, until we determine if it's the thermostat."

"Is this going to cause a problem meeting orders?"

"It shouldn't. Even if the thermostat is bad, you know we can replace it in ten minutes and have the oven back up and running in another twenty."

"All right," said Willis. "Keep me posted."

"You got it."

Twenty-five minutes later the oven technician arrived, checked the oven's heat control mechanism, and reported there was nothing wrong with it. Willis, Swanson, and Rodriguez discussed the matter briefly and decided to reheat the oven and bake another batch to replace the burned loaves.

Shortly after midnight, Wanda Parnell bolted into Swanson's office. "Ted, you better come and see this!"

"What is it?" Swanson sprang from his chair and followed Parnell out into the bakery.

"Crew One overbaked another batch, and now Crew Three has done it, too, though not as bad."

The two jogged past the Crew 1 area, where Fernie and his people were again hauling out blackened loaves, and arrived at the Crew 3 area. There they found Bobby Lanham, the crew's baker, glowering, his hands clasped behind him, silently shaking his head, looking over worktables covered with fifty pans of hot bread just removed from Crew 3's number four oven.

"What's the problem, Bobby?" asked Swanson.

"Overbaked 'em. I can't explain it. Fernie's burned two batches, and now I've almost done the same. They aren't burned like his, but they're too crusty to ship to the stores. Okay with you to pitch 'em?"

"Might as well," said Swanson with obvious resignation.

At that moment Willis joined them. "Another ruined batch?" he said, gazing unhappily at the dark brown loaves.

"Three batches," replied Swanson, pointing to Fernie's area.

"Three!" he exclaimed. "What the hell is going on around here?" The look on his face and the inflection and tone of his voice implied he suspected these were not accidents or oversights.

The others looked at him, first with surprise, then with a mixture of concern and resentment. "We don't know yet," said Swanson, "but we've gotta find out pronto." He started walking toward his office. "I'm calling the technician back here. There's got to be something wrong with these ovens. Maybe the gas pressure's fluctuating. Let's shut both those ovens down, and don't reheat Crew One's number three. We need some answers first."

Twenty minutes later, Willis entered Swanson's office and sat down. "I don't like it, Ted. Not one bit. Something's going on here. Experienced bakers don't *accidentally* overbake bread. Not like this. Not three batches."

"What are you suggesting? Sabotage?"

"Not suggesting. Declaring!"

"Impossible! Fernie and Bobby would never do that."

"Oh, yeah? Bobby's a hothead and has made his unhappiness with my management very clear over the past few weeks, and he and Fernie are best friends."

Swanson could not take issue with either point. The Bakery Workers Union had been putting a lot of pressure on Willis concerning the contract renegotiations in two weeks. In a meeting with Willis and Swanson just two days before, Wanda Parnell had presented the union's demands for a significant increase in employee benefits including additional sick leave. Willis had been dead set against granting any further benefits, insisting the company couldn't afford it.

Willis continued, "What better time to foul things up than just before Thanksgiving? I'd fire the both of them if I had proof."

"There could be other explanations," said Swanson.

"Like what?"

"You know bread making. Could be the oven racks turning too slowly, too much voltage to the oven blowers, maybe bad yeast or other stale ingredients. Lots of things the bakers have no control over."

"All right. Let's look at the facts. Bobby's been wound up tight as a drum ever since I fired Juan Menendez two weeks ago for being drunk on the job. That was the third time I caught him. I had warned him twice before, but the third time . . . that was the last straw. So Bobby keeps yammering about no evidence, no blood test, like I was a cop who arrested

Menendez for drunk driving and forgot to read him his rights. This is a business, not a police station. And I know a drunk when I see one. Now Bobby's got the crews all steamed up about it, including Fernie."

"Okay, you're right about Fernie," said Swanson. "He *has* spoken to me a few times about Menendez, but always polite and reasonable, not high-strung like Bobby."

"And didn't Fernie help Bobby hold a special union meeting over the weekend to discuss the benefits package? Remember what one of the guys on Crew One said to you Monday?"

"I remember. 'The union's gonna get the new benefits come hell or high water.' "

"Right. It wouldn't surprise me if Crew Two burns the next batch. Union people call it *solidarity!*"

"Oh, come on, Hank. Frank Moreau? Neither he nor anyone on his crew would deliberately do such a thing. Frank is antiunion."

"But still a union member!" said Willis, shaking his finger.

"Frank explained all that. He *had* to join if he was to build team-work on his crew."

"Baloney. I was a baker for ten years, and I never felt obliged to join the damn union."

"Times are different."

"Did you know Menendez was here yesterday?"

"No! Where?"

"Behind the bakery in the parking lot. And guess who I saw him talking to!"

Swanson shrugged.

"Frank Moreau. What do you make of that little rendezvous?"

Swanson was shocked and remained silent for a moment. Then he got up. "I'm gonna check on the ovens. The technician is looking at them right now. I'll speak with Frank about all this."

"While you're at it," said Willis smirking, "ask him how his *leg* is."

"His leg? What's wrong with it?"

"He claims he dropped a sack of flour on his foot this morning unloading that shipment from the new supplier. Nothing broken, he said, but he was limping badly . . . or pretending to limp. Maybe he'll file for workers' comp."

Swanson shot him a disdainful look and departed.

Swanson found Frank in the Crew 2 area checking the temperature gauges on his ovens. "So what's your opinion, Frank? Are the gauges going funny?"

"Nope. The service guy just finished his tests. The gauges are fine and so are the rack and blower mechanisms. And if the problem was pressure fluctuations on the gas lines, then *all* of the ovens would have been affected."

"How's the leg?"

"Could be better. Damn sacks. I was helping Wanda unload the truck this morning. She usually forklifts the entire load into the warehouse, but at the end of our shift yesterday Bobby gave her all kinds of hell because there was no more flour. With the Thanksgiving rush and one sack for every two batches, it's a wonder we didn't run out sooner. So I helped her move some sacks directly to the crew areas so each would have enough for the day's baking."

"Any problems?"

"Nope, but I don't recommend dropping one of those hundred-pound babies on your foot. The shipment arrived just in time. It was two days late, you know." Moreau laughed. "Did Willis think the union was behind the delay? Like maybe someone pulled strings with the teamsters?"

Swanson shook his head and frowned. "Of course not." But he knew Moreau was right. Willis suspected union interference.

"I'll bet he *did.* It was a close call. Like always, we use up old ingredients before starting with the new. When we finished yesterday, I had two of the old sacks left, Bobby was down to one and a half, and Fernie had only one. I could see Willis pacing up and down in his office yelling into the phone to the shipper. Willis knew we were right on the edge of disaster. He probably thinks we planned to run short just to make his life miserable."

"Can you blame him? It's Thanksgiving, our busiest time."

"I suppose not. But the mood around here is pretty nasty. I don't think the crews would feel sorry for Willis if this place were shut down for a day or so."

"Whaddaya mean by that?" Swanson was shocked. It sounded like a threat.

"I mean people are angry. They don't get the standard benefits other bakeries give."

"Are you siding with the union on this thing?"

Moreau scowled. "What's the union got to do with it? I thought we were talking about the mood around here. People want what they think they're entitled to. The union's just taking advantage of it, like unions always do. You know I'm not fond of unions. But the facts are the facts. Willis better wake up or he's going to have real problems, and his firing Menendez didn't help the situation."

"Are there really hard feelings about the Menendez thing?"

"Naturally. He was very popular with the crews. And he was older, kind of a father figure for some of the younger people. Willis should have thought of that."

"I hear Menendez stopped by here yesterday. Did you talk to him?"

"Would it make a difference if I did?"

"That depends on what you talked about."

"Well, for your information, we just talked. Nothing special."

"Did he talk with anyone else?"

"Look, Ted, I'm not your informant. If you want to know that, ask them." Moreau abruptly turned his back and redirected his attention to the ovens.

Swanson checked his watch. It was a quarter of one. He hurried away to talk with Willis.

What's the problem? What caused the three batches to be overbaked? What was behind it? Was it accidental or intentional? What do you think? On a sheet of paper write what you think "the problem" is. *Don't write more than one problem statement!*

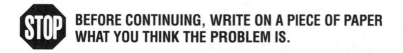 **BEFORE CONTINUING, WRITE ON A PIECE OF PAPER WHAT YOU THINK THE PROBLEM IS.**

Most people who work a problem of this type do all of the analysis in their heads, thinking it through, reasoning out the different possible explanations, and focusing on the first one they can confidently defend.

But would they *structure* their analysis? Probably not, because, as I said in the beginning of this book, most people don't know how. Let me show you how to structure the analysis of "The Bakery" problem.

First, we think of as many different explanations as we can for the bread being overcooked. We call that *diverging*. We then sort the explanations (cluster them) into definable groups, which we'll call categories, for want of a better term. As we analyze the situation, we discern four fundamental categories: human, mechanical, materials, and combinations thereof. We also discern ten basic explanations (you may have thought up more), which I have listed below by category:

### *Human*
- ☐ Sabotage
- ☐ Careless error
- ☐ Fatigue
- ☐ Drunkenness
- ☐ Flaws in the work plan

### *Mechanical*
- ☐ Malfunctioning of the oven temperature gauge
- ☐ Malfunctioning of the rotating oven racks
- ☐ Malfunctioning of the oven blower
- ☐ Malfunctioning of the gas pressure gauge

### *Materials*
- ☐ Spoiled or otherwise unsuitable ingredients

### *Combinations* (of the three categories above)

Let's examine each category. Remember, that's what *structuring analysis* does: it enables us to analyze each element of a problem *separately*, *systematically*, and *sufficiently*.

In the "Human" category, the text did not furnish any information upon which to conclude that carelessness, fatigue, drunkenness, or flaws in the work routine would explain the overbaking. To consider these possibilities, we need to gather more information. There is, however, plenty of evidence to support *sabotage*. One could spin a number of plausible scenarios involving the bakery's angry, disgruntled employ-ees. That's what Willis was doing. He focused on sabotage as the expla-nation and was interpreting each new event through the prism of that bias.

The text essentially ruled out the "Mechanical" category, but here again we could probably benefit from gathering more information.

There were a number of references, of course, to "Materials": the ingredients used to make the bread. Three ingredients were mentioned: milk and yeast (but only once each) and flour (numerous times). What did the text say about flour?

☐ As a matter of practice, the crews used up old ingredients (in this case, flour) before starting with the new.
☐ At close of business the day before, there was no flour in the ware-house, and the crews would not have had enough that day had a shipment not been delivered that morning. Crew 1 had one sack of flour left, Crew 2 had two, and Crew 3 had one and a half.
☐ The shipment of flour that arrived that morning was from a *new* supplier.
☐ The shipment was two days late; it arrived just in time.
☐ Moreau helped Wanda Parnell move some sacks directly to the crew areas so each crew would have enough for the day's baking.
☐ Each batch of bread consumed one-half sack of flour.

Could using the new flour explain the overbaked loaves? It's con-ceivable there was something wrong with the flour delivered that morn-ing from the new supplier. We can find out by determining whether there was a correlation between use of the new flour and the incidents of overbaking. To analyze this question, I have constructed chronolo-gies using a *matrix*.

# What's a Matrix?

As shown in Figure 8-1, a matrix is nothing more than a grid with as many cells as needed for whatever problem is being analyzed. A matrix is one of the handiest, clearest methods of sorting information. Anytime

FIGURE 8-1

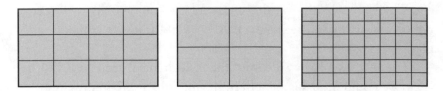

I can reduce information to a matrix, I find it analytically illuminating. Like sorting pieces of a jigsaw puzzle, a matrix enables us, among other things, to:

☐ Separate elements of a problem
☐ Categorize information by type
☐ Compare one type of information with another
☐ Compare pieces of information of the same type
☐ See correlations (patterns) among the information

The matrices in Figures 8-2 through 8-4 show when each crew started each of its first five batches, when each batch was removed from an oven, and which batches used the new flour. Each crew prepared one batch every hour, using its ovens sequentially.

As Figure 8-2 indicates, Crew 1 had one sack of old flour left when work began at 4:00 P.M. It used that sack for its first and second batches (each batch required a half sack of flour). That means the third batch

FIGURE 8-2    Batch Chronology: Crew 1

| Batch/Oven | Time | | | | | | | | | |
|---|---|---|---|---|---|---|---|---|---|---|
| | 4 P.M. | 5 P.M. | 6 P.M. | 7 P.M. | 8 P.M. | 9 P.M. | 10 P.M. | 11 P.M. | 12 A.M. | 1 A.M. |
| 1/1 | ├─── Old flour ───┤ | | | | | | | | | |
| 2/2 | | ├─── Old flour ───┤ | | | | | | | | |
| 3/3 | | | ├─── New flour ───┤ | | | | | | | |
| 4/4 | | | | ├─── New flour ───┤ | | | | | | |
| 5/5 | | | | | ├─── New flour ───┤ | | | | | |

(begun at 6:00 P.M.) and each subsequent batch used the new flour. Crew 1's first and second batches (with the old flour) came out all right, but the third and fourth (using the new flour), removed from the ovens at 11:00 P.M. and midnight, were overbaked. This pattern is consistent with the new flour's causing the overbaking.

Crew 2 (Figure 8-3) had two sacks of old flour. It didn't begin using the new flour until the fifth batch at 8:00 P.M. If that batch were overbaked, it wouldn't be known until the loaves were removed at 1:00 A.M. Nevertheless, this pattern is consistent with the new flour being the source of the problem.

Crew 3 (Figure 8-4) had one and a half sacks of old flour when work began at 4:00 P.M. It used up those sacks on the first three batches. The dough for the fourth and fifth batches used the new flour. The fourth batch, which was begun at 7:00 P.M. and removed at midnight, was overbaked. This pattern, too, is consistent with the new flour being the source of the problem.

On the basis of these three chronologies, we can conclude with high confidence that the new flour is very likely the cause of the overbaking. Tests of the flour are needed to confirm this finding.

What did you think the problem was? Very few people consider the flour to be the culprit. Most believe that sabotage is *probably* behind the overbaking, and for two reasons: there is plenty of evidence for sabotage, and most people don't know how to use a matrix or a chronology to analyze a problem.

**FIGURE 8-3**  Batch Chronology: Crew 2

| Batch/Oven | Time | | | | | | | | | |
|---|---|---|---|---|---|---|---|---|---|---|
| | 4 P.M. | 5 P.M. | 6 P.M. | 7 P.M. | 8 P.M. | 9 P.M. | 10 P.M. | 11 P.M. | 12 A.M. | 1 A.M. |
| 1/1 | ├──── Old flour ────┤ | | | | | | | | | |
| 2/2 | | ├──── Old flour ────┤ | | | | | | | | |
| 3/3 | | | ├──── Old flour ────┤ | | | | | | | |
| 4/4 | | | | ├──── Old flour ────┤ | | | | | | |
| 5/5 | | | | | ├──── **New flour** ────┤ | | | | | |

**FIGURE 8-4**   Batch Chronology: Crew 3

| Batch/Oven | Time | | | | | | | | | |
|---|---|---|---|---|---|---|---|---|---|---|
| | 4 P.M. | 5 P.M. | 6 P.M. | 7 P.M. | 8 P.M. | 9 P.M. | 10 P.M. | 11 P.M. | 12 A.M. | 1 A.M. |
| 1/1 | ├──── Old flour ────┤ | | | | | | | | | |
| 2/2 | | ├──── Old flour ────┤ | | | | | | | | |
| 3/3 | | | ├──── Old flour ────┤ | | | | | | | |
| 4/4 | | | | ├──── **New flour** ────┤ | | | | | | |
| 5/5 | | | | | ├──── **New flour** ────┤ | | | | | |

There are endless ways of employing a matrix; combining the matrix and chronology techniques is only one. Let's look at another example of how a matrix can facilitate analysis.

## EXERCISE 13   Symptom and Disease

On a sheet of paper create a matrix out of the following information (excerpted from *The Universe Within*):

37 patients with a particular symptom had a disease.

33 patients with the same symptom did not have the disease.

17 patients without the symptom had the disease.

13 patients without the symptom did not have the disease.

This is good practice in constructing a matrix. Don't be upset if you have difficulty doing it. The more you use matrices, the easier it will become.

 **BEFORE CONTINUING, FINISH CONSTRUCTING YOUR MATRIX.**

The matrix should appear as shown in Part 1 of the solution to Exercise 13.

Creating a matrix is a piece of cake once you get the hang of it. See how putting the numerical data into matrix form has the effect of isolating the data so they can be analyzed more easily, both separately and in combination. See how much easier it is to focus on the data when they are in a matrix than when they are presented in sentences?

The question to which these data are to be applied is the following:

Is there a correlation between the symptom and the disease? In medical terms that means: Do people who display the symptom have the disease?

Based on the data in the matrix, what do you think? Think about it for a moment, then write your answer on a sheet of paper.

 **BEFORE CONTINUING, WRITE DOWN YOUR ANSWER.**

When a group of nurses was given this problem, 85 percent of them concluded there *was* a correlation, pointing out that there were more cases with both symptom and disease (37) than in any of the other three categories or that twice as many people had the symptom (37) as didn't (17). But the nurses were wrong! For even among people *without* the disease, about the same majority had the symptom (33 had it, 13 didn't). This becomes clearer when viewed as percentages from the standpoint of symptoms (Part 2 of the solution to Exercise 13). The percentage of those *with* symptom and *with* disease is roughly the same as those *without* symptom and *with* disease. If the proportion is the same in both cases, there's no correlation.

Looked at from the standpoint of disease (Part 3 of the solution to Exercise 13), the percentage of those *with* disease and *with* symptom was roughly comparable to those *without* disease and *with* symptom. Again the numbers are too close: there is no correlation.

Putting the numbers into a matrix allows us to *structure* the analysis of the data easily and meaningfully. Learn to use a matrix. It's a marvelous analytic tool.

Let's do another matrix exercise.

## EXERCISE 14    Hats and Coats

This one is a simple brainteaser and demonstrates graphically how a matrix can help us solve a problem. Here are the clues:

> Smith, Brown, Jones, and Williams had dinner together. When they parted, each of them, by mistake, wore the hat belonging to one other member of the party and the coat belonging to yet another member. The man who took Williams's hat took Jones's coat. Smith took Brown's hat. The hat taken by Jones belonged to the owner of the coat taken by Williams.
>
> Who took Smith's coat?

Try to find the answer by working up a matrix on a sheet of paper.

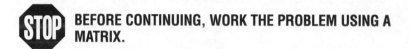 **BEFORE CONTINUING, WORK THE PROBLEM USING A MATRIX.**

Figure 8-5 shows the matrix you should have constructed. Let's work the problem together and see how well you did. Our objective is to identify the four members represented by the numbers 1, 2, 3, and 4. Let's go through the clues and fill out the matrix as we go.

*The man who took Williams's hat took Jones's coat.* So we enter "Williams" in "Hat 1" and "Jones" in "Coat 1" (Figure 8-6). We don't know yet who Member No. 1 is, but we *do* know it is neither Williams nor Jones, because neither could take his own hat or coat. So we place their names at the tops of columns 2 and 3 (Figure 8-7).

*Smith took Brown's hat.* So, Smith, too, cannot be at the top of column 1. Ergo (Figure 8-8), Smith is atop column 4, and Brown is atop column 1. And, of course, Brown goes into "Hat" under "Smith." Since Jones cannot take his own hat, the only hat left for him is Smith's, so (Figure 8-9) Smith goes into "Hat" under "Jones." Ergo, Jones goes into "Hat" under "Williams."

*The hat taken by Jones belonged to the owner of the coat taken by Williams.* The matrix shows that the hat taken by Jones was Smith's. So we have the answer (Figure 8-10): *the coat taken by Williams was Smith's.*

**FIGURE 8-5**

| Member | 1 | 2 | 3 | 4 |
|--------|---|---|---|---|
| Hat | | | | |
| Coat | | | | |

**FIGURE 8-6**

| Member | 1 | 2 | 3 | 4 |
|--------|---|---|---|---|
| Hat | *Williams* | | | |
| Coat | *Jones* | | | |

**FIGURE 8-7**

| Member | 1 | *Williams* | *Jones* | 4 |
|--------|---|------------|---------|---|
| Hat | Williams | | | |
| Coat | Jones | | | |

**FIGURE 8-8**

| Member | *Brown* | Williams | Jones | *Smith* |
|--------|---------|----------|-------|---------|
| Hat | Williams | | | *Brown* |
| Coat | Jones | | | |

**FIGURE 8-9**

| Member | Brown | Williams | Jones | Smith |
|--------|-------|----------|-------|-------|
| Hat | Williams | *Jones* | *Smith* | Brown |
| Coat | Jones | | | |

**FIGURE 8-10**

| Member | Brown | Williams | Jones | Smith |
|--------|-------|----------|-------|-------|
| Hat | Williams | Jones | Smith | Brown |
| Coat | Jones | *Smith* | | |

Wasn't that easy? Could you have done that in your head? I certainly couldn't, and doing it with a matrix is quick and simple.

Just for the fun of it, let's fill in the other two squares. The only coats left for Smith to have taken are Brown's and Williams's, but Smith took Brown's hat, so he had to take another member's coat. That means Smith took Williams's coat. Which leaves Brown's coat for Jones (Figure 8-11).

**FIGURE 8-11**

| Member | Brown | Williams | Jones | Smith |
|--------|-------|----------|-------|-------|
| Hat | Williams | Jones | Smith | Brown |
| Coat | Jones | Smith | **Brown** | **Williams** |

As I said, a matrix is a marvelous analytic structuring tool. Try your hand again at using a matrix on a different problem.

## EXERCISE 15    Weather Forecaster's Dilemma I

If you were a TV weatherperson, which one of the following circumstances would be best from the standpoint of your reputation among viewers as a forecaster? For a normal midweek workday:

☐ You predict it will snow, and it snows.
☐ You predict it will snow, but it doesn't snow.
☐ You predict it will not snow, but it does.
☐ You predict it will not snow, and it doesn't.

Construct a matrix to represent this problem, but don't analyze it! Just construct the matrix.

 **BEFORE CONTINUING, CONSTRUCT THE MATRIX.**

The solution to Exercise 15 shows the matrix you should have constructed. See how nicely the matrix organizes (structures) analysis of the problem? There are four possible outcomes—four cells where the predictions and outcomes intersect. The matrix facilitates our thinking by stripping away the superfluous language that surrounded the key words "snow" and "not snow" in the four sentences. The matrix also juxtaposes these key words in a way that enables us to isolate their connections in the cells and to perceive more easily and clearly the distinctions among them. We will return to this problem later in another analytic context.

## EXERCISE 16    Staff Size

Your personal services budget for next year is currently under review by your organization's leadership. You have requested additional funds with which to enlarge your staff. But funds are tight; you may not be granted an increase. Indeed, your budget could be cut. Complicating matters is your recent request to move your staff to a larger building because your present office space is crowded. Tomorrow at a meeting with management you will defend your request for a larger staff. To prepare your defense, you are holding a meeting today with your five assistants to review the arguments, pro and con, for a larger staff. Construct a matrix that relates the three possible outcomes for your personal services budget to the possibilities of moving to a larger building or remaining in your current offices.

 **BEFORE CONTINUING, CONSTRUCT THE MATRIX.**

The solution to Exercise 16 shows one way of representing this situation in a matrix. Such a matrix, displayed on a screen as a slide or transparency for all of your assistants to see, would facilitate discussion of the six possible scenarios (alternative outcomes) to ensure that the pros and cons of each were analyzed separately, systematically, and sufficiently.

The more you use a matrix in your analysis, the easier it is. I'm so accustomed to using matrices that the first thing I do, when confronted with a problem, is to ask myself how I can represent the problem in a matrix. And I find that, when I can portray it in a matrix, the problem immediately opens itself to analysis, like the petals of a flower opening up to reveal its inner parts. Moreover, displaying a matrix like this one on a screen to guide discussion at a meeting can be extremely helpful.

For good measure, let's do one more matrix problem.

### EXERCISE 17    Candidates for Supervisory Positions

You are to attend a personnel meeting that will consider three candidates for promotion to three supervisory positions. Construct a matrix that relates the three candidates to the three positions.

 **BEFORE CONTINUING, CONSTRUCT THE MATRIX.**

The solution to Exercise 17 is my version of the matrix. Here again the matrix technique facilitates analysis of the nine possible options. By providing a visual means of focusing our mind on each option, one at a time, the matrix enables us to easily compare and rank the employees by their qualifications for each position.

# 9

# The Decision/Event Tree

Another superb structuring technique is what I call a "Decision/Event Tree." A decision/event tree is a diagram that graphically shows choices and their outcomes at different junctures in alternative sequences or chains of events. Each sequence or chain of events is a separate scenario.

The ancient enigma in which a man must choose between two doors, one leading to a beautiful lady, the other to a ravenous tiger, serves admirably to illustrate the decision/event tree (Figure 9-1).

**FIGURE 9-1**   The Lady or the Tiger: Decision/Event Tree

This tree portrays two alternative scenarios, or sequences of events:

*Scenario* A: Chooses door—opens Door 1—gets lady (lives).

*Scenario* B: Chooses door—opens Door 2—gets tiger (dies).

This example demonstrates the two immutable, universal characteristics of a decision/event tree:

**113**

1. The branches of the tree are *mutually exclusive*, meaning that, if the *actor* (the person making the choice) picks Door 1, he can't also pick Door 2. And if he picks Door 1, he gets the lady, not the tiger.
2. The branches are *collectively exhaustive*, meaning that the alternatives at each branch incorporate all possibilities; no other options (other decisions or events) are possible at that point in the sequence or scenario. (There is no third door, nor is there anything other than a lady or a tiger waiting behind the two doors.)

Here's another example of a decision/event tree (Figure 9-2). Make a purchase, buy a raincoat/umbrella, and keep it/return it are all both decisions and events, but repels rain/leaks are events, not decisions.

**FIGURE 9-2** Decision/Event Tree

Let's review the principles involved in constructing and using a decision/event tree by examining another example. This particular diagram (Figure 9-3) portrays an admittedly oversimplified sequence of possible decisions/events following a woman's blind date with a man. Each branch of the tree presents alternative options that are *mutually exclusive* (if we pick one, we can't pick the other) and *collectively exhaustive* (all available options are considered; there are no other possibilities). The diagram represents a total of five alternative scenarios:

1. Go on blind date—date him no more.
2. Go on blind date—date him again—stop dating.
3. Go on blind date—date him again—get engaged—break engagement.
4. Go on blind date—date him again—get engaged—get married—get divorced.

5. Go on blind date—date him again—get engaged—get married—
stay married.

**FIGURE 9-3**   Decision/Event Tree

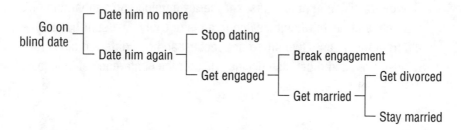

Note that the tip of each branch marks the end of a scenario; there
are five tip ends and five scenarios.

By graphically representing points in a chain of decisions or events,
the decision/event tree enables us to structure analysis of a problem in a
way no other technique offers:

☐   It dissects a scenario into its sequential events.
☐   It shows clearly the cause-and-effect linkages, indicating which
    decisions and events precede and follow others.
☐   It shows which decisions or events are dependent on others.
☐   It shows where the linkages are strongest and weakest.
☐   It enables us to visually compare how one scenario differs from
    another.
☐   Most important of all, it reveals alternatives we might otherwise
    not perceive and enables us to analyze them—separately, systemat-
    ically, and sufficiently.

A decision/event tree is, indeed, a powerful analytic tool. Let me
demonstrate this power with an exercise.

## EXERCISE 18   Executive Leadership Conference

Construct a decision/event tree that portrays all of the possible scenarios to be considered in the following problem:

The administrative staff of a large corporation is planning to conduct an executive leadership conference at one of three locations. The choice of site depends largely on the recreational activities to which attendees would have access. Three sites are under consideration. One offers hiking in mountains, another swimming and sunbathing on a beach, and the third sightseeing in a historic city. The staff has two different mountains, two different beaches, and two different cities to choose from and must also decide whether the conference should last two days or three.

## BEFORE CONTINUING, DRAW YOUR DECISION/EVENT TREE.

The solution to Exercise 18 shows two versions of a tree that incorporates all of the possible scenarios. Without a tree, most staffs would discuss, more likely argue, about which site to pick by hopping back and forth among the options. Some of the options would receive greater attention than others, and some would be ignored altogether. The discussion would be unstructured and thus highly vulnerable to those fallibilities of human reasoning I keep mentioning.

A decision/event tree displayed on a screen for all members of the staff to see simultaneously is a simple, uncomplicated way of structuring such a discussion to ensure that all options are given due consideration. Some options can, of course, be eliminated instantly as undesirable, but even these deserve serious, if only momentary, attention. Other options will require lengthy deliberation. The decision/event tree helps the staff focus its discussion on a single decision or event point. Being able to focus visually on a decision or event helps the mind focus its thinking. Remember: the mind instinctively focuses. Focusing will facilitate and empower the staff's analysis of the alternative conference sites.

Let's look in on the staff members as their discussion to select a conference site begins. Dolores, who is the staff director, runs the meeting. "Before we discuss the sites," she says, "let's address the issue of whether the conference should last two or three days. The duration of the conference could influence our thinking about which site and which form of recreation are preferable."

The group discusses the relative importance of the length of the conference and determines that the decision on length should be based solely on the time needed to cover the subjects on the conference agenda. Recreational considerations are secondary.

"That being the case," says Dolores, who is versed in analytic structuring techniques, "let's use this tree to structure our discussion." She projects the decision tree from Part 1 of the solution from a transparency onto a screen facing the staff members.

Discerning that the PROs-CONs-and-FIXes technique is well suited for this discussion, Dolores asks the staffers, "What are the pros and cons of a two-day conference?" The group quickly identifies a dozen positive aspects and a number of negatives and then thinks of several ways to offset the negatives. Dolores lists all of these items on flip charts.

"Two days is long enough to get in some great hiking," says Tom, an outdoors enthusiast.

"I'm sure it is," says Dolores smiling, "but let's keep focused on the issue of two or three days. We'll get to hiking in a minute. Okay?"

"No problem," replies Tom.

Dolores now shifts the focus. "What are the pros and cons of a three-day conference?"

The group generates lists of positives and negatives and ways of eliminating or neutralizing the negatives.

"So," says Dolores, "it appears there is unanimous support for three days." The members all nod in agreement. "Okay, let's eliminate the two-day option." As all members of the staff watch the screen, she marks the transparency with a large black felt-tip pen, crossing out the branch of the tree flowing from "2 days."

"As you can all see, there are three sites: one in the mountains, one on the seashore, and one in the city. Let's first discuss hiking in the mountains as the principal form of recreation during the conference."

"Mountain A would be perfect for hiking," says Bill, eager to support the hiking option. "I've been there a number of times. We could—"

"Please hold that thought," says Dolores, cutting him off. "It sounds like a good one, but first I want us to keep focused on the three basic forms of recreation we're dealing with."

"Please do," replies Bill. "I'll reserve my support for Mountain A for later."

"Good. Now let's consider the pros and cons of hiking."

The participants quickly generate the incentives and disincentives of hiking for the executives who will be attending the conference. One of the major negatives is the long-range weather forecast predicting rain and heavy cloud cover for the appointed days of the conference. "Sightseeing," says George, "would be more suitable in that kind of weather. It goes without saying that—"

Again Dolores interrupts. "Excuse me, George, but I'd like to defer discussion of sightseeing until we've exhausted our thoughts on hiking and swimming. We'll get to sightseeing in a moment. Please make your point about the weather at that time. Thank you."

Now the group turns its attention first to swimming and sunbathing and then to sightseeing, discussing the pros and cons of each and thinking of viable ways of offsetting the negatives.

"All right, then," says Dolores, "the sentiment, after considering the pros and cons of each alternative recreation, appears to be leaning toward swimming and sunbathing. Does anyone disagree?" All members shake their heads. "Okay, let's eliminate hiking and sightseeing." Again, as the members watch the screen, Dolores crosses out the branches of the tree flowing from "Hiking" and "Sightseeing." All that remains for discussion are "Beach A" and "Beach B." A brief discussion of the pros and cons of each results in a unanimous decision to eliminate Beach B. Thus the staff selects Beach A for a three-day conference.

If no tree had been used, Dolores would have had a more difficult time focusing the thinking of all staff members on one option at a time and eliminating options from consideration. The tree enabled the staff to consider each option *separately* and *systematically* and to narrow the choices by *visually* eliminating those that didn't meet the needs of the conference.

Think for a moment of instances in your own work or personal life when using a decision/event tree would have been helpful and where it might be helpful in the future.

### EXERCISE 19   Securities Investment I

Construct a decision/event tree to structure the following problem:

> Your company is planning to invest a goodly sum of money in stocks or bonds. Three options are under consideration: high-risk, high-return stocks (HI/HI); medium-risk, medium-return stocks (MED/MED); and no-risk, low-return bonds (NO/LOW). Looking ahead, the company foresees four major developments that will affect the viability and profitability of each of these three investment opportunities: war or peace, and prosperity or depression.

 **BEFORE CONTINUING, DRAW YOUR DECISION/EVENT TREE.**

The solution to Exercise 19 is one rendition of the tree. I'm always amused by people who reject using such a structuring technique on the grounds that it's too complicated. Do they mean to say that analyzing this problem in their heads is *less* complicated? The truth is, as I mentioned earlier—and it bears repeating—the human mind doesn't like to be structured. It prefers to operate as a free spirit, jumping compulsively from one thought to another . . . *just messing around.* The inevitable result is that some of the scenarios depicted in the tree above would never be considered, and that is precisely the deficiency in human problem solving that the structuring techniques in this book remedy.

You may be wondering how one would use this tree to analyze and determine which of the investment options is best. I explain how in Exercise 42 in Chapter 14. For now, let's stay focused on the technique of constructing the tree itself. To that end, let's do another exercise.

## EXERCISE 20   Disgruntled Employee

A middle-aged employee of a large manufacturing plant was fired, allegedly because of unsatisfactory performance. A week later, armed with an automatic rifle, he returned to the plant and shot his former supervisor to death. The employee was arrested and indicted for premeditated murder, to which he pleaded innocent by reason of temporary insanity. Three issues dominated his trial: (1) whether he was by nature prone to be violent, (2) whether the supervisor's allegedly cruel and unwarranted treatment of him could have destabilized his mind, and (3) whether he was, from the moment he seized the rifle until he killed the supervisor, in such a state of dementia that he was unaware of his actions and unable to distinguish right from wrong. Construct a decision/event tree to represent these three issues.

 **BEFORE TURNING THE PAGE,
DRAW YOUR DECISION/EVENT TREE.**

Part 1 of the solution to Exercise 20 shows my rendition of the tree. This tree does exactly what structuring is supposed to do: it separates the elements of the problem in an organized way so that we can see and analyze each element separately. It allows us to view the entire range of possible scenarios at a glance. There is absolutely no other way to do this without such a diagram. Doing it in one's head is virtually impossible.

Whether we are the defense lawyer or the prosecutor, this diagram serves as a guide for our strategy, showing us—given whatever evidence there is for and against our position—where our strengths and weaknesses are.

Settling the issue of the employee's violent nature ("prone to violence") was vital to both sides, for the outcome in either case eliminates four scenarios, or half of the tree. As it happened, the defense proved conclusively that the defendant was a quiet, peaceful, law-abiding person not normally prone to violence. Consequently, the tree at that point could be revised as in Part 2.

Subsequently, the defense presented compelling evidence that the supervisor's treatment of the employee had been so cruel and unwarranted that it could have caused temporary derangement. Now the tree could be revised as in Part 3.

The verdict thus hinged on whether the defense could persuade the jury that at the time of the incident the employee was so deranged he was unaware of his actions and unable to distinguish right from wrong. The jury was so persuaded and consequently found him innocent.

## EXERCISE 21   Survey of Workers

This problem is more difficult to diagram in a tree than the previous three, so be creative. Try more than one design. It usually takes me three or four tries before I figure out how to depict a complex problem in a tree. Our aim, as with every other structuring technique, is to construct a tree that facilitates analysis of the problem. Different tree designs yield different insights. Which tree design is "best" depends entirely upon what the analyst is seeking to determine. Read the following article and construct a decision/event tree that illustrates alternative scenarios related to some important aspect of the situation.

# Groping Toward a Way to Share the Reins
# Major Survey Finds Most Employees Want Cooperation and a Voice, if Not a Union, on the Job

### by Frank Swoboda
WASHINGTON POST STAFF WRITER

If most American workers don't want to belong to a union, but they don't really trust their boss to protect their interests, just what do they want?

The answer may lie in the fog of statistics compiled in a new survey of employee attitudes toward workplace decision making.

The authors . . . interviewed 2,400 workers nationwide to find out whether employees want greater participation in the workplace; what kind of involvement and representation they desire; and whether they have any ideas for closing the gap between their desires to participate and the reality of their own jobs.

A major finding . . . is the existence of a "participation gap" between the representation workers have on the job and what they want.

According to the study, "most employees want more say in how their companies are run and how key decisions affecting them are made. They want more individual say, and more say as a group, and believe greater worker involvement in firm decision making is good for the company as well as for them."

While 40 percent ... said they would vote to join a union ... the majority of the workers said they believed it was essential to have employee work organizations on the job even if those organizations had no real power to determine the outcome of decision making.

But ... the survey shows a substantial majority of the workers would prefer a weak employee involvement program that had management's approval to a strong organization, such as a union, that management opposed. This ... simply reflects the reality of most modern work sites, where management sets the rules. It doesn't mean the average worker wants to be a doormat.... When workers in the survey were asked to specify the attributes they would like to see in an employee organization, "most employees want cooperative joint committees with some independent standing inside their companies, and many want unions or union-like organizations."

"In a question format offering laws, joint committees, or unions that negotiate or bargain with management over issues, 63 percent chose joint committees, 20 percent chose unions, and 15 percent chose laws" ...

Asked to consider any kind of employee organizations on the assumption that it was the respondents' decision alone to make and everybody went along with it, 85 percent ... opted for an organization run jointly by employees and management, and only 10 percent chose one run by employees alone. Union members involved in the survey split almost identically on the issue.

How would workers involved in these joint committees propose settling decision-making disputes with management? Nearly 60 percent ... said in such cases an outside arbitrator should make final decisions.

"In a nutshell" ... the survey "shows that most American employees want more involvement and greater say in their jobs ... some form of workplace organization or policy that provides them with group as well as individual voice. Employees wish such organization or policy to give them independent input into workplace decisions."

 **BEFORE CONTINUING, DRAW YOUR DECISION/EVENT TREE.**

My rendition of the tree is shown in the solution to Exercise 21, which outlines all of the possible outcomes connecting the degree of employee involvement in management and the four alternative means of bargaining.

These examples demonstrate the impressive power of a decision/event tree to clearly and easily delineate the various paths that events can take in a given situation. Yet as I mentioned early on, our educational system does not, as a rule, teach students to use trees routinely when analyzing problems. That is an immense loss for each individual and an even greater one for the nation. How much easier it would be to solve some of the many problems our society faces if people knew how to "diagram" these problems in trees. Whenever I can depict a problem in a decision/event tree (or in a matrix), I take a giant step in understanding the problem and a major step toward a solution. At times, a decision/event tree (again like a matrix) literally points the way to a solution. In either case, such structuring techniques can be indispensable to effective problem solving.

## Should You Use a Matrix or a Tree?

There are, of course, trade-offs between trees and matrices. These trade-offs become evident when we convert a matrix into a decision/event tree and vice versa. For example, we can easily convert the matrix on "Symptom and Disease" (Exercise 13, page 106) into either of two trees (Figure 9-4).

**FIGURE 9-4**   Symptom and Disease Matrix

|         |     | Disease | |
|---------|-----|------|------|
|         |     | **Yes** | **No** |
| **Symptom** | Yes | 37 | 33 |
|         | No  | 17 | 13 |

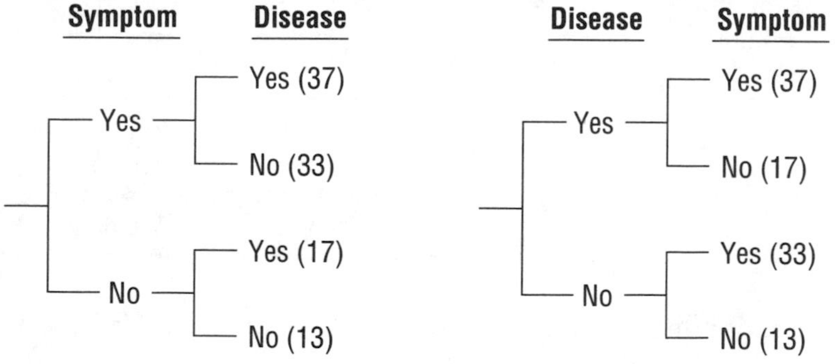

Try converting the matrix in Figure 9-5 into a decision/event tree. (This is the "Weather Forecaster's Dilemma" we addressed in Chapter 8.)

**FIGURE 9-5**

|  |  | Outcomes | |
|---|---|---|---|
|  |  | **Snow** | **Not snow** |
| **Prediction** | Snow |  |  |
|  | Not snow |  |  |

 **STOP** **BEFORE CONTINUING, DRAW YOUR DECISION/EVENT TREE.**

My rendition of the tree is shown in Figure 9-7.

It is likewise possible to convert a decision/event tree into a matrix, but doing so is practical only if the resulting matrix is two-dimensional. Going beyond two dimensions makes for a somewhat complicated diagram, as we can see if we convert the "Disgruntled Employee" tree into a matrix (Figure 9-6). Although the matrix does visually organize the

**FIGURE 9-6**

|  |  | Prone to Violence | | | |
|---|---|---|---|---|---|
|  |  | **Yes** | | **No** | |
| **Treatment Deranged Him** | Yes |  |  |  |  |
|  | No |  |  |  |  |
|  |  | Yes | No | Yes | No |
|  |  | Aware of Actions | | Aware of Actions | |

problem and focus our analysis on the interconnections of the three main issues, it confuses the problem. The beauty of the "Disgruntled

Employee" tree was depicting the various scenarios. The matrix is devoid of scenarios and is therefore, in my opinion, ill suited to analyzing this particular case.

I personally find a tree less insightful than a matrix for analyzing the forecaster's dilemma. But, again, it's a matter of personal choice. Which is preferable, a matrix or a tree, depends on the nature of the problem and what the analyst is seeking. I always recommend experimenting with both techniques, because the advantages and disadvantages of each then become clear and will inform our decision as to which is more useful in analyzing a given problem.

I hope you have learned from these exercises how easy it is to capture the elements of a problem in a matrix or tree. The challenge, of course, comes in analyzing a problem once you've captured it in either of these structuring techniques. I can't help you there. *Structuring* is the first step; it organizes the elements of the problem; it doesn't analyze them. For that, you have to use your mind; but structuring makes that a whole lot easier.

**FIGURE 9-7**

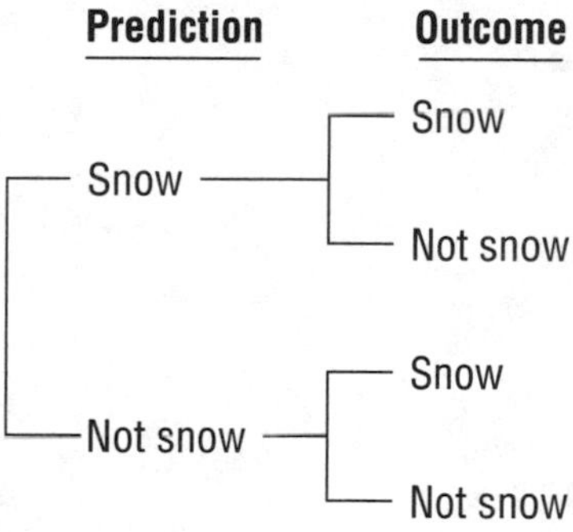

# 10
# Weighted Ranking

 We may not realize it, but we humans are constantly ranking things: the food we buy in the grocery, the clothes we wear each day, the route we drive to work, the TV programs we watch, the sections of the newspaper we read, and so on. Like most of what we do mentally, this ranking is an unconscious but instinctive process that facilitates (perhaps even enables) our decision making. Because these everyday decisions are unconscious, we aren't aware that they involve *ranking*. To rank means to assign a position to something relative to other things. In deciding what to wear to work in the morning, we open our closet, scan our wardrobe, eye several different outfits or suits, and select one. Is that ranking? Absolutely! We select—prefer—one article *over* the others; that is, we rank it higher and them lower. Our instinctive (we're born with it) ability to rank things quickly and effortlessly is indeed a blessing. As with our other mental traits, we would be in serious trouble making decisions without this built-in software for ranking.

A simple exercise in ranking movies will serve to demonstrate our instinctive method. I have selected movies as the subject because your preference in movies is highly subjective, even arbitrary, and you have no stake in the rankings. Therefore, your method of ranking and the decisions you make won't be distorted or hamstrung by concerns about putting the movies into the "right" order. There is no right or wrong order here. Whatever you think and feel about each movie is correct.

## EXERCISE 22    Movies

In a column on a sheet of paper write fifteen movies you have seen and about which you can make reasoned judgments. The list below will give you some ideas.

| | | |
|---|---|---|
| *Gone With the Wind* | *From Here to Eternity* | *The Godfather* |
| *Back to the Future* | *Ghostbusters* | *The Great Escape* |
| *Gandhi* | *Star Wars* | *The Silence of the Lambs* |
| *Ben Hur* | *Patton* | *E.T.* |
| *The Ten Commandments* | *The Bridge on the River Kwai* | *Schindler's List* |
| *The Sound of Music* | *Dances with Wolves* | *Platoon* |
| *The African Queen* | *The Treasure of the Sierra Madre* | *Aladdin* |
| *Superman* | *On Golden Pond* | *Chariots of Fire* |
| *Driving Miss Daisy* | *Amadeus* | *Rain Man* |
| *My Fair Lady* | *A Man for All Seasons* | *Stalag 17* |
| *The Graduate* | *Rocky* | *An Officer and a Gentleman* |
| *Terms of Endearment* | *Moonstruck* | *Scent of a Woman* |

Now rank these fifteen movies from best to worst according to your personal likes and dislikes.

 **BEFORE CONTINUING, LIST AND RANK 15 MOVIES.**

On a second sheet of paper, copy the matrix in Figure 10-1. In the first
column, write in your fifteen movies as you initially listed them. I have
entered my own list of movies as an example. Enter your rankings in
the next column, as I have done with mine, and write "Instinctive
Ranking" at the head of that column.

**STOP** BEFORE CONTINUING, CONSTRUCT A MATRIX AND
ENTER FIFTEEN MOVIES AND THEIR RANKINGS.

**FIGURE 10-1**

| Movie | Ranking Techniques Matrix | | |
|---|---|---|---|
| | Instinctive Ranking | | |
| Gone With the Wind | 2 | | |
| From Here to Eternity | 12 | | |
| Back to the Future | 14 | | |
| Ghostbusters | 15 | | |
| The Great Escape | 10 | | |
| Star Wars | 13 | | |
| Schindler's List | 3 | | |
| Patton | 6 | | |
| The Godfather | 5 | | |
| Gandhi | 1 | | |
| The Silence of the Lambs | 11 | | |
| Ben Hur | 8 | | |
| The Ten Commandments | 7 | | |
| The Bridge on the River Kwai | 9 | | |
| Dances with Wolves | 4 | | |

Now, write down the reason(s) why you ranked your top choice at the top. Then write down the reason(s) why you ranked your bottom choice at the bottom.

 **BEFORE CONTINUING, WRITE THE REASONS FOR YOUR TOP AND BOTTOM CHOICES.**

I would guess that the reason(s) you gave for making your top and bottom choices are distinctly different. For example, you may have put *The Silence of the Lambs* first because you love scary movies and put *From Here to Eternity* last because you dislike black-and-white films. "What's wrong with that?" you ask. "After all, these are legitimate reasons: *Silence* is scary and *Eternity* is in black and white." That's true enough, but there are other factors—other criteria—to be considered. Scariness and film color are only two.

The main defect in our instinctive method lies in our tendency (addressed in Chapter 1) to view problems one-dimensionally . . . to focus on (glom on to) the first solution that makes sense, that offers an explanation. Thus, the moment we think of a reason—any sound, persuasive reason—to like or dislike one of the movies on our list, we tend to latch on to that reason, make our ranking decision on that basis, and move on without considering our other likes and dislikes, which may actually be more important to us.

Imagine ten female dancers standing side by side at the rear of a stage waiting to audition for selection for a chorus line in a Broadway musical. The dance director walks onto the stage, glances at the line of dancers, instantly points at a lanky blonde, and announces, "You're first!" As that dancer steps to the center of the stage to demonstrate her talents, the director quickly surveys the line again and, nodding to a short brunette, declares, "You may go! We won't need you." Crestfallen, the dancer leaves, while the director, retreating several paces, begins to study the remaining candidates with great care, striding up and down the line, first in front, then behind. She* stops and crosses her arms, pondering her next decision.

---

*You thought the director was a "he," didn't you! It's those bothersome mental traits again.

What are all of the yet-to-be-chosen dancers thinking about at that moment? I'll tell you. They're trying to guess what the director saw in the dancer chosen first and the one sent home. They're thinking, "Should I stand up straight to look taller? Is my goose cooked because I'm a brunette? Should I smile? Should I look her in the eye? Is my makeup too heavy?" Each is trying to guess what *criteria* the director used in making her first two selections.

The director picked the lanky blonde first because she was strikingly attractive and had a well-proportioned figure and slender legs, perfect for a chorus line. The director sent the brunette packing because her overly high forehead made her look bald. But whereas the criteria the director used for her first two decisions were clear-cut, the water quickly muddied when she considered the other candidates. Some had slender legs but chunky figures; some had chunky legs but slender figures; some faces were bland, some distinctive. It was difficult ranking one over another. So she was forced to come up with other rationales—*other criteria*—on which to make her decisions.

We all do the same thing when we rank things, such as when we select a place in which to reside. We survey several neighborhoods and dislike this one because the traffic is too heavy, like that one because it's close to an elementary school, dislike this one because it lacks city sewers, like that one because the residences are attractive and well kept, and so on. We make our decision and, after moving in, are disappointed because the roof of the house leaks and the heating bills are too expensive. It is well and good to use stringent criteria in making decisions, but we should be sure we have considered all relevant criteria and have applied all of the criteria equitably to all of the decisions. As for the dance director, she ultimately dismissed the lanky blonde; although she was a talented dancer, she couldn't remember the dance routines.

By applying different criteria to different ranking decisions, we distort our analysis, which can lead to gravely disappointing outcomes that later make us wonder what went wrong.

This phenomenon was brought home to me when my wife and I spent a couple of days in North Carolina looking at possible sites on which to build a home. As we went from one lot to another, we noted the acreage, whether city sewers were available, where the house would best be situated, whether the rear of the house would face south, and so on. As the day went on, we focused more and more on the landscape—the number, kinds, and placement of trees and bushes. When we returned to our hotel to mull over our findings, we discovered that we had eliminated several otherwise attractive lots simply because the landscape was not ideal. Suspecting that something was wrong with our methodology, we wrote down all of our major concerns (the major factors) about the suitability of a lot for our home. Then we ranked the concerns. It turned out that landscaping was far down on the list, so we reevaluated the lots we had excluded and moved a couple of them to the top of our list.

There are two inherent weaknesses in our instinctive method. First, we tend to apply different criteria to the different items being ranked. Second, we tend to regard all of our criteria as having equal importance to us, when one can easily demonstrate (as in my experience in North Carolina) that this is not the case.

For that reason, rankings generated with our instinctive method tend to be inconsistent and are thus unreliable. But the degree of error (the extent to which the rankings are out of order) is rarely a problem for us, because most of the things we rank, such as the clothes we wear, the route we drive to work, or the movies listed above, are of a mundane, commonplace nature. But when the decisions we make in ranking are crucial, as in, say, selecting one of several lawyers to represent us or our company in a damage suit or choosing among sites for building a home or a multimillion-dollar office complex, our instinctive method poses hazardous pitfalls.

"But," you say, "when I rank really important things, things in which I have a vital stake, I don't use the method I did to rank the movies. I'm more careful and systematic. I use a different, more reliable method."

I seriously doubt it. If you are like most members of our species—and I include myself in that number—your mind doesn't distinguish between vital and nonvital matters when it comes to ranking. We tend in every case to use our instinctive method—the one we're born with, the one we've used all our lives.

But we shouldn't! When we have a great deal invested personally or corporately in the results of a ranking, we should employ an unwaveringly consistent method whose results we can rely upon unconditionally. The only way I know to ensure reliable results is to impose a systematic structure on the process. But how do we do that? What systematic technique will enable us to determine which criteria are the most important and apply them equitably to all the items being ranked? The answer is a technique called *"weighted ranking."*

The paramount feature of weighted ranking is its method of ranking each item against every other. It's very simple. It's called *"pair ranking."* Here's how it works.

Let's say we are ranking four options: A, B, C, and D. To pair-rank these options, we list them in a column one beneath the other:

Option A

Option B

Option C

Option D

We then ask ourselves:

Which is better, A or B? We put a pencil mark after the one we decide is better.

Which is better, A or C? We put another pencil mark after the better one.

Which is better, A or D? A pencil mark.

Which is better, B or C? A pencil mark.

Which is better, B or D? A pencil mark.

Which is better, C or D? A pencil mark.

We thus systematically compare each item with every other item. If we have been consistent in our rankings, one of the items will have three marks, one will have two, one will have one, and one will have none. The item with three marks is the most favored and thus is ranked first. The item with two marks is second; one mark—third; no marks—fourth. If, by chance, two items end up with the same number of marks because our analysis was inconsistent, we simply rank these two items head to head to break the tie. The benefits of pair ranking aren't noticeable with short lists of four or five items, but with longer lists they are unmistakable.

So let's try it. Pair-rank your list of fifteen movies and enter your rankings in the next column of the Ranking Techniques Matrix and label that column "Pair Ranking."

**BEFORE CONTINUING, PAIR-RANK THE MOVIES, ENTER YOUR PAIR RANKINGS IN THE RANKING TECHNIQUES MATRIX, AND LABEL THE COLUMN "PAIR RANKING."**

See my pair rankings in Figure 10-2.

You may feel uncomfortable with pair ranking and think that it's too mechanical and laborious. Well, your discomfort is only natural. It's a manifestation of your mind sending you signals telling you, "I don't like to work this way. I prefer my loosey-goosey, unfettered, mental-messing-around instinctive approach." Ignore these signals. What's happening here is that we're running against the mind's grain, against the way it prefers to operate, so of course it feels uncomfortable. Once it becomes accustomed to pair ranking, it will feel at home with the technique and won't want to rank things any other way. And neither will you.

But is it really "mechanical and laborious"? Mechanical, yes. That's its beauty. It's systematic: 1 against 2, 1 against 3, 1 against 4, 2 against 3, 2 against 4, 3 against 4. But is it "laborious"? Yes again. One has to methodically, over and over again, reason out each pair to be ranked. But that's what makes pair ranking so valuable analytically. It doesn't permit us to take analytic shortcuts that shortchange our analysis. We *must analyze and make a decision on **each member** of **every pair**.*

Pair ranking, by comparing one thing against another, conforms to the one-track, ever-focusing nature of our minds. It narrows the mind's field of attention first to a single pair and then separately to each of the items in the pair. Ranking things in pairs is something the mind can do easily, quickly, and effectively. The mind does love to focus.

FIGURE 10-2

| Movie | Ranking Techniques Matrix | | |
| --- | --- | --- | --- |
| | Instinctive Ranking | Pair Ranking | |
| Gone With the Wind | 2 | 4 | |
| From Here to Eternity | 12 | 15 | |
| Back to the Future | 14 | 11 | |
| Ghostbusters | 15 | 14 | |
| The Great Escape | 10 | 6 | |
| Star Wars | 13 | 5 | |
| Schindler's List | 3 | 2 | |
| Patton | 6 | 7 | |
| The Godfather | 5 | 10 | |
| Gandhi | 1 | 1 | |
| The Silence of the Lambs | 11 | 12 | |
| Ben Hur | 8 | 3 | |
| The Ten Commandments | 7 | 13 | |
| The Bridge on the River Kwai | 9 | 9 | |
| Dances with Wolves | 4 | 8 | |

Pair ranking offers a simple, reliable way to rank items, regardless of the subject matter. By focusing on individual items, pair ranking separates the elements of the task—the problem—in an organized way that, like all effective structuring techniques, allows us to analyze each element *separately*, *systematically*, and *sufficiently*. Pair ranking also provides reliability. By measuring every item against every other, it provides an absolutely reliable indicator of where each item ranks. What happens is that the *process* delivers the rankings. We don't have to decide which movie is fifth and which is sixth or which is eleventh and which is twelfth. Instead, we rank them in pairs and the process puts them into order. With instinctive ranking we can only guess whether each item being ranked is in its proper place. With pair ranking we are certain.

Now, take a look at the Ranking Techniques Matrix and compare the results of your instinctive ranking with the results of your pair ranking. Do you note any differences? Twelve of my rankings changed by an average of nearly four places. Two movies moved five places, and one (*Star Wars*) went from thirteenth to fifth.

Having learned what pair ranking is all about, we are now ready to review the nine steps of weighted ranking, still using movies as our working example.

# The Nine Steps of Weighted Ranking

*Step 1:* List all of the major criteria for ranking.

Write down in a column on a sheet of paper eight criteria for ranking movies, for example, type of plot, strength of plot, degree of excitement, level of violence, cinematography, music, the cast, the director, whether a film has won an Oscar, and so on.

 **BEFORE CONTINUING, WRITE DOWN EIGHT CRITERIA FOR RANKING MOVIES.**

*Step 2:* Pair-rank the criteria.

We now must determine which of these criteria are the most important. To do that we simply pair-rank them: the first against the second, first against the third, and so on. Add up the votes you give to each criterion. The one with the most votes is the top criterion, the one with the second most votes is second, and so on.

As you practice pair ranking, you'll discover that sometimes you can quickly determine with certainty which item is going to be first or which last. When you do, make a note of it and don't include that item anymore as you rank the others.

 **BEFORE CONTINUING, PAIR-RANK THE CRITERIA.**

Figure 10-3 shows my pair ranking of eight criteria.

*Step* 3: Select the top several criteria and weight them in percentiles (their sum must equal 1.0).

For this exercise alone, use only your top three criteria. Of course, when you apply this structuring technique to your own business or personal problems, you can employ as many criteria as you wish.

Weight your three criteria by dividing 100 points among them according to the importance you assign to each. Convert these points to percentiles; their total must equal 1.0.

**FIGURE 10-3**

| Criterion | Votes from Pair Ranking | Final Ranking |
|---|---|---|
| Pageantry | 3 | 5 |
| Cast | 5 | 3 |
| Strength of plot | 7 | 1 |
| Type of plot | 6 | 2 |
| Music | 4 | 4 |
| Script | 2 | 6 |
| Cinematography | 1 | 7 |
| Realism | 0 | 8 |

**FIGURE 10-4**

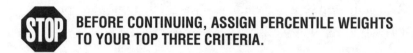

| Strength of plot | 50 | or | .5 |
| Type of plot | 30 | or | .3 |
| Cast | 20 | or | .2 |
| | 100 | or | 1.0 |

Figure 10-4 shows my weightings of my top three criteria.

For me, "strength of plot" is significantly more important than "type of plot" and more than twice as important as "cast."

🛑 **BEFORE CONTINUING, ASSIGN PERCENTILE WEIGHTS TO YOUR TOP THREE CRITERIA.**

*Step 4*: Construct a Weighted Ranking Matrix and enter the items to be ranked, the selected criteria, and the criteria weights.

Use the matrix in Figure 10-5 as a guide.

🛑 **BEFORE CONTINUING, CONSTRUCT A WEIGHTED RANKING MATRIX AND ENTER YOUR FIFTEEN MOVIES AND YOUR TOP THREE CRITERIA AND THEIR WEIGHTS.**

Figure 10-6 shows my Weighted Ranking Matrix, the movies to be ranked, my three criteria, and their weights.

**FIGURE 10-5**

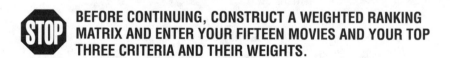

| Items to Be Ranked | Criteria | | | Total Votes | Final Ranking |
|---|---|---|---|---|---|
| | | | | | |
| | | | | | |
| | | | | | |

**FIGURE 10-6**

| | Criteria | | | | |
|---|---|---|---|---|---|
| **Items to Be Ranked** | **Strength of Plot, Weight: .5** | **Type of Plot, Weight: .3** | **Cast, Weight: .2** | **Total Votes** | **Final Ranking** |
| *Gone With the Wind* | | | | | |
| *From Here to Eternity* | | | | | |
| *Back to the Future* | | | | | |
| *Ghostbusters* | | | | | |
| *The Great Escape* | | | | | |
| *Star Wars* | | | | | |
| *Schindler's List* | | | | | |
| *Patton* | | | | | |
| *The Godfather* | | | | | |
| *Gandhi* | | | | | |
| *The Silence of the Lambs* | | | | | |
| *Ben Hur* | | | | | |
| *The Ten Commandments* | | | | | |
| *The Bridge on the River Kwai* | | | | | |
| *Dances with Wolves* | | | | | |

*Step 5:* Pair-rank all of the items by each criterion, recording in the appropriate spaces the number of "votes" each item receives.

At this juncture, the technique gets a bit more complicated, but there's no way around it if we are to rank all options equitably. What we're going to do is pair-rank the movies by each of three criteria, which means performing three separate rankings.

*If you feel a panic attack coming on, remember it's only your subconscious screaming, "I don't like this! I don't analyze this way!" Don't listen to it. Just stick with me. This technique, once you understand it, is really quite simple.*

Rank the fifteen movies by the first criterion and enter the number of votes each movie receives. Repeat the same process for the second and third criteria. See my example in Figure 10-7.

**FIGURE 10-7**

| Items to Be Ranked | Criteria | | | Total Votes | Final Ranking |
|---|---|---|---|---|---|
| | Strength of Plot, Weight: .5 | Type of Plot, Weight: .3 | Cast, Weight: .2 | | |
| Gone With the Wind | 9 | 1 | 2 | | |
| From Here to Eternity | 1 | 0 | 0 | | |
| Back to the Future | 2 | 5 | 3 | | |
| Ghostbusters | 0 | 2 | 1 | | |
| The Great Escape | 8 | 9 | 9 | | |
| Star Wars | 4 | 12 | 8 | | |
| Schindler's List | 13 | 6 | 13 | | |
| Patton | 3 | 7 | 7 | | |
| The Godfather | 11 | 8 | 10 | | |
| Gandhi | 14 | 14 | 14 | | |
| The Silence of the Lambs | 5 | 10 | 4 | | |
| Ben Hur | 12 | 13 | 12 | | |
| The Ten Commandments | 6 | 3 | 5 | | |
| The Bridge on the River Kwai | 10 | 11 | 11 | | |
| Dances with Wolves | 7 | 4 | 6 | | |

**STOP** **BEFORE CONTINUING, RANK THE MOVIES BY EACH CRITERION AND ENTER THE NUMBER OF VOTES.**

*Step 6:* Multiply the number of votes by the respective criterion's weight.

Multiply the number of votes for each entry under each criterion by that criterion's weight. See how I did it in Figure 10-8.

**FIGURE 10-8**

| Items to Be Ranked | Criteria | | | Total Votes | Final Ranking |
|---|---|---|---|---|---|
| | Strength of Plot, Weight: .5 | Type of Plot, Weight: .3 | Cast, Weight: .2 | | |
| Gone With the Wind | 9 × .5 = 4.5 | 1 × .3 = 0.3 | 2 × .2 = 0.4 | | |
| From Here to Eternity | 1 × .5 = 0.5 | 0 × .3 = 0 | 0 × .2 = 0 | | |
| Back to the Future | 2 × .5 = 1.0 | 5 × .3 = 1.5 | 3 × .2 = 0.6 | | |
| Ghostbusters | 0 × .5 = 0 | 2 × .3 = 0.6 | 1 × .2 = 0.2 | | |
| The Great Escape | 8 × .5 = 4.0 | 9 × .3 = 2.7 | 9 × .2 = 1.8 | | |
| Star Wars | 4 × .5 = 2.0 | 12 × .3 = 3.6 | 8 × .2 = 1.6 | | |
| Schindler's List | 13 × .5 = 6.5 | 6 × .3 = 1.8 | 13 × .2 = 2.6 | | |
| Patton | 3 × .5 = 1.5 | 7 × .3 = 2.1 | 7 × .2 = 1.4 | | |
| The Godfather | 11 × .5 = 5.5 | 8 × .3 = 2.4 | 10 × .2 = 2.0 | | |
| Gandhi | 14 × .5 = 7.0 | 14 × .3 = 4.2 | 14 × .2 = 2.8 | | |
| The Silence of the Lambs | 5 × .5 = 2.5 | 10 × .3 = 3.0 | 4 × .2 = 0.8 | | |
| Ben Hur | 12 × .5 = 6.0 | 13 × .3 = 3.9 | 12 × .2 = 2.4 | | |
| The Ten Commandments | 6 × .5 = 3.0 | 3 × .3 = 0.9 | 5 × .2 = 1.0 | | |
| The Bridge on the River Kwai | 10 × .5 = 5.0 | 11 × .3 = 3.3 | 11 × .2 = 2.2 | | |
| Dances with Wolves | 7 × .5 = 3.5 | 4 × .3 = 1.2 | 6 × .2 = 1.2 | | |

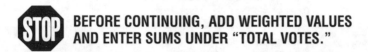 **BEFORE CONTINUING, MULTIPLY THE NUMBER OF VOTES BY CRITERION WEIGHTS.**

*Step* 7: Add the weighted values for each item and enter the sums in the column labeled "Total Votes."

Add up the number of votes each movie receives under all three criteria and enter the sums under "Total Votes." See how I did it in Figure 10-9.

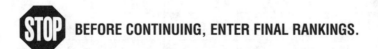 **BEFORE CONTINUING, ADD WEIGHTED VALUES AND ENTER SUMS UNDER "TOTAL VOTES."**

*Step* 8: Determine the final rankings and enter them in the last column, labeled "Final Ranking." (The item with the most points is ranked highest.)

The movie with the highest number of votes is ranked first, second highest second, and so on (Figure 10-10).

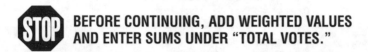 **BEFORE CONTINUING, ENTER FINAL RANKINGS.**

*Step* 9: Perform a sanity check.

Do the results make intuitive sense? If not, go back and check the rankings, the weights, and the arithmetic. Don't be surprised if the results are discomforting. Our instinctive ranking approach still drives our intuition, so we may feel uncomfortable with the results of weighted ranking.

Now copy the final rankings into the last column of the Ranking Techniques Matrix, and label that column "Weighted Ranking," as in Figure 10-11. The Ranking Techniques Matrix reveals rather impressively how the positions of the movies shift as the technique becomes

**FIGURE 10-9**

| Items to Be Ranked | Criteria | | | Total Votes | Final Ranking |
| --- | --- | --- | --- | --- | --- |
| | Strength of Plot, Weight: .5 | Type of Plot, Weight: .3 | Cast, Weight: .2 | | |
| *Gone With the Wind* | 9 × .5 = 4.5 | 1 × .3 = 0.3 | 2 × .2 = 0.4 | *5.2* | |
| *From Here to Eternity* | 1 × .5 = 0.5 | 0 × .3 = 0 | 0 × .2 = 0 | *0.5* | |
| *Back to the Future* | 2 × .5 = 1.0 | 5 × .3 = 1.5 | 3 × .2 = 0.6 | *3.1* | |
| *Ghostbusters* | 0 × .5 = 0 | 2 × .3 = 0.6 | 1 × .2 = 0.2 | *0.8* | |
| *The Great Escape* | 8 × .5 = 4.0 | 9 × .3 = 2.7 | 9 × .2 = 1.8 | *8.5* | |
| *Star Wars* | 4 × .5 = 2.0 | 12 × .3 = 3.6 | 8 × .2 = 1.6 | *7.2* | |
| *Schindler's List* | 13 × .5 = 6.5 | 6 × .3 = 1.8 | 13 × .2 = 2.6 | *10.9* | |
| *Patton* | 3 × .5 = 1.5 | 7 × .3 = 2.1 | 7 × .2 = 1.4 | *5.0* | |
| *The Godfather* | 11 × .5 = 5.5 | 8 × .3 = 2.4 | 10 × .2 = 2.0 | *9.9* | |
| *Gandhi* | 14 × .5 = 7.0 | 14 × .3 = 4.2 | 14 × .2 = 2.8 | *14.0* | |
| *The Silence of the Lambs* | 5 × .5 = 2.5 | 10 × .3 = 3.0 | 4 × .2 = 0.8 | *6.3* | |
| *Ben Hur* | 12 × .5 = 6.0 | 13 × .3 = 3.9 | 12 × .2 = 2.4 | *12.3* | |
| *The Ten Commandments* | 6 × .5 = 3.0 | 3 × .3 = 0.9 | 5 × .2 = 1.0 | *4.9* | |
| *The Bridge on the River Kwai* | 10 × .5 = 5.0 | 11 × .3 = 3.3 | 11 × .2 = 2.2 | *10.5* | |
| *Dances with Wolves* | 7 × .5 = 3.5 | 4 × .3 = 1.2 | 6 × .2 = 1.2 | *5.9* | |

more definitive and thus more reliable as we incorporate first pair ranking and finally weighted ranking. Compare the positions under "Instinctive Ranking" and "Weighted Ranking." How significant were the changes? *Gandhi* remained my top choice, but *Gone With the Wind* (*instinctively* second) dropped to tenth, while *Ben Hur* (instinctively eighth) moved up to second.

You may argue that these changes in rankings between the two techniques are only superficial; that is, they show only that weighted

**FIGURE 10-10**

| Items to Be Ranked | Criteria | | | Total Votes | Final Ranking |
| | Strength of Plot, Weight: .5 | Type of Plot, Weight: .3 | Cast, Weight: .2 | | |
|---|---|---|---|---|---|
| *Gone With the Wind* | 9 × .5 = 4.5 | 1 × .3 = 0.3 | 2 × .2 = 0.4 | 5.2 | *10* |
| *From Here to Eternity* | 1 × .5 = 0.5 | 0 × .3 = 0 | 0 × .2 = 0 | 0.5 | *15* |
| *Back to the Future* | 2 × .5 = 1.0 | 5 × .3 = 1.5 | 3 × .2 = 0.6 | 3.1 | *13* |
| *Ghostbusters* | 0 × .5 = 0 | 2 × .3 = 0.6 | 1 × .2 = 0.2 | 0.8 | *14* |
| *The Great Escape* | 8 × .5 = 4.0 | 9 × .3 = 2.7 | 9 × .2 = 1.8 | 8.5 | *6/7* |
| *Star Wars* | 4 × .5 = 2.0 | 12 × .3 = 3.6 | 8 × .2 = 1.6 | 7.2 | *8* |
| *Schindler's List* | 13 × .5 = 6.5 | 6 × .3 = 1.8 | 13 × .2 = 2.6 | 10.9 | *3* |
| *Patton* | 3 × .5 = 1.5 | 7 × .3 = 2.1 | 7 × .2 = 1.4 | 5.0 | *11* |
| *The Godfather* | 11 × .5 = 5.5 | 8 × .3 = 2.4 | 10 × .2 = 2.0 | 9.9 | *5* |
| *Gandhi* | 14 × .5 = 7.0 | 14 × .3 = 4.2 | 14 × .2 = 2.8 | 14.0 | *1* |
| *The Silence of the Lambs* | 5 × .5 = 2.5 | 10 × .3 = 3.0 | 4 × .2 = 0.8 | 6.3 | *6/7* |
| *Ben Hur* | 12 × .5 = 6.0 | 13 × .3 = 3.9 | 12 × .2 = 2.4 | 12.3 | *2* |
| *The Ten Commandments* | 6 × .5 = 3.0 | 3 × .3 = 0.9 | 5 × .2 = 1.0 | 4.9 | *12* |
| *The Bridge on the River Kwai* | 10 × .5 = 5.0 | 11 × .3 = 3.3 | 11 × .2 = 2.2 | 10.5 | *4* |
| *Dances with Wolves* | 7 × .5 = 3.5 | 4 × .3 = 1.2 | 6 × .2 = 1.2 | 5.9 | *9* |

ranking results in a *different* order than instinctive ranking. Indeed, my rankings of some of the movies changed very little or not at all. For example, *Gandhi* was my top-ranked movie in both the instinctive and weighted rankings. So what did weighted ranking buy me over instinctive ranking? I got the same result: *Gandhi* was number one.

The answer is *confidence in the validity of the rankings.* What if we really had a vital interest in how these movies were ranked? What if millions of dollars were at stake? In that case, the validity of the rankings would be critical, and validity is what weighted ranking ensures.

## FIGURE 10-11

| Movie | Ranking Techniques Matrix | | |
|---|---|---|---|
| | Instinctive Ranking | Pair Ranking | Weighted Ranking |
| Gone With the Wind | 2 | 4 | 10 |
| From Here to Eternity | 12 | 15 | 15 |
| Back to the Future | 14 | 11 | 13 |
| Ghostbusters | 15 | 14 | 14 |
| The Great Escape | 10 | 6 | 6/7 |
| Star Wars | 13 | 5 | 8 |
| Schindler's List | 3 | 2 | 3 |
| Patton | 6 | 7 | 11 |
| The Godfather | 5 | 10 | 5 |
| Gandhi | 1 | 1 | 1 |
| The Silence of the Lambs | 11 | 12 | 6/7 |
| Ben Hur | 8 | 3 | 2 |
| The Ten Commandments | 7 | 13 | 12 |
| The Bridge on the River Kwai | 9 | 9 | 4 |
| Dances with Wolves | 4 | 8 | 9 |

How can one place any trust in the results of instinctive ranking, which is inherently flawed? It is an unsystematic approach that is flagrantly vulnerable to our fallible reasoning traits and that applies criteria inconsistently, without giving equal consideration to each item being ranked. In short, instinctive ranking is a disaster waiting to happen.

Therefore, at a minimum, always use pair ranking. Pair ranking is reliable and so easy that a child can do it. But if you are faced with a situation in which ranking is important, you would be well advised to employ weighted ranking—an unwaveringly consistent method on whose results we can rely unconditionally.

As with anything in life, if you practice the weighted ranking technique, you will gain confidence in using it, and what at first seems foreign, awkward, and unwieldy will become second nature. Practice, practice, practice. What more can I say? I promise you won't regret it.

## EXERCISE 23   Automobiles

As a prelude to purchasing a new car, we are going to rank ten different makes and models. I'll walk you through the steps, working the problem myself as we go.

*Step 1:* List all of the major criteria for ranking.

I list all the criteria I think might be important, combining those that are similar. My criteria are as follows: price, mileage, reliability, ease of driving, attractiveness of styling, safety record, insurance cost, fuel tank capacity, luggage compartment capacity, engine horsepower, and turning radius.

*Step 2:* Pair-rank the criteria.

I pair-rank the criteria, comparing the first in the list against the second, against the third, and so on. I then count the votes each criterion received and write that number adjacent to the criterion. Figure 10-12 shows the results of my pair rankings.

*Step 3:* Select the top several criteria and weight them in percentiles (their sum must equal 1.0).

Price, attractiveness, and reliability are my top three criteria, which I weight as .5, .3, and .2 respectively.

*Step 4:* Construct a Weighted Ranking Matrix and enter the items to be ranked, the selected criteria, and the criteria weights.

I construct the matrix in Figure 10-13.

**FIGURE 10-12**

| | Times Won in Pairings | Votes |
|---|---|---|
| Price | \| \| \| \| \| \| \| \| \| \| | 10 |
| Mileage | \| \| \| \| | 4 |
| Reliability | \| \| \| \| \| \| \| \| | 8 |
| Ease of driving | \| \| \| \| \| | 5 |
| Attractiveness | \| \| \| \| \| \| \| \| \| | 9 |
| Safety record | | 0 |
| Insurance cost | \| \| \| | 3 |
| Fuel tank capacity | \| | 1 |
| Luggage compartment capacity | \| \| | 2 |
| Engine horsepower | \| \| \| \| \| \| \| | 7 |
| Turning circle | \| \| \| \| \| \| | 6 |

*Step 5:* Pair-rank all of the items by each criterion, recording in the appropriate spaces the number of "votes" each item receives.

Figure 10-14 shows my pair rankings.

*Step 6:* Multiply the votes by the respective criterion's weight.

Figure 10-15 shows my weighted votes.

*Step 7:* Add the weighted values for each item and enter the sums in the column labeled "Total Votes."

Figure 10-16 shows my total weighted votes.

*Step 8:* Determine the final rankings and enter them in the last column, labeled "Final Ranking." (The option with the most points is ranked highest.)

**FIGURE 10-13**

| Items to Be Ranked | Criteria | | | Total Votes | Final Ranking |
|---|---|---|---|---|---|
| | Price, Weight: .5 | Attractiveness, Weight: .3 | Reliability, Weight: .2 | | |
| Acura Vigor | | | | | |
| Chrysler Concorde | | | | | |
| Dodge Intrepid | | | | | |
| Chevrolet Geo Prizm | | | | | |
| Infiniti G20 | | | | | |
| Lexus ES300 | | | | | |
| Mazda 626 | | | | | |
| Nissan Maxima | | | | | |
| Saturn | | | | | |
| Toyota Camry | | | | | |

Figure 10-17 shows my final rankings. My analysis indicates that, according to my preferences, Saturn is my first choice and Chevrolet Geo Prizm a close second.

*Step* 9: Perform a sanity check.

I am intuitively comfortable with this finding.

**FIGURE 10-14**

| Items to Be Ranked | Criteria | | | Total Votes | Final Ranking |
|---|---|---|---|---|---|
| | Price, Weight: .5 | Attractiveness, Weight: .3 | Reliability, Weight: .2 | | |
| Acura Vigor | 1 | 4 | 4 | | |
| Chrysler Concorde | 5 | 9 | 2 | | |
| Dodge Intrepid | 6 | 5 | 1 | | |
| Chevrolet Geo Prizm | 9 | 3 | 6 | | |
| Infiniti G20 | 2 | 0 | 7 | | |
| Lexus ES300 | 0 | 6 | 9 | | |
| Mazda 626 | 7 | 7 | 0 | | |
| Nissan Maxima | 3 | 1 | 8 | | |
| Saturn | 8 | 8 | 3 | | |
| Toyota Camry | 4 | 2 | 5 | | |

## EXERCISE 24   Personnel

The process of making personnel decisions is usually driven by highly subjective mind-sets, uneven and inequitable consideration of personal qualifications (usually based on formal performance evaluations), and, worst of all, slipshod adherence to standards (criteria) of performance. Because the weighted ranking technique goes a long way toward eliminating these undesirable influences, it is ideally suited for analyzing

**FIGURE 10-15**

| Items to Be Ranked | Criteria | | | Total Votes | Final Ranking |
|---|---|---|---|---|---|
| | Price, Weight: .5 | Attractiveness, Weight: .3 | Reliability, Weight: .2 | | |
| Acura Vigor | .5 × 1 = 0.5 | .3 × 4 = 1.2 | .2 × 4 = 0.8 | | |
| Chrysler Concorde | .5 × 5 = 2.5 | .3 × 9 = 2.7 | .2 × 2 = 0.4 | | |
| Dodge Intrepid | .5 × 6 = 3.0 | .3 × 5 = 1.5 | .2 × 1 = 0.2 | | |
| Chevrolet Geo Prizm | .5 × 9 = 4.5 | .3 × 3 = 0.9 | .2 × 6 = 1.2 | | |
| Infiniti G20 | .5 × 2 = 1.0 | .3 × 0 = 0 | .2 × 7 = 1.4 | | |
| Lexus ES300 | .5 × 0 = 0 | .3 × 6 = 1.8 | .2 × 9 = 1.8 | | |
| Mazda 626 | .5 × 7 = 3.5 | .3 × 7 = 2.1 | .2 × 0 = 0 | | |
| Nissan Maxima | .5 × 3 = 1.5 | .3 × 1 = 0.3 | .2 × 8 = 1.6 | | |
| Saturn | .5 × 8 = 4.0 | .3 × 8 = 2.4 | .2 × 3 = 0.6 | | |
| Toyota Camry | .5 × 4 = 2.0 | .3 × 2 = 0.6 | .2 × 5 = 1.0 | | |

personnel decisions such as choosing among applicants for hiring, selecting among candidates for advancement to a more senior position, and so on.

Consider, for example, how weighted ranking can be used for *ranking employees for promotion*—a standard, prevalent, and ever-contentious function of management. To illustrate the technique's effectiveness in this application, I will use four (out of ten) criteria to

**FIGURE 10-16**

| | Criteria | | | | |
|---|---|---|---|---|---|
| Items to Be Ranked | Price, Weight: .5 | Attractiveness, Weight: .3 | Reliability, Weight: .2 | Total Votes | Final Ranking |
| Acura Vigor | .5 × 1 = 0.5 | .3 × 4 = 1.2 | .2 × 4 = 0.8 | 2.5 | |
| Chrysler Concorde | .5 × 5 = 2.5 | .3 × 9 = 2.7 | .2 × 2 = 0.4 | 5.6 | |
| Dodge Intrepid | .5 × 6 = 3.0 | .3 × 5 = 1.5 | .2 × 1 = 0.2 | 4.7 | |
| Chevrolet Geo Prizm | .5 × 9 = 4.5 | .3 × 3 = 0.9 | .2 × 6 = 1.2 | 6.6 | |
| Infiniti G20 | .5 × 2 = 1.0 | .3 × 0 = 0 | .2 × 7 = 1.4 | 2.4 | |
| Lexus ES300 | .5 × 0 = 0 | .3 × 6 = 1.8 | .2 × 9 = 1.8 | 3.6 | |
| Mazda 626 | .5 × 7 = 3.5 | .3 × 7 = 2.1 | .2 × 0 = 0 | 5.6 | |
| Nissan Maxima | .5 × 3 = 1.5 | .3 × 1 = 0.3 | .2 × 8 = 1.6 | 3.4 | |
| Saturn | .5 × 8 = 4.0 | .3 × 8 = 2.4 | .2 × 3 = 0.6 | 7.0 | |
| Toyota Camry | .5 × 4 = 2.0 | .3 × 2 = 0.6 | .2 × 5 = 1.0 | 3.6 | |

rank ten salespeople being considered for promotion to the position of regional sales manager in a hypothetical manufacturing company.

*Step 1:* List all of the major criteria for ranking.

I will stipulate, for the purpose of this demonstration, the following ten criteria for promotion: the candidate's supervisory experience, knowledge of the company's products, salesmanship, communication

**FIGURE 10-17**

| Items to Be Ranked | Criteria | | | Total Votes | Final Ranking |
| | Price, Weight: .5 | Attractiveness, Weight: .3 | Reliability, Weight: .2 | | |
|---|---|---|---|---|---|
| Acura Vigor | $.5 \times 1 = 0.5$ | $.3 \times 4 = 1.2$ | $.2 \times 4 = 0.8$ | 2.5 | 9 |
| Chrysler Concorde | $.5 \times 5 = 2.5$ | $.3 \times 9 = 2.7$ | $.2 \times 2 = 0.4$ | 5.6 | 3/4 |
| Dodge Intrepid | $.5 \times 6 = 3.0$ | $.3 \times 5 = 1.5$ | $.2 \times 1 = 0.2$ | 4.7 | 5 |
| Chevrolet Geo Prizm | $.5 \times 9 = 4.5$ | $.3 \times 3 = 0.9$ | $.2 \times 6 = 1.2$ | 6.6 | 2 |
| Infiniti G20 | $.5 \times 2 = 1.0$ | $.3 \times 0 = 0$ | $.2 \times 7 = 1.4$ | 2.4 | 10 |
| Lexus ES300 | $.5 \times 0 = 0$ | $.3 \times 6 = 1.8$ | $.2 \times 9 = 1.8$ | 3.6 | 6/7 |
| Mazda 626 | $.5 \times 7 = 3.5$ | $.3 \times 7 = 2.1$ | $.2 \times 0 = 0$ | 5.6 | 3/4 |
| Nissan Maxima | $.5 \times 3 = 1.5$ | $.3 \times 1 = 0.3$ | $.2 \times 8 = 1.6$ | 3.4 | 8 |
| Saturn | $.5 \times 8 = 4.0$ | $.3 \times 8 = 2.4$ | $.2 \times 3 = 0.6$ | 7.0 | 1 |
| Toyota Camry | $.5 \times 4 = 2.0$ | $.3 \times 2 = 0.6$ | $.2 \times 5 = 1.0$ | 3.6 | 6/7 |

skills (speaking and writing), budget management, creativity (in all aspects of responsibility), dedication, image (of the candidate as seen by employees and management alike), personal integrity, and earnings for the company through sales.

*Step* 2: Pair-rank the criteria.

Figure 10-18 shows my pair ranking of the criteria.

*Step* 3: Select the top several criteria and weight them in percentiles (their sum must equal 1.0).

Product knowledge, communication skills, image, and budget management are my four criteria, which I weight as .4, .3, .2, and .1 respectively.

*Step* 4: Construct a Weighted Ranking Matrix and enter the items to be ranked, the selected criteria, and the criteria weights.

I construct the matrix in Figure 10-19.

*Step* 5: Pair-rank all of the items by each criterion, recording in the appropriate spaces the number of "votes" each item receives.

Figure 10-20 shows the votes each item received from my pair rankings by each criterion.

*Step* 6: Multiply the votes by the respective criterion's weight.

**FIGURE 10-18**

| | Times Won in Pairings | Votes |
|---|---|---|
| Supervisory experience | &#124; &#124; &#124; | 3 |
| Product knowledge | &#124; &#124; &#124; &#124; &#124; &#124; &#124; &#124; &#124; | 9 |
| Salesmanship | &#124; | 1 |
| Communication skills | &#124; &#124; &#124; &#124; &#124; &#124; &#124; &#124; | 8 |
| Budget management | &#124; &#124; &#124; &#124; &#124; &#124; | 6 |
| Creativity | &#124; &#124; &#124; &#124; &#124; | 5 |
| Dedication | &#124; &#124; &#124; &#124; | 4 |
| Image | &#124; &#124; &#124; &#124; &#124; &#124; &#124; | 7 |
| Integrity | &#124; &#124; | 2 |
| Earnings | | 0 |

**FIGURE 10-19**

| | Criteria | | | | | |
|---|---|---|---|---|---|---|
| Items to Be Ranked | Product Knowledge, Weight: .4 | Communica- tion Skills, Weight: .3 | Image, Weight: .2 | Budget Management, Weight: .1 | Total Votes | Final Ranking |
| Martha | | | | | | |
| Tom | | | | | | |
| Patricia | | | | | | |
| Susan | | | | | | |
| George | | | | | | |
| Frank | | | | | | |
| Bill | | | | | | |
| Cynthia | | | | | | |
| Willard | | | | | | |
| Randy | | | | | | |

Figure 10-21 shows the weighted votes.

*Step* 7: Add the weighted values for each option and enter the sums in the column headed "Total Votes."

Figure 10-22 shows the total weighted votes for each item.

*Step* 8: Determine the final rankings and enter them in the last column, headed "Final Ranking." (The option with the most points is ranked highest.)

Figure 10-23 shows the final rankings. This analysis indicates that Susan should be my first choice, edging out Cynthia by a slim margin. However, because the top four rankings are very close, ranging from 6.7 to 7.3, it would pay to repeat the ranking process with just those four indi-

**FIGURE 10-20**

| Items to Be Ranked | Criteria | | | | Total Votes | Final Ranking |
|---|---|---|---|---|---|---|
| | Product Knowledge, Weight: .4 | Communica- tion Skills, Weight: .3 | Image, Weight: .2 | Budget Management, Weight: .1 | | |
| Martha | 1 | 4 | 1 | 3 | | |
| Tom | 9 | 5 | 6 | 5 | | |
| Patricia | 2 | 3 | 2 | 7 | | |
| Susan | 8 | 6 | 7 | 9 | | |
| George | 3 | 2 | 3 | 1 | | |
| Frank | 7 | 7 | 8 | 2 | | |
| Bill | 4 | 1 | 4 | 4 | | |
| Cynthia | 6 | 8 | 9 | 6 | | |
| Willard | 5 | 0 | 5 | 8 | | |
| Randy | 0 | 9 | 0 | 0 | | |

viduals, as in a runoff election—just to be sure. There's a lot riding on this analysis, and I want to be fair as well as accurate in my judgments.

*Step* 9: Perform a sanity check.

Here, for your review and reference, are the nine steps of weighted ranking:

# The Nine Steps of Weighted Ranking

*Step* 1: List all of the major criteria for ranking.

*Step* 2: Pair-rank the criteria.

*Step* 3: Select the top several criteria and weight them in percentiles (their sum must equal 1.0).

**FIGURE 10-21**

| Items to Be Ranked | Product Knowledge, Weight: .4 | Communica-tion Skills, Weight: .3 | Image, Weight: .2 | Budget Management, Weight: .1 | Total Votes | Final Ranking |
|---|---|---|---|---|---|---|
| | | | Criteria | | | |
| Martha | $1 \times .4 = 0.4$ | $4 \times .3 = 1.2$ | $1 \times .2 = 0.2$ | $3 \times .1 = 0.3$ | | |
| Tom | $9 \times .4 = 3.6$ | $5 \times .3 = 1.5$ | $6 \times .2 = 1.2$ | $5 \times .1 = 0.5$ | | |
| Patricia | $2 \times .4 = 0.8$ | $3 \times .3 = 0.9$ | $2 \times .2 = 0.4$ | $7 \times .1 = 0.7$ | | |
| Susan | $8 \times .4 = 3.2$ | $6 \times .3 = 1.8$ | $7 \times .2 = 1.4$ | $9 \times .1 = 0.9$ | | |
| George | $3 \times .4 = 1.2$ | $2 \times .3 = 0.6$ | $3 \times .2 = 0.6$ | $1 \times .1 = 0.1$ | | |
| Frank | $7 \times .4 = 2.8$ | $7 \times .3 = 2.1$ | $8 \times .2 = 1.6$ | $2 \times .1 = 0.2$ | | |
| Bill | $4 \times .4 = 1.6$ | $1 \times .3 = 0.3$ | $4 \times .2 = 0.8$ | $4 \times .1 = 0.4$ | | |
| Cynthia | $6 \times .4 = 2.4$ | $8 \times .3 = 2.4$ | $9 \times .2 = 1.8$ | $6 \times .1 = 0.6$ | | |
| Willard | $5 \times .4 = 2.0$ | $0 \times .3 = 0$ | $5 \times .2 = 1.0$ | $8 \times .1 = 0.8$ | | |
| Randy | $0 \times .4 = 0$ | $9 \times .3 = 2.7$ | $0 \times .2 = 0$ | $0 \times .1 = 0$ | | |

*Step 4*: Construct a Weighted Ranking Matrix (see Figure 10-24) and enter the items to be ranked, the selected criteria, and the criteria weights.

*Step 5*: Pair-rank all of the items by each criterion, recording in the appropriate spaces the number of "votes" each item receives.

*Step 6*: Multiply the votes by the respective criterion's weight.

*Step 7*: Add the weighted values for each item and enter the sums in the column headed "Total Votes."

*Step 8*: Determine the final rankings and enter them in the last column, headed "Final Ranking." (The item with the most points is ranked highest.)

*Step 9*: Perform a sanity check.

Using the above steps as a guide, practice the weighted ranking technique on the following two problems.

**FIGURE 10-22**

| Items to Be Ranked | Criteria | | | | Total Votes | Final Ranking |
|---|---|---|---|---|---|---|
| | Product Knowledge, Weight: .4 | Communication Skills, Weight: .3 | Image, Weight: .2 | Budget Management, Weight: .1 | | |
| Martha | 1 × .4 = 0.4 | 4 × .3 = 1.2 | 1 × .2 = 0.2 | 3 × .1 = 0.3 | 2.1 | |
| Tom | 9 × .4 = 3.6 | 5 × .3 = 1.5 | 6 × .2 = 1.2 | 5 × .1 = 0.5 | 6.8 | |
| Patricia | 2 × .4 = 0.8 | 3 × .3 = 0.9 | 2 × .2 = 0.4 | 7 × .1 = 0.7 | 2.8 | |
| Susan | 8 × .4 = 3.2 | 6 × .3 = 1.8 | 7 × .2 = 1.4 | 9 × .1 = 0.9 | 7.3 | |
| George | 3 × .4 = 1.2 | 2 × .3 = 0.6 | 3 × .2 = 0.6 | 1 × .1 = 0.1 | 2.5 | |
| Frank | 7 × .4 = 2.8 | 7 × .3 = 2.1 | 8 × .2 = 1.6 | 2 × .1 = 0.2 | 6.7 | |
| Bill | 4 × .4 = 1.6 | 1 × .3 = 0.3 | 4 × .2 = 0.8 | 4 × .1 = 0.4 | 3.1 | |
| Cynthia | 6 × .4 = 2.4 | 8 × .3 = 2.4 | 9 × .2 = 1.8 | 6 × .1 = 0.6 | 7.2 | |
| Willard | 5 × .4 = 2.0 | 0 × .3 = 0 | 5 × .2 = 1.0 | 8 × .1 = 0.8 | 3.8 | |
| Randy | 0 × .4 = 0 | 9 × .3 = 2.7 | 0 × .2 = 0 | 0 × .1 = 0 | 2.7 | |

## EXERCISE 25   Restaurants

You are planning to take a client to dinner this evening with several of your business associates and wish to make a good impression on him. Because you have never met him before, you are uncertain about his tastes in cuisine and dining atmosphere. But there has been no time to find out. He is arriving by plane in a matter of hours, and a dinner reservation must be made now. Think of five restaurants of different cuisine that you have patronized and that you believe would impress such a visitor. Based entirely on your own experience and preferences, rank the five restaurants based on the following four criteria: price of food, quality of food (meaning appearance and taste), quality of service, and the degree to which the general atmosphere in the restaurant adds to the pleasure of the meal.

 **BEFORE CONTINUING, COMPLETE THE RESTAURANTS PROBLEM.**

**FIGURE 10-23**

| Items to Be Ranked | Criteria | | | | Total Votes | Final Ranking |
|---|---|---|---|---|---|---|
| | Product Knowledge, Weight: .4 | Communication Skills, Weight: .3 | Image, Weight: .2 | Budget Management, Weight: .1 | | |
| Martha | 1 × .4 = 0.4 | 4 × .3 = 1.2 | 1 × .2 = 0.2 | 3 × .1 = 0.3 | 2.1 | 10 |
| Tom | 9 × .4 = 3.6 | 5 × .3 = 1.5 | 6 × .2 = 1.2 | 5 × .1 = 0.5 | 6.8 | 3 |
| Patricia | 2 × .4 = 0.8 | 3 × .3 = 0.9 | 2 × .2 = 0.4 | 7 × .1 = 0.7 | 2.8 | 7 |
| Susan | 8 × .4 = 3.2 | 6 × .3 = 1.8 | 7 × .2 = 1.4 | 9 × .1 = 0.9 | 7.3 | 1 |
| George | 3 × .4 = 1.2 | 2 × .3 = 0.6 | 3 × .2 = 0.6 | 1 × .1 = 0.1 | 2.5 | 9 |
| Frank | 7 × .4 = 2.8 | 7 × .3 = 2.1 | 8 × .2 = 1.6 | 2 × .1 = 0.2 | 6.7 | 4 |
| Bill | 4 × .4 = 1.6 | 1 × .3 = 0.3 | 4 × .2 = 0.8 | 4 × .1 = 0.4 | 3.1 | 6 |
| Cynthia | 6 × .4 = 2.4 | 8 × .3 = 2.4 | 9 × .2 = 1.8 | 6 × .1 = 0.6 | 7.2 | 2 |
| Willard | 5 × .4 = 2.0 | 0 × .3 = 0 | 5 × .2 = 1.0 | 8 × .1 = 0.8 | 3.8 | 5 |
| Randy | 0 × .4 = 0 | 9 × .3 = 2.7 | 0 × .2 = 0 | 0 × .1 = 0 | 2.7 | 8 |

The solution to Exercise 25 shows the matrix you should have constructed.

## EXERCISE 26   Business Magnates

Using the weighted ranking technique, determine which of the following famous business magnates is the most inspiring role model for young people interested in business careers: Ross Perot, Donald Trump, Lee Iacocca (Ford and Chrysler), Bill Gates (Microsoft), and Michael Eisner (Disney).

Here are eight criteria for your consideration in Step 1: innovative projects that they managed or in which they were involved, business accomplishments, philanthropic activities, moral standards, political activities, importance of their business activities to the nation's welfare, public image of the corporations they have headed, and personal life (as portrayed in the news media).

**FIGURE 10-24**

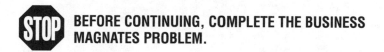

| Items to Be Ranked | (Criterion) (Weight) | Total Votes | Final Ranking |
|---|---|---|---|
|  |  |  |  |

Please add other criteria you believe would be relevant and eliminate any criteria on which you lack sufficient knowledge. Remember, this is just an exercise; there is no right or wrong answer. Limit your list of criteria to no fewer than six and no more than eight. In Step 3, select only the top *three* criteria.

**STOP** **BEFORE CONTINUING, COMPLETE THE BUSINESS MAGNATES PROBLEM.**

The solution to Exercise 26 shows the matrix you should have constructed.

# 11

# Hypothesis Testing

 Do you believe in UFOs? That is, do you believe that so-called unidentified flying objects are spacecraft controlled by aliens from another solar system or galaxy? Why? Think about it for a moment.

If you flat out don't believe a word about UFOs being aliens from outer space, have you ever considered the alternative? Has it ever occurred to you that you might be wrong—that UFOs might actually be extraterrestrial vehicles?

If, on the other hand, you are a true believer in their extraterrestrial origin, have you ever given serious thought to the notion that UFOs may not exist at all, that they are, as some leading scientists argue, purely imaginings and illusions?

The study of the UFO phenomenon and public reactions to it illustrate how humans customarily analyze possible scenarios that would explain a given situation. In keeping with our troublesome instinctive mental traits, we first select the scenario we intuitively believe is most likely correct, say, "UFOs are from another solar system." Next, we look for evidence to support that scenario. Because we tend to find what we look for, we begin to gather supporting evidence. As this evidence accumulates, we become more and more convinced of our hypothesis and more and more resistant to, and contemptuous of, contradictory evidence and the alternative scenarios such evidence supports. When we come across contradictory evidence (as the two interviewers on *Prime Time Live*'s segment on age discrimination did when shown a videotape of the interviews), we either ignore it, belittle it, or construe it in a way that renders it, if not supportive, at least neutral.

Some notable examples of this get-off-at-the-first-stop approach to analyzing problems have occurred in criminal investigations by law enforcement organizations. A major TV investigative news program reported a year ago on just such a case: A young man accused of rape was arrested by the police, tried, and convicted. He lived near the victim, was identified by her in a lineup as her assailant, and had no alibi. When the police apprehended him shortly after the rape, they halted their investigation and looked no further. A year or so later, the real rapist, who also lived in the victim's neighborhood, confessed to the crime, and the first man arrested was released. Had the police continued their investigation, they would probably have discovered the look-alike.

What the police did is called "satisficing"—picking the first solution that seems satisfactory, rather than examining all of the alternative hypotheses to identify not simply one that fits the evidence but the one that fits *best*. The problem is that most evidence is consistent with several hypotheses. That my cat's fur is wet is consistent with the cat having been outside in the rain, having fallen into a water-filled sink, having been sprayed by one of the children, and so on. Thus, the wet fur, as evidence, is of no value whatever in determining which of these hypotheses is true.

# Hypotheses

A hypothesis is a declarative statement that has not been established as true. (If we knew it to be true, it wouldn't be a hypothesis.) We assert the truth of a hypothesis by offering supporting evidence. But, as the late philosopher Karl Popper established in his writings in the 1930s, we can never really prove a hypothesis true. We can and do, however, for countless reasons, accept hypotheses as true until they are proven to be false. The enduring belief five centuries ago that the earth was flat could not be proven true no matter how much evidence its adherents presented. Yet it took only one item of contradictory evidence—Magellan's voyage—to prove the hypothesis false.

We disprove a hypothesis with *evidence*. "Information" becomes "evidence" only when we connect it with a hypothesis. Thus, we scan "information" looking for "evidence."

When we find "evidence," we should try to establish its validity by answering four questions:

1. *Who or what was the source?*
2. *What was the source's access?* How did the source obtain the information? Was that method plausible? For example, if the source of the information claims he or she read the information in a certain document, is it reasonable that the source had access to that document?
3. *What is the source's reliability?* Is the source reputable? Has other information from the source proven to be accurate?
4. *Is the information plausible?* From the standpoint of everything we know about the problem and from just plain old common sense, does the information seem to make sense? Is such information common or rare?

Illustrative of the problems and issues associated with source validation was the controversy reported in *The Washington Post* surrounding a Soviet document alleging that the government of North Vietnam had lied about the number of U.S. prisoners of war it held at the end of the Vietnam conflict. In April 1993, U.S. Department of Defense officials and intelligence analysts accepted the document as authentic—that is, it was determined to be a genuine official Soviet intelligence document. But according to press articles, they challenged the validity of the information it contained because it conflicted with strong evidence from reliable sources. The Harvard-based researcher who obtained the document from the Russian government's archives in Moscow reportedly based the credibility of his research on the validity of Soviet intelligence and categorically denied that the Soviet intelligence on which he planned to base his book was flawed. He was quoted as saying, "If this story is flawed ... then the whole Soviet Politburo was misinformed about the Vietnam conflict [in] which they invested billions of rubles." It was apparently inconceivable to the researcher that an official intelligence document, and a Soviet document as well, could be inaccurate. In short, he seemed to have difficulty distinguishing between the authenticity of a document and the accuracy of the information it contains.

Hypotheses play a vital role in analysis. By yielding to the mind's proclivity to focus on one solution, a hypothesis helps to narrow the scope of our thinking. It thus provides a framework—a mind-set—within which to analyze and interpret information. While this focusing is normally beneficial to analysis, it can have dramatically negative effects if it leads to satisficing—to focusing on one hypothesis to the exclusion of alternatives.

So what can we do to offset our natural tendency to satisfice? You know the answer. All together, now: *structure!* And how might we structure analysis to ensure that all hypotheses are considered sufficiently to test their degree of validity? By using a technique called, strangely enough, "hypothesis testing."

What the technique does is to rank competing hypotheses by the degree to which relevant evidence is *inconsistent.* The favored hypothesis is the one with the *least inconsistent* evidence, not the one with the *most consistent* evidence. Let me say that again. The favored hypothesis has the least inconsistent evidence, not the most consistent evidence. Consistent evidence proves nothing, because evidence can, and usually does, support more than one hypothesis.

This insight concerning the inherent, inescapable limitations of consistent evidence is profound but regrettably not widely known or applied. Time and again, all around us, in every walk of life, people make judgments based on a preponderance of evidence consistent with (in favor of) a particular course of action only to be blindsided by unforeseen adverse circumstances (inconsistent evidence) that prevent a satisfactory outcome. Only *inconsistent* evidence has any real value in determining the credibility of a hypothesis and in ranking hypotheses by the degree of their credibility. Let me demonstrate.

Figure 11-1 presents what is called a Hypothesis-Testing Matrix. Its structural components are elementary. The pieces of *key* evidence (not

**FIGURE 11-1**   Hypothesis-Testing Matrix

| Evidence | Hypotheses | | |
|---|---|---|---|
| | **A** | **B** | **C** |
| 1. | | | |
| 2. | | | |
| 3. | | | |
| 4. | | | |

just *any* evidence but the important items) are listed down the left; the competing hypotheses are labeled and entered at the top right.

# The Seven Steps of Hypothesis Testing

There are seven steps in hypothesis testing, and they may appear a bit complicated at first, but practice will show they really aren't. Let me demonstrate the steps by applying them to "The Bakery" problem cited in Chapter 8. To get the most out of this exercise, please perform all seven steps on a sheet of paper as we go through them. (As someone once said, you can't learn to play the piano by watching someone else practice.)

The three sudden episodes of overbaked bread faced Henry Willis, the bakery manager, with the grim prospect of not meeting deliveries during the biggest grocery shopping week of the year. The loss of revenue and, if the overbaking continued, the eventual loss of customers would be a staggering setback, just when the bakery had begun to post solid profits for the first time in six months. Frantic for a solution, Willis phoned a management research firm, which immediately dispatched Connie Stewart, a consultant trained in analytic structuring techniques, to investigate the problem.

For an hour Stewart interviewed all of the principals involved, recording on yellow pads and cassette tapes the information they provided. Then, withdrawing to a vacant office, she began to analyze her findings. First, she wrote down as many hypotheses as she could think of to explain how the bread had come to be overbaked. Eliminating the implausible and combining several that were similar, she narrowed the list to three: sabotage by employees (meaning they had intentionally baked the bread too long or at too hot a temperature or had added something to the batter to cause overbaking), malfunctioning of the ovens' gas gauges, and fluctuations in the gas pressure being supplied to the bakery. She then performed the first step in hypothesis testing: construction of a matrix.

*Step 1*: Construct a matrix. Label the first column "Evidence." Label the other columns to the right "Hypotheses," and enter descriptors of the hypotheses atop the columns. The hypotheses must be mutually exclusive.

The hypotheses need *not* be collectively exhaustive. In some cases, it may serve our analytic purpose to test only selected hypotheses. Figure 11-2 shows what the matrix should look like.

*Step 2*: List "significant" evidence down the left-hand margin, including "absent" evidence.

In keeping with the principal of major factors, list only significant evidence.

Because we are prone to satisfice, we often don't dig deep or far enough in gathering evidence. Asking ourselves questions about absent evidence is a divergent way of breaking this tendency.

Include the *absence* of evidence one would expect if the hypothesis were true as well as the absence of evidence one would expect if it were untrue. For example, if the hypothesis "a drought" were true, one would expect the absence of rain puddles. If it were untrue, one would expect the absence of dry, crusty soil.

Ask "Alexander's question": What evidence *not* included in the matrix would refute one or more of the hypotheses? Determine if such evidence exists. If it does, acquire it and incorporate it into the matrix.

**FIGURE 11- 2**

| Evidence | Hypotheses | | |
|---|---|---|---|
| | Sabotage by employees | Malfunction of the ovens' gas gauges | Fluctuations in gas pressure |
| | | | |
| | | | |
| | | | |
| | | | |
| | | | |
| | | | |
| | | | |
| | | | |
| | | | |

Neustadt and May refer to Alexander's question in their book *Thinking in Time*. They relate that in 1976 President Gerald Ford consulted an ad hoc advisory committee regarding the advisability of approving a program to immunize the U.S. population against swine flu. Dr. Russell Alexander, a public health professor at the University of Washington and a member of the committee, wished to know *what fresh data from anywhere would cause his colleagues to reverse their support for the immunization program.* In other words, what evidence, not currently in hand and whose existence was purely conjectural, would be *inconsistent* with immunizing the U.S. population. If such evidence were plausible, a concerted effort should be made to determine if it existed and, if it did, to acquire it. That is Alexander's question: *What fresh information from anywhere would be inconsistent with a certain hypothesis?* It is a divergent analytic technique that can be applied advantageously to analysis of any problem.

Stewart listed nine items of evidence in the left-hand column of the matrix:

Three batches of bread were overbaked.

Only the specially prepared bread was overbaked.

Only two ovens overbaked bread.

The maintenance man found nothing wrong with the heat gauges.

Overbaking took place during the bakery's busiest season of the year.

Employees are unhappy over poor benefits.

Employees are angry over the Menendez firing.

Frank Moreau [the baker of Crew 2] was seen talking with Menendez in the parking lot.

Flour deliveries from the new supplier were delayed.

Figure 11-3 shows the matrix with the evidence listed.

*Step 3:* Working across the matrix, test the evidence for consistency with each hypothesis, one item of evidence at a time.

**FIGURE 11-3**

| Evidence | Hypotheses | | |
| --- | --- | --- | --- |
| | **Sabotage by employees** | **Malfunction of the ovens' gas gauges** | **Fluctuations in gas pressure** |
| Three batches of bread were overbaked. | | | |
| Only specially prepared bread was overbaked. | | | |
| Only two ovens overbaked bread. | | | |
| The maintenance man found nothing wrong with the heat gauges. | | | |
| Overbaking took place during the bakery's busiest season of the year. | | | |
| Employees are unhappy over poor benefits. | | | |
| Employees are angry over the Menendez firing. | | | |
| Frank Moreau was seen talking with Menendez in the parking lot. | | | |
| Flour deliveries from the new supplier were delayed. | | | |

Experience shows that working horizontally (weighing each item of evidence against all of the hypotheses) is more effective than working vertically (weighing all of the evidence against one hypothesis at a time).

Work one item of evidence at a time, determine with respect to each hypothesis whether the evidence is *consistent* (C), *inconsistent* (I), or *ambiguous* (?).

"Consistency" does not mean the evidence necessarily validates the hypothesis. It means the evidence is compatible—i.e., not inconsistent—with the hypothesis.

You may wish to indicate varying degrees of consistency, inconsistency, or ambiguity by annotating the letters with −, +, or * (e.g., C− for "consistent in part"; I+ for "inconsistent in many respects"; and C* for "absolutely consistent"). I also recommend writing succinct comments in the cells, again as you think necessary, explaining your reasoning. These annotations are important because they force us to explain and record our decisions at the time we make them, and they later serve as valuable references.

Stewart then tested the consistency or inconsistency of the evidence with each hypothesis:

☐   Is the fact that three batches of bread were overbaked consistent or inconsistent with "Sabotage by employees"? Consistent . . . meaning that sabotage is compatible with three batches of bread being overbaked. It does not mean there is necessarily a relationship between the overcooking and the sabotage—that three batches being overbaked is "proof" of sabotage. Rather, it means that both sabotage and the overbaking of three batches could have occurred.
☐   Is overbaking three batches consistent or inconsistent with "Malfunction of the ovens' gas gauges"? Consistent.
☐   Is the overbaking consistent or inconsistent with "Fluctuations in gas pressure"? Consistent.

And so on.

Figure 11-4 shows the entries in each cell of the matrix.

**FIGURE 11-4**

| Evidence | Hypotheses | | |
| --- | --- | --- | --- |
| | Sabotage by employees | Malfunction of the ovens' gas gauges | Fluctuations in gas pressure |
| Three batches of bread were overbaked. | C | C | C |
| Only specially prepared bread was overbaked. | C | C | C |
| Only two ovens overbaked bread. | C | C | I |
| The maintenance man found nothing wrong with the heat gauges. | C | I | C |
| Overbaking took place during the bakery's busiest season of the year. | C | C | C |
| Employees are unhappy over poor benefits. | C | C | C |
| Employees are angry over the Menendez firing. | C | C | C |
| Frank Moreau was seen talking with Menendez in the parking lot. | C | C | C |
| Flour deliveries from the new supplier were delayed. | C | C | C |

Stewart found only two inconsistencies:

The fact that only two ovens overbaked bread is inconsistent with the
hypothesis that the gas pressure fluctuated. Had the pressure fluctuated, all of the ovens (not just two) would have experienced overbaking.

The fact that the maintenance man found nothing wrong with the
heat gauges is inconsistent with the hypothesis that the oven
gauges malfunctioned.

*Step 4*: Refine the matrix.
  *a*. Add or reword hypotheses.

Sometimes we discover other alternative hypotheses that should be
considered along with the ones already in the matrix.

As Stewart studied the matrix and reviewed her notes, it occurred to her
that the delivery of flour from the new supplier had coincided with the
onset of overbaked bread. Could there be a connection? If so, a fourth
hypothesis—"The new flour is defective"—should be added to the
matrix, which Stewart did, entering a C in each of its cells.

Sometimes in the course of our analysis we find it useful to define a
hypothesis more clearly.

None of the four hypotheses required revision. Figure 11-5 shows these
additions.

  *b*. Add "significant" evidence relevant to any new or reworded
      hypothesis and test it against all hypotheses.

Considering the newly added hypothesis, Stewart wondered if only
batches made with the flour from the new supplier had overbaked. If
that were the case, it would be inconsistent with sabotage. Why would
employees bent on sabotaging the bakery's operations overbake only
batches made from the new flour? That didn't make sense. Nor was this

**FIGURE 11-5**

| Evidence | Hypotheses | | | |
| --- | --- | --- | --- | --- |
| | Sabotage by employees | Malfunction of the ovens' gas gauges | Fluctuations in gas pressure | The new flour is defective |
| Three batches of bread were overbaked. | C | C | C | C |
| Only specially prepared bread was overbaked. | C | C | C | C |
| Only two ovens overbaked bread. | C | C | I | C |
| The maintenance man found nothing wrong with the heat gauges. | C | I | C | C |
| Overbaking took place during the bakery's busiest season of the year. | C | C | C | C |
| Employees are unhappy over poor benefits. | C | C | C | C |
| Employees are angry over the Menendez firing. | C | C | C | C |
| Frank Moreau was seen talking with Menendez in the parking lot. | C | C | C | C |
| Flour deliveries from the new supplier were delayed. | C | C | C | C |

new evidence consistent with the heat gauge and gas fluctuation hypotheses. So she added this new item as evidence and entered I's for the first three hypotheses and a C for the fourth. Figure 11-6 shows these additions.

c. Delete, but keep a record of, evidence that is consistent with all of the hypotheses. It has no diagnostic value.

Stewart deleted the seven items of evidence that were consistent with all three hypotheses, leaving three (Figure 11-7): "Only two ovens over-baked bread," "The maintenance man found nothing wrong with the heat gauges," and "Only batches made with the new flour overbaked." For future reference, she kept a separate record of the deleted evidence, as you should when you do hypothesis testing.

*Step 5:* Working downward, evaluate each hypothesis.

Delete any hypothesis for which there is significant inconsistent evidence. Confirm the validity of evidence that is decisive in contradicting a hypothesis. Also identify, and check the validity of, the principal underlying assumptions.

Stewart reviewed her findings. Was there sufficient inconsistent evidence to refute any hypothesis? There were three—all but "The new flour is defective"—so she promptly deleted them. Figure 11-8 shows the deletion of the three hypotheses.

*Step 6:* Rank the hypotheses by the strength of inconsistent evidence.

Normally, the hypothesis with the least inconsistent evidence should be ranked first. But it's rarely as cut and dried as that. This is not an arithmetical process of simply adding up the I's. The degree of inconsistency of evidence can vary widely from cell to cell and is subject to interpretation—but that's what analysis is all about, isn't it.

Stewart observed that only one hypothesis—"The new flour is defective"—had no inconsistent evidence. Because she knew that consistent

**FIGURE 11-6**

| Evidence | Hypotheses | | | |
|---|---|---|---|---|
| | Sabotage by employees | Malfunction of the ovens' gas gauges | Fluctuations in gas pressure | The new flour is defective |
| Three batches of bread were overbaked. | C | C | C | C |
| Only specially prepared bread was overbaked. | C | C | C | C |
| Only two ovens overbaked bread. | C | C | I | C |
| The maintenance man found nothing wrong with the heat gauges. | C | I | C | C |
| Overbaking took place during the bakery's busiest season of the year. | C | C | C | C |
| Employees are unhappy over poor benefits. | C | C | C | C |
| Employees are angry over the Menendez firing. | C | C | C | C |
| Frank Moreau was seen talking with Menendez in the parking lot. | C | C | C | C |
| Flour deliveries from the new supplier were delayed. | C | C | C | C |
| Only batches made with the new flour overbaked. | I | I | I | C |

**FIGURE 11-7**

| Evidence | Hypotheses | | | |
|---|---|---|---|---|
| | Sabotage by employees | Malfunction of the ovens' gas gauges | Fluctuations in gas pressure | The new flour is defective |
| Only two ovens overbaked bread. | C | C | I | C |
| The maintenance man found nothing wrong with the heat gauges. | C | I | C | C |
| Only batches made with the new flour overbaked. | I | I | I | C |

**FIGURE 11-8**

| Evidence | Hypotheses | | | |
|---|---|---|---|---|
| | ~~Sabotage by employees~~ | ~~Malfunction of the ovens' gas gauges~~ | ~~Fluctuations in gas pressure~~ | The new flour is defective |
| Only two ovens overbaked bread. | C | C | I | C |
| The maintenance man found nothing wrong with the heat gauges. | C | I | C | C |
| Only batches made with the new flour overbaked. | I | I | I | C |

evidence has no diagnostic value, she did not leap to the conclusion that the new flour was the cause of the overbaking. Instead, she analyzed the relationship between the new flour and the overbaked batches, sorting the data chronologically in matrices (see Chapter 8). The matrices showed a conclusive correlation.

*Step* 7: Perform a sanity check.

Stewart reviewed her findings, the hypotheses, the evidence, and the principal underlying assumptions and was comfortable with her conclusion that the new flour had caused the overbaking.

## The Case of Disney's America

An example of how hypothesis testing could have made a significant difference in the outcome of a business investment was the Walt Disney Company's failed attempt to build a major theme park, Disney's America, in Prince William County, Virginia, fifty miles west of Washington, D.C. The company announced its theme park project in late 1993, then glumly canceled it ten months later, culminating what *The Washingtonian* magazine described as "an epic struggle . . . over complicated issues ranging from how much real estate development is ideal on metropolitan Washington's western fringe to the proper place of history in American life."

Landowners and residents in Prince William and adjacent counties, caught unawares by Disney's behind-the-scenes activities to acquire land for the park, were slow to mount effective opposition when the plan became known. Although the park's opponents gradually amassed considerable funding and professional talent, theirs was a losing cause until the powerful National Trust for Historic Preservation (NTHP) entered the fray late in the game, persuading Disney CEO Michael Eisner that Disney's America was an unwise investment.

Disney planners were taken aback by the ferocity of the opposition. According to *The Washingtonian*, Eisner declared, "I'm shocked [by the opposition to the project] because I thought we were doing good. I expected to be taken around on people's shoulders." The article stated he was surprised that so many wealthy people with such deep attachment to their land lived west of Washington. "But," it continued, "it was hardly a surprise to anyone who drove along the back roads. . . . The landscape suggested the presence of wealth around every turn. . . . It was the horse that gave the region its distinction. There were 15,000 horses stabled in [Fauquier and Loudoun] counties, about half of Virginia's total and enough to rank the area as one of the greatest concentrations of equine flesh outside Kentucky."

It is too easy in hindsight to say what Disney *should* have done and *why*. But there is no question that the Disney planners miscalculated both the nature and power of the opposition the project would face. Another way of putting it is that Disney was persuaded to proceed with the project by evidence *consistent* with the company's objectives, while misunderstanding, underestimating, or ignoring *inconsistent* evidence. It was the latter evidence that spelled the project's demise.

One approach Disney's planners could have used with hypothesis testing was to examine two basic propositions: The plan for Disney's America *will be* approved; the plan *will not be* approved. The evidence to be tested against these two hypotheses would have consisted of anticipated actions, forces, beliefs, and attitudes for and against the plan. By following the steps of this technique, especially by asking Alexander's question, the nature and strength of potential opposition to the plan would almost certainly have emerged as key evidence and would have brought to light the plan's major vulnerabilities.

Had Disney planners taken this approach to structuring their analysis of the project early in the planning process, they would, I am confident, have better understood the vitality and durability of the opposition they would face and would have been better prepared to deal with it. A small group of creative divergent planners could have conceived of a dozen ways to preempt and overcome this opposition long before it could coalesce into the formidable force it ultimately became. For example, had Disney's decision makers foreseen the role the NTHP might play on behalf of the opposition, they could have enlisted the NTHP's scholarly assistance and professional advice from the start, even before a site for the theme park had been selected. The NTHP and various leading historians would then have had a direct, leading role in determining which historic themes would be portrayed in the park and how these portrayals could be made both educational and entertaining for the public. (Indeed, from the negative public reaction that some of Disney's ideas for themes received, Disney could have used the NTHP's help.) Having therefore acquired an intellectual stake—"intellectual ownership"—in the park, the historians and the NTHP would have been less well positioned later to oppose the park's concepts, and the opposition could very well have been deprived of the central argument that, in the actual event, carried the day—namely, protection of America's sacred heritage: the Civil War battlefields near Manassas.

# The Seven Steps of Hypothesis Testing, One More Time

Let's review the seven steps of hypothesis testing. You will need to refer to them as you undertake the practice exercises that follow.

*Step 1:* Construct a matrix. Label the first column "Evidence." Label the other columns to the right "Hypotheses," and enter descriptors of the hypotheses atop the columns. The hypotheses must be mutually exclusive.

*Step 2:* List "significant" evidence down the left-hand margin.
- ☐ Include "absent" evidence.
- ☐ Ask Alexander's question.

*Step 3:* Working across the matrix, test the evidence for consistency with each hypothesis, one item of evidence at a time.
- ☐ C, I, or ?

*Step 4:* Refine the matrix.
- ☐ Add or reword hypotheses.
- ☐ Add "significant" evidence relevant to new or reworded hypotheses and test it against all hypotheses.
- ☐ Delete, but keep a record of, evidence that is consistent with all hypotheses.

*Step* 5: Working downward, evaluate each hypothesis.
- ☐ Delete hypotheses for which there is significant inconsistent evidence.
- ☐ Confirm the validity of evidence that is decisive in contradicting a hypothesis.

*Step* 6: Rank the hypotheses by the strength of inconsistent evidence.
- ☐ The hypothesis with the least inconsistent evidence is normally ranked first.

*Step* 7: Perform a sanity check.

# A Versatile Analytic Tool

Like the weighted ranking technique, hypothesis testing can be both a diagnostic and a decision-making tool. At times it plays the role of decision maker by eliminating all but one hypothesis. But even when it doesn't point decisively to a solution, the results of hypothesis testing inform and sharpen our analytic judgments about the likelihood of the alternatives being considered. Remember that the cardinal strength of hypothesis testing lies in its function, which is to *disprove, not prove, hypotheses.*

Hypothesis testing mirrors the PROs, CONs, and FIXes technique. Consistent evidence equates to pros, while inconsistent evidence equates to cons. Just as cons represent the burden one must bear if one implements a particular option, so inconsistent evidence is the incongruity one must live with if one "buys" a particular hypothesis. Both techniques illuminate and focus our attention on the factors (pro and con) and the evidence (consistent and inconsistent) that are critical to our analysis.

Hypothesis testing is, in sum, a powerful and highly versatile technique that can be used to analyze past, current, and even future events. Two examples of applying hypothesis testing to a future situation are:

Will Russia's free-market economy evolve and prosper or lead to societal chaos? (We can hypothesize two alternative scenarios: the Russian market economy will fail or it will succeed.)

Will the cost of city services grow in the next five years? (We can hypothesize three alternative scenarios: costs will decrease, remain the same, or increase.)

In both examples we look for significant *current* evidence relating to each alternative hypothesis, analyze the evidence in a hypothesis-testing matrix, and rank the hypotheses according to our assessment of their likelihood of occurring.

# A Consoling Word About Consistent Evidence

Lest I leave you with the erroneous impression that I believe consistent evidence has no value, permit me to digress briefly to consecrate its analytic role.

Consistent evidence is, of course, vital in the presentation of one's analytic findings. One could not sensibly champion a particular hypothesis solely on the ground that there is less inconsistent evidence for it than for the alternatives. Indeed, it is the search for consistent evidence—the reasons *favoring* something—that usually drives our analysis. To make a compelling case for a hypothesis, we must naturally offer positive, supporting evidence—that is, consistent evidence.

Take "The Bakery" problem, for example. On the basis of *inconsistent* evidence, Stewart eliminated all of the hypotheses save one: defective flour. But to make her case to the management that the flour was indeed defective and the cause of the overbaking, she had to prove it, that is, present evidence *consistent* with this hypothesis. This demonstrates very well that, in problem solving, inconsistent evidence plays the key role during the analytic phase while consistent evidence plays the key role in the summation and presentation phase.

Let's practice the hypothesis-testing technique on an analytic problem.

## EXERCISE 27   Lost Data

Sarah, the president of a small but highly successful advertising agency, was awakened at 1:00 A.M. by the ringing of her bedside phone. Her hand easily found the receiver in the dark and lifted it to her ear.

"Yes?" she said groggily, struggling to clear her mind.

"Sarah, this is Gerald. I'm at the office. Something terrible has happened!" Gerald was one of her three account executives.

Her mind slowly clearing, she mumbled, "What? What's wrong?"

"I was working late on the Anderson job, and, when I went into the computer for the latest cost figures, they weren't there."

"Not there?"

"No. They're gone. Deleted."

Sarah was now fully awake, her mind racing to assess the situation and the problem it presented and to think of a quick solution. "Isn't there a backup? I thought it was automatic."

"I've checked the backup. The Anderson records have been deleted there, too."

"I don't understand," she said. "How could they be deleted? Was it a computer virus? I thought we were protected from that."

"We are. The system is programmed to automatically check for viruses in any program loaded into the computer. Just to be sure, I ran a special virus check a few minutes ago and it found none. It wasn't a virus."

"Then what? Someone deleted the records on purpose?"

"It looks that way, Sarah."

"But who?"

In the momentary silence while they both pondered her question, another thought occurred to her. "Are the cost records the only ones deleted?"

She heard Gerald sigh.

"That's the really bad part. I looked. *All* the Anderson files are gone, and on the backup as well."

"You mean our proposals on future projects, the planning documents, everything?"

"Sorry, Sarah. They're all gone. It's a major loss. A horrible setback. It took us months to put that together, and it will take months to redo it."

Switching on her bed lamp, Sarah started to get up, then slumped down on the edge of the bed, too shaken to stand. There wasn't time to redo the proposals. The submission deadline was in two weeks. There was no way she could make it. They were dead.

"You all right, Sarah?" asked Gerald softly, breaking the silence.

"No . . . but what can I do?"

"Nothing, I guess."

"Who do you think did it?" she asked. "Someone working for one of our competitors?"

"I have no idea."

"I don't either, but I will!" A sharp, determined businesswoman, Sarah resolved that minute to find out who the culprit was. "There's nothing we can do about it right now, but I'm going to interview everyone first thing in the morning and try to get to the bottom of this."

As soon as she arrived at her desk, Sarah interviewed Gerald and her other four employees: her secretary, Lisa; her administrative assistant, Chuck; and the other two account executives, Sam and Edward. Based on the information she obtained, she constructed the matrix in Figure 11-9 showing the hours each staff member had been present in the office and had had access to one of the computer terminals. She determined that at least one staff member had been in the office from 4:00 P.M., when the Anderson files had last been accessed, until midnight, when they were gone. At least one staff member had been present the whole time, meaning no one had broken into the office to commit this

**FIGURE 11-9**

| Staff Member | 4 P.M. | 5 P.M. | 6 P.M. | 7 P.M. | 8 P.M. | 9 P.M. | 10 P.M. | 11 P.M. | 12 A.M. |
|---|---|---|---|---|---|---|---|---|---|
| Edward | | | | | | | | | |
| Sam | X | | | | X | X | X | | |
| Gerald | X | X | X | | X | X | X | X | |
| Lisa | X | X | X | | | | | | |
| Chuck | | | | X | | | X | | |

heinous act. She also ascertained that, when two or more staffers were present, it would have been impossible (because of the way the computer was set up) for anyone to access the backup system without the others present knowing it.

She further determined that all of the staff members except Sam knew how to operate the computer well enough to delete the Anderson records. Sam was averse to computers, and, though he had attended several computer training courses, he had never quite got the hang of it and whenever possible studiously avoided using the "infernal contraption."

Sam suggested that perhaps someone had deleted the files remotely over a phone line. But Gerald dispelled that idea, assuring her that their computer was electronically isolated; no phone-line connections.

Upon further questioning, Sarah learned that, aside from herself, only Gerald and Chuck knew the password to the files stored in the computer's automatic backup system.

Using the hypothesis-testing technique, try to determine from all of this information who deleted the Anderson records.

*Step 1:* Construct a matrix.

Complete only the upper portion, identifying the various hypotheses.

 **BEFORE CONTINUING, PERFORM STEP 1.**

Based on the evidence she had gathered, Sarah quickly eliminated three explanations for the deletion of the computer files:

A computer virus had destroyed the records.

Someone had deleted the records by gaining remote access to the computer via a phone line.

Some outsider, not a member of her staff, either visiting or breaking into the office, had deleted the records.

Therefore, the perpetrator had to be one of her five staff members, in which case the matrix should have five hypotheses, one for each suspect. Figure 11-10 shows the upper part of the matrix you should have constructed.

*Step 2:* List "significant" evidence down the left-hand margin.

For the sake of simplicity, let us forgo the consideration of "absent" evidence.

Sarah identified three items of significant evidence: the perpetrator had been alone in the office, was computer smart, and knew the password (to access the Anderson files). Enter these items into your matrix.

 **BEFORE CONTINUING, PERFORM STEP 2.**

Figure 11-11 shows the amended matrix.

*Step 3:* Working across the matrix, test the evidence for consistency with each hypothesis, one item of evidence at a time.

**FIGURE 11-10**

| Evidence | Hypotheses | | | | |
|---|---|---|---|---|---|
| | Edward | Sam | Gerald | Lisa | Chuck |
| | | | | | |

**FIGURE 11-11**

| Evidence | Hypotheses | | | | |
|---|---|---|---|---|---|
| | Edward | Sam | Gerald | Lisa | Chuck |
| Alone in the office | | | | | |
| Computer smart | | | | | |
| Knew the password | | | | | |

**BEFORE CONTINUING, PERFORM STEP 3.**

Figure 11-12 shows the consistency and inconsistency of the items of evidence with each hypothesis.

*Step 4*: Refine the matrix.

Are there any hypotheses to be added or reworded? No. Is there any evidence to be deleted because it is consistent with all hypotheses? No. Let us then move on to the next step.

*Step 5*: Working downward, evaluate each hypothesis.

Delete hypotheses for which there is significant inconsistent evidence, but in doing so confirm the validity of decisive evidence.

 **BEFORE CONTINUING, PERFORM STEP 5.**

All three items of evidence are inconsistent with Sam: he was never alone in the office, he did not know how to operate the computer well enough to delete the files, and he did not know the password to the backup system. Sam can therefore be eliminated as a suspect.

Both Edward and Lisa can be eliminated because neither was ever alone in the office or knew the backup system password.

**FIGURE 11-12**

| Evidence | Hypotheses | | | | |
|---|---|---|---|---|---|
| | **Edward** | **Sam** | **Gerald** | **Lisa** | **Chuck** |
| Alone in the office | *I* | *I* | *C* | *I* | *C* |
| Computer smart | *C* | *I* | *C* | *C* | *C* |
| Knew the password | *I* | *I* | *C* | *I* | *C* |

**FIGURE 11-13**

| Evidence | Hypotheses | |
|---|---|---|
| | Gerald | Chuck |
| Alone in the office | C | C |
| Computer smart | C | C |
| Knew the password | C | C |

Figure 11-13 shows the matrix with these three hypotheses removed.

*Step* 6: Rank the hypotheses by the strength of inconsistent evidence.

As the evidence is not inconsistent with either the Gerald or Chuck hypotheses, we must rate them as equal possibilities.

*Step* 7: Perform a sanity check.

Are our findings intuitively reasonable? I believe they are.

## EXERCISE 28 The Jane Bolding Case (based on an article in *Regardie's,* May 1988)

"Jane Bolding was a smart, committed, exemplary nurse, but her patients died more often than other nurses'. And when the results of a shocking statistical study were released, the police said she was a killer."

Raised a Catholic in a poor blue-collar family in Bladensburg, Maryland, she was active in high school (student government, drama club, broadcasting club, and school newspaper), a neat girl, funny, easy to talk to, and a great shoulder to cry on. Her father was an alcoholic, and her mother, a large woman, always had a vicious look on her face and verbally abused her. Bolding was adopted, something she learned at age fourteen during a fight with her parents. She was a bright, serious student who breezed through math and science. She worked as a candy striper at the Prince George's Hospital Center and aspired to become a doctor, but she was bitterly disappointed that her parents could not afford to send her to college. Two months after graduating from high school in 1975, she got a job as a blood collector in the hospital's pathology lab.

Three years later she transferred to the Intensive Care Unit (ICU) as a low-level nursing assistant, and later she became a critical care technician. Soon afterward her performance was rated exemplary: intelligent, sound medical judgment, superconscientious, did the best for her patients. Enrolled part-time in a two-year nursing program, she graduated in May 1983 as a registered nurse. Her job was her life. She kept up with nursing research, taught classes in critical care, worked extra shifts, stayed late to write meticulous notes about her patients, rarely charged overtime, and was especially adept at reconciling families to the death or permanent handicap of a loved one.

In May 1988, Bolding was tried before a jury for murdering her patients. The jury acquitted her of the charges.

There are three principal hypotheses that explain the deaths of patients under Bolding's care:

1. She murdered the patients (either alone or in collusion with another person or persons).
2. Someone else murdered them.
3. They died of natural causes or some unknown phenomenon or force.

Following the seven steps of hypothesis testing, determine which of these hypotheses is most likely correct based solely on the following evidence.

## The Evidence

1. Between 1983 and 1985, twenty-eight people in Bolding's care died in the ICU of the Prince George's Hospital Center in Maryland. Most of the 194 other nurses who worked in the ICU at some point during that period had only two or three patients die, or none at all.

2. There was a surge in cardiac arrests in the ICU between January 1984 and March 1985. Bolding's patients suffered fifty-seven fatal or nonfatal arrests. The nurse with the next highest number was present at only five, while most other ICU nurses saw only one or two.

3. During the fifteen-month epidemic, ten patients suffered two or three arrests in an evening, even though they had been fine during the day and night shifts. Eight of those ten were Bolding's patients. Those in bed, who were least visible from the nurse's station, were especially prone to unexpected arrests.

4. The epidemic began in January 1984, grew and gathered speed, then stopped cold when she was dismissed.

5. The deaths left no telltale evidence of murder.

6. The probability that pure chance created the epidemic is less than one in 100 million.

7. When Bolding was on duty, the ICU averaged a cardiac arrest every four days. When she was off duty, there was one every fifteen days.

8. By five measures of illness used by the ICU, her patients were no more critically ill than those of the other nurses and had similar prognoses.

9. There had been twenty-one arrests on the evening shift in 1983. Based on that figure, about thirty-one arrests would have been expected over the next fifteen months. In fact, there were eighty-eight, more than twice as many as on the day and night shifts combined. Bolding was the attending nurse in fifty-seven of the eighty-eight. If one subtracts those fifty-seven cases from the total eighty-eight, the result is thirty-one, the number that would have been expected statistically.

10. People who would ordinarily be less likely to have heart failure became, in her presence, more likely to. A woman had a 51 percent chance of an arrest under her care versus 6.7 percent under the average nurse. A man had a 32.4 percent chance under her care versus 8.3 percent under the average nurse. A patient under the age of thirty had a 41 percent chance versus 4.4 percent.

11. Her patients did not have arrests during shifts when other nurses cared for them.

12. No medication, procedure, intravenous fluid, blood product, or other health care worker was as strongly associated with cardiac arrests as was Bolding.

13. There were no witnesses or physical evidence that any crime had been committed.

14. Bolding performed well on "codes" (emergency treatment of cardiac arrests) and seemed to like being part of a cardiac arrest resuscitation team.

15. There was no evidence that Bolding had a lower threshold for calling a "code."

16. Bolding didn't work more hours than the other nurses.

17. Right after she was arrested for the murders, she admitted to police interrogators—and later recanted—that she had killed two patients.

18. She failed a polygraph during her police interrogation.

19. The hospital was her first accuser, but later hospital attorneys pooh-poohed the charges. Their turnabout may have sprung from the eight multimillion-dollar civil suits, claiming negligence, that were filed against the hospital over the deaths.

20. Police suspected the deaths were caused by administration of potassium chloride, which in large dosages can cause cardiac arrest. Potassium chloride was one of the most commonly used substances in the ICU. The majority of ICU patients received supplemental doses of potassium chloride through an IV bag over a period of hours. It was never injected all at once undiluted—in a "push," as doctors call it. Thus, patients seldom experienced a high level of potassium chloride.

21. If a patient were injected with a rich dosage of potassium chloride and survived, the excess potassium would be rapidly excreted by the blood's circulation, leaving no evidence of an overdose. Nor would an overdose be revealed by a postmortem examination.

22. Most ICU patients received medication every hour.

23. It was commonplace to see a nurse at bedside administering medicine into an intravenous bag.

24. About thirteen patients were usually in the ICU, overseen by a revolving crew of six to seven physicians. Medical residents, fellows, respiratory therapists, and other personnel also worked there.

But day in, day out, particularly late at night, the ICU was the domain of ten to eleven nurses on duty, each assigned two patients at most.

25. The nurses generally chose the patients they wanted to care for and followed their progress till they were released. Most patients remained in ICU only a week or two.

26. Although many ICU patients were semicomatose and most were so ill that death was a possibility all the time, they were by no means all expected to die.

27. Like many ICU nurses, Bolding preferred more challenging patients, those most grievously ill or injured. Less experienced or less confident nurses were happy to let her take the responsibility for those patients.

28. Medications were left in open areas.

29. One physician's assistant was on duty during 70 percent of Bolding's patients' fatal episodes, yet he also worked during other shifts when there was no epidemic. And the evening-shift epidemic continued when he was off duty and Bolding was on.

30. Three other nurses were on duty during many of the arrests, yet the epidemic continued when they weren't in the unit.

31. None of the other nurses was present during all of Bolding's patients' arrests.

 **BEFORE CONTINUING, ANALYZE THE JANE BOLDING PROBLEM USING THE HYPOTHESIS-TESTING TECHNIQUE AND MAKE A JUDGMENT CONCERNING WHICH HYPOTHESIS IS MORE LIKELY CORRECT.**

## EXERCISE 29   The U.S.S. *Iowa* Explosion

On April 19, 1989, forty-seven sailors died when five 94-pound bags of powder exploded while being pushed by a hydraulic ram into a sixteen-inch gun of Turret 2 aboard the battleship U.S.S. *Iowa*. At the time of the incident the ship was taking part in a live-fire exercise off the coast of Puerto Rico. Fires burned in the turret for ninety minutes.

The Navy's initial investigation, in which more than fifty experts from seven military laboratories took part, assumed that the explosion was accidental. The investigation therefore looked for evidence of (1) mechanical malfunction of the gun, (2) electrostatic sparking that could have set off gunpowder, and (3) spontaneous ignition of the propellant. The investigation quickly became a criminal investigation, however, when it was discovered that a member of the gun crew, Seaman Clayton Hartwig, had made a fellow seaman on the ship the beneficiary of his Navy credit union life insurance policy worth $50,000 if death were by natural causes and $100,000 if it were accidental.

The Navy contends that Hartwig was responsible for the explosion. Hartwig's relatives and friends argue that the Navy's analysis is flawed and that the Navy used Hartwig as a scapegoat to shield the Navy against criticism for faulty equipment and undertraining of the *Iowa* crew.

What do you think?

Using the seven steps of the hypothesis-testing technique, determine which of the following four hypotheses regarding why the gunpowder exploded is most likely correct:

1. Mechanical failure of the loading equipment
2. Electrostatic discharge
3. Accidental overextension of the rammer
4. Incendiary device emplaced by Seaman Clayton Hartwig

According to the last hypothesis, Hartwig inserted an incendiary device in place of the small packet of lead gun-cleaning foils the gun captain places between Powder Bags 1 and 2 closest to the projectile during loading. Hartwig then ordered the inexperienced seaman operating the rammer to overram the bags, crushing the incendiary device and igniting the propellant.

### Evidence (taken from *U.S. News & World Report*, April 23, 1990, and *Washington Post* articles 1989–1990)

1. As the three guns of Turret 2 were loading in preparation to fire, a crewman on the center gun yelled into the phone, "I have a prob-

lem here. I'm not ready yet. I have a problem here. I'm not ready yet." Then the propellant exploded.

2. The gun crew were killed in unnatural crouching positions, suggesting they knew an explosion was coming.

## The Propellant

3. The propellant used was made from World War II–era nitrocellulose chunks that had been repackaged in 1987 in bags made in 1945. A patch on the bottom of each bag was filled with granular black powder which, when the gun was fired, ignited, acting as a primer to start the nitrocellulose burning.
4. The bags of propellant that exploded had been stored for three months the previous summer in closed metal barges in the hot sun. It was initially suspected that this storage might have reduced the powder's stability. But later testing of samples from 387 bags used on the *Iowa* showed that, even though the propellant had been stored in the sun, premature ignition was improbable. Overexposure to heat reduces the effective life of powder but does not make it more dangerous to handle and use.
5. To see if the powder used on the *Iowa* that day would ignite accidentally, technicians crushed it under weighted drums, ground it beneath a weighted friction slider, and dropped the 94-pound powder bags from 40-foot and 100-foot towers. The technicians sheared the propellant, ground it, rubbed it against a rotating drum, and burned it with cigarette lighters. They found that with enough stress the propellant or the black powder would ignite, but not under conditions that would have existed on the *Iowa*.
6. On the day of the explosion, the *Iowa* was engaged in "kitchen-sink research" to test the accuracy of five full-power bags of propellant instead of the six reduced-power bags that Navy policy called for.
7. The Navy tests showed that accidental ignition of the propellant was improbable but not impossible, though such an explosion had never before occurred in all of the tens of thousands of practice and live firings of the Navy's sixteen-inch guns.

## Static Electricity

8. Some experts maintained that static electricity, generated by rubbing the powder bags against a metal surface, could have caused the explosion, yet no such explosion had ever occurred before in the Navy's sixteen-inch guns.

## Mechanical Problems

9. The Navy's sixteen-inch guns have experienced no major mechanical problems since a mishap in 1943. Sixteen-inch gun technology has changed little over the years. The *Iowa* had fired thousands of sixteen-inch shells without incident.

## The Rammer

10. The five crewmen manning the gun had never worked together before. The sailor assigned to ram the 470 pounds of propellant into the breech had never rammed live powder before and had been shown how to do it only two days earlier. Hartwig, an experienced gunner, was put in charge of the crew at the last minute.
11. Through painstaking reconstruction of the shattered rammer, naval investigators found it had inexplicably pushed the propellant twenty-one inches too far into the gun.
12. Using the reconstructed rammer, technicians rammed powder bags like those used in the explosion into the breech of a sixteen-inch test gun over and over in an attempt to trigger a reaction, but none resulted.
13. Scientists from Sandia National Laboratories told the Senate Armed Services Committee that tests had shown that improper operation of the hydraulic ram—accidentally pushing five bags of gunpowder with too much speed and pressure—could have caused the explosion. The finding was based on repeated experiments in which a number of gunpowder bags (equivalent to the amount used during the *Iowa* explosion) were attached to 860 pounds of weights and dropped onto a steel plate to simulate the

pressure of an "overram." It was not until the eighteenth repetition of the experiment that the powder ignited. The experiment represented the maximum energy the rammer system could deliver. The Sandia lab defended this approach as necessary to establish that accidental ignition in the loading process was possible, even though such an event had never happened in tens of thousands of sixteen-inch gun firings over the decades.

## Hartwig

14. Hartwig didn't exactly fit in with the crew. He came from a religious household and didn't drink, smoke, or party. He had a few close friends, including three seamen, all gunner's mates, one of whom had joined the *Iowa* three weeks prior to the explosion. Only one of the three was in the turret, below the gun; he was not injured in the blast.

15. Hartwig and one of the three seamen had been close friends for two years. They had once been seen wrestling with each other on watch, prompting sailors to tease them about being homosexual. Following the explosion, the Naval Investigative Service (NIS) found no conclusive evidence of a homosexual relationship between them. Nevertheless, the seaman acknowledged to a House Armed Services subcommittee that such talk by shipmates had once led Hartwig to discuss committing suicide.

16. Hartwig and his close friend had feuded in the days preceding the explosion because Hartwig didn't like his friend's new wife of six months.

17. Hartwig, 6 feet 2 inches tall, liked to act tough. He owned two handguns, one of which he carried in his car, and bragged about how he could make bombs and plastic explosives.

18. At the Navy's request, the FBI's National Center for the Analysis of Violent Crime produced a psychological profile of Hartwig that portrayed him as a loner, weird, possibly gay, and the sort of quiet guy next door who one day shoots up a shopping center. His written materials portrayed him as a troubled man: deeply despondent and excessively dependent on a few people. Younger than his two

sisters, he had spent most of his childhood in his room. In his teens he had been asexual, had had only one close male friend, and had allegedly attempted suicide. In the Navy, Hartwig was close to only one friend at a time. When his close friend (the seaman cited above) married, Hartwig was deeply depressed. Lonely and shy, Hartwig lived a life of imagined power and authority and was fascinated by destruction. He often talked of death and suicide and was under stress because of personal and financial problems. He disliked the *Iowa* and was ridiculed by other crew members. In sum, he considered his life a failure. Robert Hazelwood of the aforementioned FBI Center told the House Armed Services Committee that the quality of evidence for the Center's profile was excellent, based on testimony of Hartwig's friends and relatives and his letters and other possessions. Conclusion: Hartwig was suicidal and had been rehearsing all his life for violence and death.

19. There were no documents, letters, notes, or diaries written by Hartwig stating that he wanted to kill himself or others.

20. The seaman who was Hartwig's close friend said that the night before the explosion Hartwig had made a homosexual advance that the seaman had rejected. The seaman later recanted this statement.

21. At the request of the House Armed Services Committee, twelve psychologists and two psychiatrists (collectively specialists in forensics, suicide pathology, peer review, and neuropsychology) reviewed the FBI's psychological profile of Hartwig. Ten of the fourteen disputed the FBI's conclusions and called the NIS's interview techniques "biased, prosecutorial, and potentially terribly leading." An NIS spokesman defended the techniques as standard police interrogation procedures. Some of the reviewers contended that the NIS and FBI had culled only the most damaging suggestions from hundreds of interviews while ignoring mitigating information.

22. Several of the psychologists/psychiatrists contended that Hartwig's upbeat personal letters refuted the NIS-FBI interpretation that he had been suicidal. The night before he died, Hartwig had been making a list of things to take to London for his next duty assignment. (He had told friends and family he was being transferred to London when, in fact, the Navy was only considering him for that assignment.)

23. Psychological profiles were not done on the other men in the gun room.
24. Among Hartwig's books were *Getting Even: The Complete Book of Dirty Tricks* and a U.S. Army *Improvised Munitions Handbook.*

## Electronic Detonator

25. The seaman who had been Hartwig's close friend claimed Hartwig had said he could make a pipe bomb with an electronic detonator.
26. The same seaman said he had seen an electronic timer, like a Radio Shack kitchen timer, in Hartwig's locker. Investigators found no timer in the locker, nor could they determine whether Hartwig had purchased a timer from any Radio Shack store. The seaman later recanted his statement.
27. Navy scientists examining the sixteen-inch gun involved in the explosion found chemical residue consistent with materials in a Radio Shack timer: barium, silicon, aluminum, calcium. But the FBI's crime lab, asked by the Navy for an independent analysis, could find no conclusive evidence of timer residue. Moreover, Sandia National Laboratories found residues of these chemicals throughout the entire region of both Turrets 1 and 2 of the *Iowa*, Turret 2 of the U.S.S. *New Jersey*, and Turret 2 of the U.S.S. *Wisconsin*.

## Incendiary Device

28. The seaman who was Hartwig's close friend recalled that Hartwig had been unusually quiet at breakfast the day of the explosion.
29. Hartwig was not scheduled to be in the gun turret that day. His posting there as gun captain was a last-minute decision, apparently intended to put an experienced gunner in charge of an inexperienced gun crew.
30. At the time of the explosion, which literally tore Hartwig in half, he was in an abnormal position, leaning into the gun's breech rather than standing erect as he should have been.
31. To test whether Hartwig could have made and used a chemical incendiary device described in a "terrorist cookbook" the Navy

investigators had obtained, *U.S. News & World Report* and a forensics professor from George Washington University mixed the requisite materials: small amounts of a common powdered chemical, brake fluid, and steel wool. In two and a half minutes the mixture ignited spontaneously. Next, they tested the Navy's theory that Hartwig could have created a time-delay device by putting the brake fluid into a small glass vial and placing it with the other two ingredients into a small plastic bag, which he would have inserted between propellant bags during loading of the gun. The pressure of the rammer would have smashed the vial, mixing the ingredients and triggering the explosion. *U.S. News & World Report* and the professor tested a vial-in-the-bag device, dropping a one-pound weight on it. Ninety seconds later it ignited.

32. The Navy found no chemicals or steel wool, no workshop, and no other evidence that Hartwig had experimented with chemical detonators. Nor did the Navy find evidence that he had ever seen the "terrorist cookbook" that contained the recipe for the incendiary device the Navy conjectured he could have used.

33. Vital evidence of an incendiary device could have been lost immediately after the explosion. In fighting the fire, sailors washed out the entire gun turret and dumped the residue overboard. The rear admiral who later ran the Navy's investigation had earlier authorized a complete cleanup of the turret because the turret was dangerous and the explosion had looked at first like an accident.

34. The blast of the fatal explosion moved the projectile up the gun barrel forty-four inches. Technicians at a firing range could replicate this force only by igniting the propellant way up inside the breech, between Bags 1 and 2 closest to the projectile, where Hartwig could have inserted an incendiary device.

35. Scientists at the Crane Naval Laboratory, using powerful microscopes and molecular analysis, discovered, among the residue on the projectile, tiny iron fibers resembling wire from scouring pads or steel wool, coated with calcium, chlorine, and oxygen. The laboratory produced the same coated fibers by igniting an incendiary device of brake fluid, steel wool, and a commonly available chemical.

36. A physics professor at the Massachusetts Institute of Technology reviewed the Navy's reports and was skeptical of the Navy's molecular analysis indicating "foreign matter" on the projectile fin. He noted that the projectile had been sprayed with seawater and fire-fighting foam and that the Navy had used four gallons of lubricant to remove the projectile from the gun. He said the Navy had not done an exacting enough match of chemicals and their comparative concentrations to prove the existence of brake fluid and chemicals on the fin.

37. Iron fibers similar to those discovered on the projectile were found on two other projectiles from the *Iowa*, suggesting that iron fibers were not unique to the explosion.

**BEFORE CONTINUING, ANALYZE THE U.S.S. *IOWA* PROBLEM USING THE HYPOTHESIS-TESTING TECHNIQUE AND MAKE A JUDGMENT CONCERNING WHICH HYPOTHESIS IS MOST LIKELY CORRECT.**

# 12
# Devil's Advocacy

Devil's advocacy, a technique closely related to hypothesis testing, is believed to have originated in the Roman Catholic Church as a means of critically examining a deceased person's qualifications for sainthood. Learned churchmen took *the devil's position* simply for argument's sake to challenge the rationale presented in the nomination for sainthood, the idea being that through this process the truth, perforce, would out. Similarly today, we commonly hear people say, in questioning a proposition, "Let me be the devil's advocate," meaning they wish to challenge the proposition not because they disbelieve it but simply to test its validity. Devil's advocacy does this by seeking, with either the same or other evidence, to prove the opposite of whatever the challenged view holds.

The power of devil's advocacy lies in our compulsion to focus. As I have noted, focusing tends to make us favor a particular outcome or solution early on in the analytic process, often at the very beginning, long before we can objectively analyze the evidence and reach a conclusion. Devil's advocacy is analytically useful because it by design focuses on a contrary or opposite viewpoint and in doing so activates all of the instinctive behaviors associated with focusing: viewing the problem one-dimensionally through the lens of biases connected with that viewpoint; eschewing alternative solutions; valuing evidence that supports that viewpoint; devaluing and discarding evidence that does not. Devil's advocacy thus engages the very same mental tactics employed by the primary advocate but applies them in opposition, thereby promoting objectivity. What's more, the devil's advocate goes a step further by seeking out and obtaining *new* evidence, evidence about which the prime advocate has no knowledge or curiosity or that was disbelieved and discredited. This further step is the *secret weapon* of devil's advocacy, the extra dimension that makes it a formidable analytic technique.

The tremendous potential of devil's advocacy to undermine and show weaknesses in the primary view is, regrettably, underutilized. People instinctively resist devil's advocacy *precisely because* it is designed to attack and undermine the primary view. Organizing or even proposing a devil's-advocate approach is naturally interpreted by the prime advocate as threatening. Yet if one is truly interested in achieving the most beneficial solution to a problem, devil's advocacy is unquestionably an appropriate analytic technique.

I am a big fan of Tom Clancy's novels and was delighted to see his hero, in *The Sum of All Fears*, championing devil's advocacy in the following exchange between the hero, Jack Ryan, and a colleague:

JACK:          "I want to play on this a little. The [CIA's analysts of Russian affairs] will chew on it for a couple of days. I want you and me to do our own analysis, but I want a different spin on it."

COLLEAGUE:     "Meaning what?"

JACK:          "Meaning that you think [a particular scenario] is plausible, and I have my doubts. Therefore, you will look for reasons it might not be true, and I'll look for reasons that it is."

Thank you, Tom Clancy.

Take, for example, a hypothetical case in which a large manufacturing company is faced with rapidly declining sales of its principal product.

It has essentially two options: continuing production, perhaps with modifications to improve the product, or terminating production. If I, with my knowledge of structuring techniques, were the company CEO, I would establish two competing working groups, one to seek evidence in support of continuing production and against termination, and the other to seek evidence in support of termination and against continuing production. I would charge each group with presenting their findings to me separately. I would then weigh the two views and make my decision on that basis. To assign these inherently conflicting analytic tasks to a single working group would be tantamount to letting a single lawyer both prosecute and defend an accused person.

Another example of how devil's advocacy could be used is the Walt Disney Company's aborted plan, discussed earlier, to build a theme park in northern Virginia. Here again I would have set up two analytic groups, one to show why the local and state jurisdictions would approve the plan, the other to show why they would not.

We can, of course, employ the devil's-advocate approach with good effect even when we are doing the analysis by ourselves. We simply work one view of the problem and set our conclusions aside for a day or two to let our focus, mind-sets, and biases relax and fade a bit. We then go to work on the other side, trying to prove just the opposite with the same or different evidence.

Keep in mind that, should you try this, you will experience a strong reluctance to analyze the devil's-advocate view. A little voice in your head will whisper, "Why are you doing this? You've already analyzed the problem and have drawn your conclusions. This is a waste of time. *And you know the devil's-advocate view of the problem is wrong!*" Your inhibitions against spending time on devil's-advocate analysis will be powerful and relentless. But if you steel yourself against them and proceed, you will not regret it. Devil's advocacy will, with virtual certainty, open your mind to new dimensions and perceptions of the problem, poking holes in fallacious self-serving arguments and stripping away thinly reasoned and thinly supported analysis. That's the wonder and delight of the devil's-advocate technique.

## EXERCISE 30    MiG-21

Read this article from *The Washington Post* of June 14, 1994:

# U.S., Contractors in Dogfight Over MiG Modernization

### John Mintz
WASHINGTON POST STAFF WRITER

At the height of the Vietnam War, when U.S. fighter pilots met Soviet MiG-21s in the skies over Hanoi, the American airmen were pleased to learn that those slow-moving jets had limited maneuverability and could stay aloft for only an hour.

Now comes more evidence that our world has indeed turned—some U.S. defense companies . . . want to upgrade the capabilities of these aging Soviet planes. Faced with Pentagon cutbacks, the U.S. firms see modernizing old MiGs as a growth market that could save American jobs.

The American firms . . . initially are seeking permission from federal agencies to modernize the electronics systems of 120 MiG-21s used by India's air force. The firms' proposal to be allowed to do the Indian job—worth up to $350 million—has prompted considerable controversy, and a high-level review by the National Security Council and the State, Defense, and Commerce departments.

The U.S. companies are frustrated by the delay in getting U.S. government approval, because the wait could mean foreign competitors will land the work. Whoever wins this business could be front-runners for billions of dollars worth of work upgrading the electronics and avionics systems of an additional 1,400 decrepit MiG-21s owned by Poland, the Czech Republic, Romania, Egypt, Peru and many other now friendly countries. Most don't have the money to buy new aircraft.

"Some Americans may have an aversion to upgrading the equipment we spent 20 years trying to destroy," said the international vice president for the Aerospace Industries Association, a trade group. "But this is perceived to be a potentially big business.

"And when U.S. firms sell the systems," he added, "the U.S. has some control over their capabilities, which we don't have when our competitors do the work."

But many State Department officials fear that any U.S. industry help to the Indian military could anger Pakistan, India's rival and a U.S. ally.

Other U.S. officials express fears that stem from the fact that the American firms would be subcontractors to Russian prime contractors on any MiG-21 upgrades. The Russians, French or Israelis are all bidding to be prime contractors on MiG-21 upgrades worldwide, and they would have access to the U.S. subcontractors' electronics gear. The Russians, French or Israelis could "reverse engineer" [produce exact copies of] the gear for their own use or for sale to others, some U.S. officials say.

Many U.S. officials see Russia as a potential adversary to whom they don't want to give sensitive military technology, and they see the French and Israelis as opportunists who routinely sell high-tech military gear to rogue nations for profit—although those two countries dispute that.

Play an advocatory role and list as many points as you can from the article that *support* the view that the federal government should allow U.S. industries to upgrade the MiG-21s. Also, list separately any additional points you know to be true that are *not* mentioned in the article but that support this view. Finally, list, again separately, points of information that are *not* mentioned in the article and that you *don't know* to be true but that, if they could be substantiated, would support this view. To repeat, make three lists:

1. Points in the article that support the view
2. Points you know to be true that are *not* in the article but that support the view
3. Points that are *not* in the article and that you *don't know* to be true but that, if substantiated, would support the view

 **BEFORE CONTINUING,
MAKE THE THREE LISTS.**

When you have completed the lists, take a break, walk around a bit, relax, think of other things, and then return to the article and play the devil's advocate. Again make three lists, but this time support the view that the federal government should *not* allow U.S. industries to upgrade the MiG-21s.

 **BEFORE CONTINUING,
MAKE THE SECOND THREE LISTS.**

In playing the devil's advocate, did you hear the little voice in your mind counseling against it? Did you have a sense that doing the devil's-advocate lists was a waste of time? If you did, it was your innate compulsion to focus talking to you. Your mind had already focused *in favor* of the U.S. industry's position; it had already taken a stand. Now you were asking it to disavow all that and stand *against* that position, and your mind resisted.

But as you undertook the devil's-advocate position, did you sense your perspective of the problem broadening? Didn't the process of taking a position against upgrading put thoughts into your head that you had not even considered when you took a position in favor of it? As I said, this is the wonder and delight of the devil's-advocate technique. It imposes objectivity whether or not you consciously seek it. It compels divergent thinking.

# 13
# The Probability Tree

Probability is one of the more difficult concepts for humans to understand and deal with effectively. Morton Hunt explained why in *The Universe Within*. He wrote:

Most of the concepts and patterns that are difficult for the average person to grasp and use are "nonintuitive"—that is, they cannot be derived, or are not easily derived, from everyday experience, and therefore are not part of the normal mind's repertoire. Probability is one such [concept]; most people can intuitively see the answer to only the simplest problems involving probability.

Jeremy Campbell in *The Improbable Machine* made a similar observation:

People do not seem to learn, easily or at all, the rules of probability . . . just by having repeated experiences of them. . . . [One explanation for this] seems to be that the rules of . . . probability fly in the face of common sense. And "common sense" in many cases turns out to mean the way in which human memory is organized and how it processes information.

*Thinking in Time* by Harvard professors Neustadt and May was equally discouraging:

> Judging by our students, millions of Americans are either unfamiliar with numerical notations of probability or are uncomfortable at the idea of stating a subjective judgment [in terms of probability].

Understanding and dealing with probability are crucial because probability permeates analysis both explicitly and implicitly. It lies hidden in the information we analyze and is a crutch for our analytic judgments. Unless we are sensitive to probability's influence and accurately define its meaning and significance, it can, like a computer virus devouring computerized data, devastate our analytic findings and make a mockery of our recommendations and decisions.

As I mentioned earlier, the most difficult analytic problems are of the random and indeterminate type, where, because facts are scarce, our analytic product depends heavily on subjective judgments. For that reason, *there can be no certainty* when dealing with random or indeterminate problems. No certainty at all! The moment our analysis moves from facts to judgment, we leave certainty behind and enter the arena of *estimates*. "Estimating is what we do when we run out of data. The language of estimating is probability, and the laws of probability are the grammar of that language." So said the late Sherman Kent, a U.S. intelligence officer widely regarded as the "father" of the National Intelligence Estimate.

Probability is difficult to deal with because the laws of probability, as Hunt observed, are often counterintuitive and the judgments resulting from the application of those laws are, more often than not, imprecise and ambiguous when expressed verbally.

With that ambiguity in mind, and as a prelude to further discussion of probability, do the following exercise:

## EXERCISE 31   Safecracker I

A fabulous diamond is kept in a safe behind five doors, each secured by a combination lock. You are a thief seeking to steal the diamond. All five doors have exactly the same kind of lock made by the same company but with different combinations. In your career as a thief, you have encountered this lock ten times. Only once in those ten times have you failed to open the lock. Disregarding all factors except the combination lock, what is the probability, expressed as a percentile (20%, 50%, 80%, etc.), that you will get through all five doors and steal the diamond? Write your percentile on a sheet of paper.

 **BEFORE CONTINUING, WRITE DOWN A PERCENTILE THAT REPRESENTS THE PROBABILITY YOU WILL STEAL THE DIAMOND.**

Next to your percentile, write an adjective or adverb-adjective that you think best characterizes the percentile, such as unlikely, possible, very likely, almost certain.

 **BEFORE CONTINUING, WRITE NEXT TO THE PERCENTILE AN ADJECTIVE OR ADVERB-ADJECTIVE THAT CHARACTER-IZES THE PERCENTILE. (KEEP THE SHEET OF PAPER. WE'LL REFER TO IT LATER.)**

People commonly make inordinately casual use of probability expressions, such as *most likely, in all likelihood, may, slim chance,* and *certainly,* under the mistaken assumption that these expressions mean the same thing to everyone.

"What are our chances of being on time for our appointment if we stop for dinner?" asks a wife of her husband.

"Fair," he replies.

"Okay," she says, "then let's stop here."

After dining, they arrive at their appointment a half hour late. She's upset and complains to her husband, "I thought you said we'd be on time!"

He's shocked. "I never said anything of the kind."

"You said our chances were 'fair.'"

"Yeah, like we *wouldn't* be on time!"

People unfortunately have drastically different perceptions of what nonnumeric (adjectival) expressions of probability mean. Ask people how they interpret *likely* as a numerical percentage and you'll get answers ranging from 55 to 85 percent. What's a *slight chance* of rain? To the public at large, anywhere from 1 to 15 percent. If you're skeptical of these ranges, do your own survey. Ask your family or friends what various adjectival probability terms mean to them. You'll find their responses enlightening and entertaining.

Whether we are analyzing a problem alone or collaborating with others, we should make it a rule to highlight all probability expressions and translate them into percentiles. I've italicized certain words in the following excerpt of an article in *Firehouse* magazine to show you what I mean:

> The U.S. Fire Administration's Juvenile Firesetter Programs show that the greater percentage of fires are set by young children in the five to nine age group. In addition, these programs indicate that five- and six-year-olds *may* not be capable of understanding the concept that a single match can destroy a house. Therefore, not only do young children represent the highest risk group with respect to their involvement in firestarting, but they are also the *most likely* victims of fire injury and death. . . . Unlike elementary school children, who *may* be involved in only one or two unsupervised firestarts, psychiatric patients are *more likely* to be involved in several incidents of firesetting behavior. In addition, the fires set by children with psychiatric diagnoses are *more likely* to cause serious damage requiring firefighter suppression.

This is a typical example of casual use of probability expressions. If they weren't highlighted, they would hardly be noticed. Yet because they have significant impact on the meaning of the text, it is fair to question what precise probability the authors meant to convey in each case.

> [S]ix-year-olds __may__ not [understand] that a single match can destroy a house.

What probability do the authors assign to *"may"*? Fifty percent? Ten percent? One percent? It makes a huge difference. If there's a 50 percent chance that America's six-year-olds do not appreciate the dangerous firepower of a single match, the nation's homes are in serious jeopardy. If, on the other hand, there's only a 1 percent chance, the danger is drastically reduced.

*[Y]oung children . . . are the <u>most likely</u> victims of fire.*

What does *"most likely"* mean? Sixty percent? Eighty percent? Ninety-nine percent?

I repeat my advice. When we are analyzing a problem or drafting a report, we should convert all probability expressions into percentiles . . . *but only in the analytic phase.* Never use percentiles in final written products unless—and such instances are extremely rare—the numbers are based on definitive evidence and precise calculations. The biggest challenge in dealing with probability is conveying through language what a probability represents without using a percentile. But that's a subject for a book on writing, not a book on structuring analysis. (One solution, favored by some writers and strongly opposed by some others, is to identify up front for the reader what the various probability expressions used in a written product represent in percentiles, e.g., "probable" = 85%, "unlikely" = 20%, etc.)

# Determining Probability

How do we determine probability? There are basically two ways: computation and frequency-and-experience. When we have all the facts, that is, when we have all of the data, as in a deterministic problem, we *calculate* probability by arithmetic computation. When we *don't* have all the facts, we *estimate* probability based on frequency and experience. *Frequency* is how often an event has occurred in the past; *experience* is what happened during each event. A simple example: If I drop ten lightbulbs, one at a time, on the floor and each one breaks, what's the probability that, if I drop an eleventh bulb, it too will break? Very high! Almost 100 percent. How did I reach that conclusion? *Frequency*—I repeated the event ten times. *Experience*—the bulbs broke every time.

Obviously, the more we know about the circumstances of an event whose probability we are estimating, the more accurate our estimate will be. But what if we know little or nothing about the circumstances? What if someone asked you to estimate which of three political parties will win a coming election in Tanganyika, Africa? Unless by chance you are a student of African affairs, you won't have the slightest idea. A French nobleman, the Marquis de Laplace (1749–1827), gave us sound advice about how to deal with such a situation. According to Laplace, if we're trying to determine which of two or more outcomes will occur, but we don't have reliable evidence to judge which is more likely, we should *assume the probability is equal for all outcomes*. Let me repeat: if we lack evidence to support a judgment as to which of two or more outcomes is more likely, we should assume that all are equally likely.

Fortunately, we rarely have occasion to resort to Laplace. In almost every problem we face, we recognize similarities with past events of which we have some knowledge, and we use that knowledge as the basis for making probability judgments (estimating probabilities). However, our probability estimates are as vulnerable as any other workings of the human mind to those troublesome mental traits I've been talking about. "Similarities with past events" are often among those nonexistent patterns our minds are prone to perceive. And as we are prone to value evidence that supports a favored outcome, so are we prone to believe that a favored outcome is more likely (has a greater probability of occurring) than one unfavored. And we are likely to hold fast to this belief in the face of contrary evidence. Yes, indeed, our minds can as easily mislead our probability estimates as they can any other analytic judgment.

A memorably poignant example of this tendency to inflate the probability of a desired outcome was revealed in a statement by a British Royal Navy commando who took part in the Normandy invasion in World War II. "I don't think any of us realized the danger we were in. Nobody ever went to Normandy to die; they went to fight and win a war. I don't think any man that died thought that it was him that was going to be killed." Inflating or deflating probabilities to conform to our desires is the curse of wishful thinking: it won't happen to me because I don't want it to happen. As Francis Bacon said, we prefer to believe what we prefer to be true.

Given the absolutely crucial role of probability in the analysis of problems, we must take great care in the determination of probability assessments.

## Types of Probability Events

The two most common types of events whose probability we try to determine when analyzing problems are mutually exclusive and conditionally dependent.

*Mutually exclusive events* preclude one another. For example, the tossing of a coin involves mutually exclusive events, or mutually exclusive outcomes. Because a coin has two sides, one outcome (heads or tails) precludes the other. The outcomes are thus mutually exclusive. Rolling a standard die also involves mutually exclusive events. A standard die has six faces, only one of which can "come up." One outcome thus precludes the others. Election outcomes are mutually exclusive, as is almost every decision we humans make every day. If we decide *this*, we exclude *that*.

*Conditionally dependent events* are those in which the occurrence of one event depends upon the occurrence of another. The events thus occur in sequence. Starting the engine of an automobile is a good example. We insert the key into the ignition switch, we turn the key, the starter rotates the engine, and the engine ignites. The engine won't ignite if it isn't rotated; the starter won't rotate the engine unless we turn the ignition key; we can't turn the key unless we insert it into the ignition switch. The first event—inserting the ignition key—*conditions* the second, meaning the second event occurs *on condition* that the first occurs. The second event conditions the third, and so on.

## Mutually Exclusive Probability

How do we calculate mutually exclusive probability? A useful vehicle for explaining this calculation is a jar containing 90 jelly beans: 45 red ones, 36 yellow, and 9 green. We're going to reach into the jar and pick out one bean. We can visualize this more clearly with a decision/event tree (Figure 13-1) in which we have three possible, mutually exclusive decisions or outcomes: red, yellow, and green.

Assuming the beans are distributed randomly, what is the probability, if I reach into the jar and blindly take out a single jelly bean, that it will be red? What probability yellow? What probability green?

One easy way to compute mutually exclusive probabilities is to think of them as *percentages*. For example, the probability of picking one red bean out of 90 in one try is equal to the percentage of the 90 that are red. Does that make sense? Maybe it's clearer if I rephrase the sentence. If 30 percent of the beans in the jar are red, then I have a 30 percent chance of picking a red bean on one try.

How, then, do we compute the percentage of red beans in the jar? I like to use the traditional *IS-over-OF* method: *IS* divided by *OF*. I learned it in grade school and have never found a better way to structure the arithmetic formula. (Yes, *IS-over-OF* is a structuring technique.) To do the calculation, we ask ourselves, "What percent *is* this number *of* that one?" We then divide the *IS* number by the *OF* number. For instance, what percent *is* 3 *of* 6? Or what percent *of* 6 *is* 3? *IS* (3) over *OF* (6): 3 divided by 6 equals .5 (50 percent).

One advantage in using the *IS-over-OF* formulation is that sometimes the context of a problem makes it difficult to determine which number is to be divided by which. I was taught, when encountering this dilemma, to transform the language of the problem into an *IS-over-OF* format. To whit, *a bushel contains 40 apples, 10 of which are rotten. What percentage are rotten?* Some people might be confused as to which number is the divisor and which the dividend. To find out, one simply rewords the question as follows: What percent *is* 10 *of* 40?

**FIGURE 13-1**

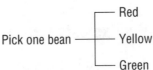

Pick one bean — Red / Yellow / Green

*IS*-over-*OF*: 10 over 40 = .25 (25 percent). I love it! (God bless my grade school teachers.)

### EXERCISE 32    Jelly Beans I

Let's apply the *IS*-over-*OF* formula to the question of what percentage of the jelly beans in the jar are red, what percentage yellow, and what percentage green. Compute the answers and write them on a sheet of paper.

 **BEFORE CONTINUING, COMPUTE THE PERCENTAGE OF RED, YELLOW, AND GREEN BEANS.**

Here are the answers:

Red—What percent is 45 of 90? *IS* (45) over *OF* (90) = .5 or 50 percent.

Yellow—What percent is 36 of 90? *IS* (36) over *OF* (90) = .4 or 40 percent.

Green—What percent is 9 of 90? *IS* (9) over *OF* (90) = .1 or 10 percent.

Now we convert the percentages to probabilities and enter the numbers in the tree (Figure 13-2).

Because the tree contains probabilities, I prefer to call it a "Probability Tree."

# The Probability Tree

There are three inviolable rules for constructing probability trees:

1. As with any decision/event tree, the events depicted must be *mutually exclusive*, meaning each event is distinct from the others.
2. Likewise, the events must be *collectively exhaustive*, meaning they must include all possible events in the scenario being analyzed.
3. The probabilities of the branches at each node (each branching of the tree) must equal 1.0.

**FIGURE 13-2**  Probability Tree

Probability

Red        .5

Pick one bean ————  Yellow     .4

Green      .1

*A point to remember for those unaccustomed to dealing with, and calculating, numerical probabilities is that an event cannot occur more times than its possibility of occurring. Therefore, probability can never be greater than 100 percent, or 1.0.*

Let's raise the complexity of the jelly bean problem a notch.

What is the probability of picking a red *or* a green jelly bean from the jar in one try?

Again, the way to solve this problem is to think in terms of percentages: what percent of the beans in the jar are red or green? There are 45 red and 9 green, which equals 54. What percent of 90 is 54? *IS* (54) over *OF* (90) = .6. So we have a .6 probability of picking red or green on one try. What we did, in effect, was to *add* the probability of picking a red (.5) and the probability of picking a green (.1).

## EXERCISE 33    Jelly Beans II

What is the probability of picking a red *or* a yellow? What is the probability of a yellow *or* a green? Write your answers on a sheet of paper.

**BEFORE CONTINUING, COMPUTE THE PROBABILITY OF PICKING RED OR YELLOW, YELLOW OR GREEN BEANS**

The probability of picking red or yellow is .5 + .4 = .9
The probability of picking yellow or green is .4 + .1 = .5

The point here is that we express *OR* in probability calculations as a plus sign; that is, we *add* the *OR* probabilities. This is one of those probability concepts that most analysts don't understand until it is called to their attention, meaning it isn't intuitively obvious. Even when the concept is pointed out, it doesn't sink in for many people. As Campbell wrote, people don't seem to remember the rules of probability simply by practicing them. That's why most of us have to reason them out every time.

Let's practice drawing a probability tree and calculating an *OR* probability.

### EXERCISE 34   Fox in the Henhouse

Fifty hens live in a henhouse: 10 are red, 5 are black, 15 are brown, and 20 are white. If a fox steals into the henhouse and randomly kills a hen, what is the probability the hen will be red or brown? On a separate sheet of paper, draw a probability tree showing each color hen's probability of being killed and then determine the answer to the problem.

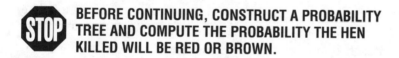

**BEFORE CONTINUING, CONSTRUCT A PROBABILITY TREE AND COMPUTE THE PROBABILITY THE HEN KILLED WILL BE RED OR BROWN.**

Figure 13-3 shows the probability tree.

The probability of killing a red hen is .2 and a brown hen is .3, so the probability of killing either a red *or* a brown is .2 + .3 = .5.

# Conditionally Dependent Probability

How do we calculate conditionally dependent probability? By *multiplying* the two probabilities that are linked conditionally. Let me explain why.

What is the probability of tossing two heads in a row with a coin?

**FIGURE 13-3**

**Probability**

| | Probability |
|---|---|
| Red | .2 |
| Black | .1 |
| Brown | .3 |
| White | .4 |

The probability tree in Figure 13-4 illustrates the possible sequences of events. The probability of getting heads on the first toss is .5. If we get tails, the sequence ends; it's over, and we're stuck on that limb of the tree. We toss the coin a second time only on condition that we get heads on the first toss. Thus, the second toss is *conditionally dependent* upon the first. If we get heads on the first toss, what is the probability of getting heads on the second toss? Still .5, so we have a 50 percent chance of a 50 percent chance (.5 times .5) of tossing two heads in a row, which equals a probability of .25.

Let's review calculating conditionally dependent probability with the jelly beans. What is the probability that we will first pick a single red bean (and return it to the jar) and then pick a green bean? The probability of picking a single red bean is .5; the probability of a single green bean is .1. So the probability of picking a red *and then* a green bean is .5 times .1, which equals .05.

## EXERCISE 35   Safecracker II

Let's go back to the "Safecracker" problem. There were five doors, each secured by a combination lock. You, the thief, had picked this kind of lock on nine of ten previous occasions. What is the probability you will unlock all five doors?

This is a problem of conditionally dependent probabilities, because opening the second door is dependent upon opening the first, opening the third is dependent upon opening the second, and so on.

What is the probability (let's call it P1) you will get through the first door? We compute it based on your previous success rate: 9 out of 10. What percent is 9 of 10? 90. So P1 is .9.

**FIGURE 13-4**

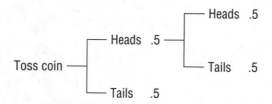

What is the probability of opening the first and second doors? Opening the second door is contingent upon opening the first. We therefore multiply the probability of opening the first door (.9) times the probability of opening the second. What is the probability of opening the second door? .9? Sorry, wrong number. That was the probability of the first door based on nine out of ten successes. But if we opened the first door we scored another success, so now our batting average is 10 divided by 11. P2 is therefore .91. The answer to the probability of opening the first two doors is .9 times .91, which is .82. Are you following this? If not, read the foregoing again.

Calculate the probability of opening the fifth door (and, of course, stealing the diamond). Write your calculations and final answer on a sheet of paper.

**BEFORE CONTINUING, CALCULATE THE PROBABILITY OF OPENING THE FIFTH DOOR.**

The following list provides the answers.

P1 is 9 divided by $10 = .9$.

P2 is .9 times 10 divided by $11 = .82$.

P3 is .82 times 11 divided by $12 = .75$.

P4 is .75 times 12 divided by $13 = .69$.

P5 is .69 times 13 divided by $14 = .64$.

Now compare .64 with the percentile you earlier selected to represent the probability of your stealing the diamond. How close were you? Most people intuitively believe the probability of stealing the diamond is quite high. If you earlier greatly miscalculated the probabilities in the Safecracker I problem, don't be upset. Most people miscalculate them because, as I said at the opening of this chapter, probability is one of the more difficult concepts for humans to understand and deal with effectively. It is unquestionably not instinctive. For that reason, we must thoroughly understand the differences in the concepts of mutually exclusive and conditionally dependent probabilities, and we must practice calculating these probabilities every chance we get. Only by doing so will they become second nature to us.

The distinction between calculating mutually exclusive and conditionally dependent probabilities is clearly apparent in how we diagram these two calculations in a probability tree.

In summary, to determine the combined probability that two or more events will occur as a result of a single decision or event (the "or" situation), we *add* their individual probabilities. To determine the probability that two or more events will occur in succession (the "and" situation), we *multiply* their individual probabilities.

In dealing with probability questions, we must carefully scrutinize how a probability statement or question is framed, that is, whether the question relates to the probability of a single (mutually exclusive) event or a series of connected (conditionally dependent) events. Wording of the probability question is critical and underlines the importance of restating any problem we analyze to ensure that we understand what the question is and that this is the right question.

Let's do an exercise that combines the calculation of mutually exclusive and conditionally dependent probabilities.

## EXERCISE 36　Karati Missile

Developers of the Karati missile are trying to meet a Defense Department deadline. To do so, they must begin production of the missile within two months. A crucial test launch of the missile is planned for tomorrow. Three outcomes are possible (the probability of each outcome is given in parentheses):

1. Total failure (.2)
2. Successful flight, but technical failure (.6)
3. Total success (.2)

If the flight is a total failure, the developers have only a .1 probability of beginning production in two months. If the flight is successful but experiences a technical failure, there is a .4 probability of beginning production in two months. If the flight is a total success, the probability of beginning production in two months is .9.

Construct a probability tree that portrays these events. Then answer the following questions:

1. What is the probability the developers will meet the deadline?
2. What is the probability they *won't* meet the deadline in the event of either a total failure or a successful flight but a technical failure?

**STOP** **BEFORE CONTINUING, CONSTRUCT A PROBABILITY TREE AND ANSWER QUESTIONS A AND B.**

The solution to Exercise 36 shows the probability tree. To answer the questions, we must first calculate the conditionally dependent probabilities of meeting the deadline for each of the six scenarios: Test Launch Failure–Production Yes, Test Launch Failure–Production No, and so on. We do this by multiplying the test launch and production probabilities and entering their products opposite each respective branch of the tree under "Probability of Meeting Deadline." Then, to answer question 1, we add the three mutually exclusive probabilities opposite the "Yes" branches (.02 + .24 + .18 = .44). To answer question 2, we add the two probabilities opposite the "No" branches for "Failure" and "Technical Failure" (.18 + .36 = .54).

You will note that, when added together, all of the probabilities of meeting and not meeting the deadline equal 1.0, as they should if the probabilities at each node of the tree also equal 1.0. Summing to 1.0 is a valid test of the accuracy of the arithmetic in computing these probabilities.

Here's another exercise that combines the calculation of these two types of probabilities.

### EXERCISE 37    Airliner Hijacking I

You are one of a group of terrorists planning to hijack an airliner to force release of several of your comrades imprisoned in a foreign capital. Your leader has asked you to calculate the probability that the imprisoned terrorists will be released as a result of the hijacking.

Construct a probability tree that considers the following:

- ☐   The success or failure of the hijacking
- ☐   An attempt (yes or no) by counterterrorist units to rescue the passengers and crew
- ☐   The success or failure of the rescue attempt
- ☐   The killing of passengers or crew (none, some, or all) during the rescue attempt

You have carefully analyzed the situation and determined there is a .9 probability of a rescue attempt; a .1 probability that all passengers and crew will be killed; a .8 probability that only some will be killed; a .1 probability that none will be killed; a 0 probability that, if all are killed, comrades will be released; a .1 probability that comrades will be released if some or none of the passengers and crew are killed; and a .9 probability that comrades will be released if there is no rescue attempt.

Calculate the total probability that all of the imprisoned terrorists will be released.

 **BEFORE CONTINUING, CONSTRUCT A PROBABILITY TREE, ASSIGN PROBABILITIES, AND CALCULATE THE TOTAL PROBABILITY ALL IMPRISONED TERRORISTS WILL BE RELEASED.**

The solution to Exercise 37 shows my interpretation of the probability tree. To determine the total probability that all imprisoned terrorists would be released, I first multiplied the probabilities of the three conditionally dependent events ("Rescue Attempt Made," "Passengers and Crew Killed During Rescue," and "Comrades Released").

I then added the results for Released–Yes (.072 + .009 + .09 = .171). To verify that the probabilities at each node equal 1.0, I added the results for Released–No (.829), which, when added to .171, equals 1.0.

## EXERCISE 38   New Product Lines

A manufacturer of electronic equipment is studying whether to invest in research and development of a new line of products. Two alternative lines are being considered:

☐ Cellular phones with computer capabilities and miniature screens
☐ Small portable antennas for receiving commercial television broadcasts via satellite

Four factors are paramount in the company's analysis:

1. Whether the new product will require retooling of existing assembly line.
2. Whether the retooling of the assembly line will be partial or total.
3. Whether the need for skilled labor to operate the retooled assembly line will be met by training current employees or by hiring new workers.
4. If retooling is required, labor costs, whether for training current employees or hiring new ones, will rise. The issue is whether they will rise slightly or significantly. If no retooling is required, labor costs will remain the same.

Figure 13-5 shows the probabilities of these various factors. Based on these factors, construct two probability trees—one for the phone, one for the antenna—and answer the following questions for each of the products, that is, give one answer for the phone, one for the antenna:
    What is the probability:

1. That the assembly line will have to be totally retooled?
2. That current employees will have to be retrained?

3. That the company will have to hire new employees?
4. That labor costs will rise slightly?
5. That labor costs will rise significantly?

### FIGURE 13-5

|  |  | Phone (%) | Antenna (%) |
|---|---|---|---|
| Retooling will be required: | Yes | 30 | 60 |
|  | No | 70 | 40 |
| If required, retooling will be: | Partial | 40 | 30 |
|  | Total | 60 | 70 |
| If partial retooling, labor will be: | Trained | 70 | 60 |
|  | Hired | 30 | 40 |
| If total retooling, labor can be: | Trained | 40 | 20 |
|  | Hired | 60 | 80 |
| Whether retooling is partial or total, if labor is trained, labor costs will rise: | Slightly | 50 | 40 |
|  | Significantly | 50 | 60 |
| Whether retooling is partial or total, if labor is hired, labor costs will rise: | Slightly | 40 | 20 |
|  | Significantly | 60 | 80 |

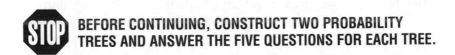 **BEFORE CONTINUING, CONSTRUCT TWO PROBABILITY TREES AND ANSWER THE FIVE QUESTIONS FOR EACH TREE.**

Part 1 of the solution to Exercise 38 shows the two probability trees. Part 2 provides the answers to the questions.

# Summary

Estimating is what we do when we run out of data. The language of estimating is probability, and the laws of probability are the grammar of that language.

Probability is one of the most important concepts covered in this book because probability permeates all analysis. Yet it's one of the least understood concepts and one of the most difficult to deal with effectively because the laws of probability are often counterintuitive.

Proper application of the laws of probability is not something that humans do instinctively.

Despite the trappings of mathematical certainty and scientific objectivity, probability is driven much more by subjective judgments than by mathematical calculation. These subjective judgments, like all others, are subject to biases and other troublesome human mental traits.

Most people can intuitively see the answer to only the most simple problems involving probability.

We determine probability in basically two ways: by computation, when we have the requisite data, and by frequency and experience, when we don't.

The two types of probability we encounter most often in analysis are mutually exclusive (the "or" type, where we *add* probabilities) and conditionally dependent (the "and" type, where we *multiply* them).

When trying to assess the probability of two or more outcomes without a sound basis for judging which is more likely, we should invoke Laplace and assume the probability is equal for all outcomes. We rarely, however, lack a basis for judging likelihood.

We diagram probability outcomes in probability trees, whose construction should follow three rules: the events depicted must be mutually exclusive (meaning each event is distinctive); they must be collectively exhaustive (meaning the tree covers all possible outcomes); and the probabilities at each node (each branching of the tree) must equal 1.0.

Because we humans have widely differing interpretations of adjectival expressions of probability, communicating probability judgments without using numerical percentiles is extremely difficult. There is no easy or right way to do it. But percentiles should be used sparingly and with great care in final reports, because percentiles imply a high degree of analytic precision, which is usually lacking.

# 14
# The
# Utility Tree

 From a purely analytic standpoint, *utility* is the benefit that someone has received, is receiving, or expects to receive from some situation. It is what that person has gained, is gaining, or expects to gain. It is the reason why that person has taken, is taking, or will take a certain action. Utility is the profit, the prize, the dividend, the trophy, the advantage, the motive, the goal, the objective, the hope. It's all these things.

Do you own a car? Why? Lots of reasons? What are they? Think about them for a moment. These reasons are the *utilities* you enjoy from owning or not owning a car.

What is your profession? Are you going to stay in it? Why? What are your reasons? Take a few moments and think about them. They are the *utilities* you expect from remaining or not remaining in your profession. I could go on and on, citing decision after decision each of us makes and the utilities we expect to gain from these decisions, but I think you get the message.

We do things for reasons. These reasons are utilities. Utilities are what's in it for us, from our most animalistic instinct to survive to our most petty, insignificant, innocuous, and idiosyncratic preferences, like the way we sit in a chair or the way we hold the steering wheel of a car. For everything we and others do, want to do, and plan to do there are reasons—and these reasons are our *utilities*. From these reasons emerges a universal truth about human behavior: normal humans, when confronted with a choice between alternative courses of action (alternative options), choose the course that offers them the greater utility, and the person making the choice defines what that utility is. The concept of utility is no stranger to us; we call it *self-interest*.

# Utility Analysis

The owner of our infamous jar of jelly beans is selling people chances to win money by drawing a bean at random from the jar. You pay one dollar a chance, deciding beforehand which color bean you will try to pick. If you pick that color, you win a prize; if you don't, you lose your dollar. The prizes vary as follows:

Red bean        $2.00
Yellow bean     $3.00
Green bean      $4.00

I'll refer to this example as I explain the three basic elements of utility analysis: *options, outcomes,* and *perspectives.*

# Options

The purpose of utility analysis is to *rank* any number of options according to how they serve the decision maker's self-interest. *Options* are alternative courses of action. To buy or sell, to move or stay, to invest or save. Life is an endless series of choices; choices are options. In our jelly bean wagering example there are three options: picking a red, yellow, or green bean. When the options are complex, utility analysis can greatly simplify making the best decision by assessing and comparing the advantages and disadvantages of each option *separately, systematically,* and *sufficiently.* This analysis not only simplifies our choosing among options but strengthens our confidence in the wisdom of our final choice.

When we analyze options, they must be mutually exclusive—distinctive enough from one another to permit meaningful comparisons. The red, yellow, and green beans are clearly mutually exclusive. Options need not, however, be collectively exhaustive, that is, encompass all possibilities. Suppose, for example, that the owner of our jelly bean jar has a second jar, one filled with multicolored jelly beans: purples, browns, pinks, oranges, and so on. Suppose further that he's giving prizes for picking only red, white, or blue beans. Were we to consider buying a chance to pick from that jar, we would restrict our analysis to the red, white, and blue options and ignore the other colored beans.

# Outcomes

The second element of utility analysis is the *outcome*. An outcome is what happens as a result of implementing a certain course of action or selecting an option.

If the San Francisco 49ers play the Dallas Cowboys (an option), there are three possible outcomes (Figure 14-1): the 49ers win, tie, or lose.

If I go to a job interview (an option), there are three possible outcomes (Figure 14-2): I don't get hired, I'm invited back for another interview, or I get hired.

Our jelly bean example is more elaborate. The options are the bets; that is, you can bet on picking a red, yellow, or green bean. For each

**FIGURE 14-1**

| Option | Outcome |
|--------|---------|
|  | Win |
| 49ers play Cowboys | Tie |
|  | Lose |

**FIGURE 14-2**

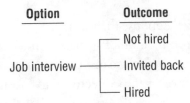

bet there are three possible outcomes: red, yellow, or green (Figure 14-3). Note that the options are disconnected from one another, resulting in three separate trees.

Outcomes are the sole basis for analyzing the utility of options. We measure one option against another—the red bean versus the yellow bean versus the green bean—based exclusively on what we postulate the results would be from executing each option. We must therefore use the identical set of outcomes in analyzing each alternative option. In contrast to options, however, *outcomes as a general rule should be collectively exhaustive*—inclusive of all possible outcomes.

**FIGURE 14-3**

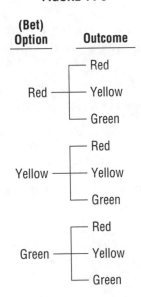

We can, if we deem it appropriate, analyze just one outcome. In the case of our jelly beans, we could consider picking only a green bean. With regard to the 49ers-Cowboys game, we could analyze only the possibility of winning or, in regard to my job interview, only the chance of my being hired. But doing so would sacrifice the huge potential of utility analysis to examine these problems in their fullest dimensions. It's our old nemesis focusing that we must beware of, lest we concentrate solely on the desired outcome and ignore, to the detriment of our analysis, the seemingly less desirable alternatives. There are, of course, rare instances when the decision maker is interested in only a single, specific, narrowly defined outcome. But, as a general rule, when doing utility analysis, we should examine the full range of possible outcomes, not just one.

The nature of the problem—the factors driving it and the solution—dictates which outcomes to consider. In gambling (betting on, say, jelly beans), the primary interest is in winning or losing money. In sports, it's winning or losing the game. In job interviews, it's being hired or not being hired. I call these groupings of alternative, closely related outcomes *classes of outcomes*. I find that in most problems the spectrum of possible outcomes is covered best by defining *three* outcomes that encompass all possibilities: one at either extreme and one in the middle, as in "win/tie/lose" or "none/some/all." In any event, always try to boil down the outcomes to as few as possible, keeping in mind the principle of major factors.

# Perspectives

*Perspectives* are "points of view" with respect to outcomes and are critical in analyzing the utility of outcomes. Most often the perspective is that of the decision maker, as in the jelly bean example. The decision maker in that case is you, the person making the bet. Alternatively, we can analyze the utility from the perspective of the owner of the jar containing the beans. What if the owner is eight years old and trying to earn money to attend summer camp? In that event we can, in a philanthropic mood, pick the option that will give the most benefit—the most utility—not to you, the bettor, but to the youngster.

We, the analyst, must decide whose perspective—whose point of view—will be reflected in our analysis. That decision is not always easy or clear. If we are analyzing other people's or organizations' options, we must "role-play" *their* perspective, trying to view the world as *they* view it, to see where *their* self-interest lies and to understand how *their* choice among options would be influenced by the perspectives of others.

When we ponder, for example, what a business competitor is likely to do, the first question we should address is *what are my competitor's utilities?* What is his or her self-interest and what is he or she likely to do to serve that interest? To make a reasonable projection of what a competitor is likely to do, we must view the world as the competitor views it, not as we *would like* the competitor to view it. That's more easily said than done, of course. It takes lots of practice. So often, when we try to role-play someone else, we simply change hats, not personas. By that I mean we view the situation as if *we*, with all our personal biases, mind-sets, likes and dislikes, were sitting in that person's seat making decisions. That isn't role playing! Role playing is when we view the situation as a professional actor would, as if we literally *were* that other person. Then, having made that transformation, we analyze what factors would influence that person and how that person would likely react, given who and what he or she is.

Nor can we forget probability analysis. That, too, must be seen through the competitor's eyes. We must ask ourselves what probability the competitor would assign to an outcome and why. That is as difficult a task as analyzing the competitor's views of utility, but it's a vital, mandatory step.

Neustadt and May's technique of "placement," mentioned in the discussion of chronologies and time lines in Chapter 6, can be of great assistance in role playing. Placement helps us to penetrate the stereotypical perceptions we have of people, organizations, and movements to discern how they experienced history and were influenced and shaped by those experiences. Neustadt and May stress the hazards inherent in placement, which they describe as "uncertain work":

> Events are all too easily misread. Personal records are prey to gaps, mistakes, and misunderstandings. Inferences are but hypotheses,

not even easily substantiated, let alone "proved." Further compli-
cations arise when placement is attempted across lines of race,
class, or country. Yet the harder placement seems, the more it may
be needed. The cruder the stereotype, the higher the returns . . .

Although placement, say Neustadt and May, gives no guarantees,
"something is better than nothing. The one thing worse than a sophisti-
cated stereotype is an unsophisticated one." As I said earlier, I strongly
recommend Neustadt's and May's book *Thinking in Time.*

To repeat, when we analyze problems that rest in part or in whole
on decisions made by other persons, groups, or organizations, we need
to replicate as best we can their viewpoints, because the latter are what
drive those decisions.

## The Seven Steps of Utility-Tree Analysis

The first step is to construct a set of decision/event trees that clearly
depicts the options and all possible outcomes. Each option is represented in a separate tree, and, as I said, the options must be mutually
exclusive but not collectively exhaustive. The outcomes, however,
must be both. Our jelly bean tree (Figure 14-3) contains the three
options (three trees, three bets) being considered and their nine possible outcomes.

The second step is to identify the perspective of the utility analysis.
We ask ourselves, "From what perspective am I analyzing the utility?"
In our example we will view the problem from the perspective of the
"bettor's profit." We write this above the tree.

### The Utility Question

In the third step, we assign a utility value to each option-outcome
combination—each scenario—by asking the Utility Question: *If we
select this option, and this outcome occurs, what is the utility from the
perspective of . . . ?* Applying the Utility Question to the first red bean
option-outcome combination, we ask: If we bet on picking a red bean

and we pick a red bean, what is the utility from the perspective of the bettor? Answer: Two dollars. We enter this value adjacent to the "Red" outcome in a column titled "Utility" (Figure 14-4). We then ask the Utility Question of the second red bean scenario (bet red, get yellow): If we bet on picking a red bean and we pick a yellow bean, what is the utility? Answer: Zero dollars. We ask the Utility Question of the seven remaining scenarios and enter their utilities.

The fact that the jelly bean outcomes are expressed in terms of dollars and cents makes calculating their utility easy, because we are accustomed to expressing values in monetary terms. Later on, we'll look at problems in which the utilities are *not* in monetary terms.

Which of the three options offers us the most benefit, the most utility? Obviously, the green bean, which is worth $4.00. But is green really the best option? Think about it. At the racetrack, do all bettors bet on the horse that offers the biggest return on their wager? Do all of them put money down to win on the filly paying 100 to 1? Of course not. They factor in the *probability of winning*. Probability. Ah, we're back to

### FIGURE 14-4

#### Perspective: Bettor's profit

| (Bet) Option | Outcome | Utility |
|---|---|---|
| Red | Red | $2 |
|  | Yellow | $0 |
|  | Green | $0 |
| Yellow | Red | $0 |
|  | Yellow | $3 |
|  | Green | $0 |
| Green | Red | $0 |
|  | Yellow | $0 |
|  | Green | $4 |

that, are we? The green bean clearly offers us the greatest utility—the biggest prize—of the three options, but to make a reasoned, judicious bet we must factor in the probability of our picking a green bean.

The prize (the utility) determines what we *want*. We want to win $4.00. But it's the probability of picking a green bean that determines whether we'll get the $4.00. Let me say it again: Utility determines what we *want*; probability determines what we *get*. Store this maxim away in memory where you'll never forget it. It is a profound teaching . . . one of the most important in this book. Would that we all, including myself, could remember this maxim and apply it when we make crucial decisions affecting our lives and those of others. Too often we lose sight of probabilities in our eagerness to gain maximum utility.

### The Probability Question

So our jelly bean analysis must take account of the *probabilities* of picking a red, yellow, or green bean. We do that in the fourth step by asking the Probability Question: *If this option is selected, what is the probability of this outcome?* Applied to the first option-outcome combination (bet red, get red), the Probability Question reads as follows: If I bet on picking a red bean, what is the probability of my picking a red bean? There are 90 beans: 45 red, 36 yellow, and 9 green. Therefore, the probability of picking a single red bean is .5, a yellow .4, and a green .1. We enter these probabilities into the tree (Figure 14-5). Note that the probabilities for the outcomes of a single option must equal 1.0.

We have established the *utilities* of the three options ($2, $3, and $4) and their respective *probabilities* (.5, .4, and .1). How can we now use these calculations to guide our decision as to which wager best serves our self-interest? We do it by means of an ingenious concept called *expected value*.

### Expected Value

Expected value is the product—the multiplication—of the utility and probability values for a given outcome. Why do we multiply them? Because the utility is *conditioned* by its probability of occurring. We get

**FIGURE 14-5**

Perspective: Bettor's profit

| (Bet) Option | Outcome | Utility | Probability |
|---|---|---|---|
| Red | Red | $2 | .5 |
| | Yellow | $0 | .4 |
| | Green | $0 | .1 |
| Yellow | Red | $0 | .5 |
| | Yellow | $3 | .4 |
| | Green | $0 | .1 |
| Green | Red | $0 | .5 |
| | Yellow | $0 | .4 |
| | Green | $4 | .1 |

the utility only *on condition* that the outcome occurs; that is, we get $4.00 only if we pick a green bean. (Utility determines what we want; probability determines what we get.) We express this conditional relationship by multiplying the utility by its probability of occurring, just as we multiplied conditionally dependent probabilities. We do this multiplication in the fifth step, entering the expected values in a column labeled "EV" (Figure 14-6). We then add the expected values for each option and enter the sums in another column labeled "Total EV" (Figure 14-7).

In the sixth step, we rank the expected values from first to last, adding yet another column (Figure 14-8). The expected values show that, if you elect to place a wager, the best decision is to buy a chance on picking a *yellow* bean.

In the seventh and last step, we do a sanity check. Does this analysis make sense? Do we understand the rationale? Let's ask ourselves whether betting on a yellow bean is reasonable. Although each of the green beans is worth $4.00, only nine of the ninety beans in

## FIGURE 14-6

**Perspective:** Bettor's profit

| (Bet) Option | Outcome | Utility | Probability | EV |
|---|---|---|---|---|
| Red | Red | $2 | .5 | **$1.00** |
| | Yellow | $0 | .4 | **0** |
| | Green | $0 | .1 | **0** |
| Yellow | Red | $0 | .5 | **0** |
| | Yellow | $3 | .4 | **$1.20** |
| | Green | $0 | .1 | **0** |
| Green | Red | $0 | .5 | **0** |
| | Yellow | $0 | .4 | **0** |
| | Green | $4 | .1 | **$0.40** |

## FIGURE 14-7

**Perspective:** Bettor's profit

| (Bet) Option | Outcome | Utility | Probability | EV | Total EV |
|---|---|---|---|---|---|
| Red | Red | $2 | .5 | $1.00 | |
| | Yellow | $0 | .4 | 0 | **$1.00** |
| | Green | $0 | .1 | 0 | |
| Yellow | Red | $0 | .5 | 0 | |
| | Yellow | $3 | .4 | $1.20 | **$1.20** |
| | Green | $0 | .1 | 0 | |
| Green | Red | $0 | .5 | 0 | |
| | Yellow | $0 | .4 | 0 | **$0.40** |
| | Green | $4 | .1 | $0.40 | |

FIGURE 14-8

**Perspective: Bettor's profit**

| (Bet) Option | Outcome | Utility | Probability | EV | Total EV | Rank |
|---|---|---|---|---|---|---|
| Red | Red | $2 | .5 | $1.00 | $1.00 | 2 |
| | Yellow | $0 | .4 | 0 | | |
| | Green | $0 | .1 | 0 | | |
| Yellow | Red | $0 | .5 | 0 | $1.20 | 1 |
| | Yellow | $3 | .4 | $1.20 | | |
| | Green | $0 | .1 | 0 | | |
| Green | Red | $0 | .5 | 0 | $0.40 | 3 |
| | Yellow | $0 | .4 | 0 | | |
| | Green | $4 | .1 | $0.40 | | |

the jar are green. And while half the beans are red, the number of yellows is only slightly less than half and the yellows are worth more. It makes sense.

You will note how the use of headers simplifies the language in the tree and greatly facilitates the analysis by graphically portraying the sequence of events of each scenario.

Our tree actually could have dispensed with all of the scenarios except bet red–pick red, bet yellow–pick yellow, and bet green–pick green. These are the only option-outcome combinations in which we are interested. Although dispensing with the others violates the rule to analyze all possible outcomes, doing so makes sense here.

When performing utility analysis, the differences we perceive in expected values among the options should prompt us to ask: Why the difference? Why is the expected value for this option greater or lesser than for that one? Analyzing these questions will unearth answers that enrich our analysis and strengthen our conclusions. We can, of course, blindly obey the numbers and adopt the option with the greatest expected value without bothering to understand the rationale that favors that option over the alternatives. But we do so at the peril of our analysis, because the purpose of utility analysis is not only to assist us in selecting the best option but also to gain a better understanding of the rationale for our selection.

These then are the seven steps of utility-tree analysis:

*Step 1:* Construct a decision/event tree for each option.

*Step 2:* Identify the perspective of the utility analysis.

*Step 3:* Assign a utility value to each option-outcome combination— each branch (scenario) of the tree—by asking the Utility Question: *If we select this option, and this outcome occurs, what is the utility from the perspective of . . . ?*

*Step 4:* Assign a probability to each outcome. Determine or estimate this probability by asking the Probability Question: *If this option is selected, what is the probability this outcome will occur?* The probabilities of all outcomes for a single option must add up to 1.0.

*Step 5:* Determine the expected values by multiplying each utility by its probability and then adding the expected values for each option.

*Step 6:* Determine the ranking of the alternative options.

*Step 7:* Perform a sanity check.

Apply these seven steps in the exercises that follow.

## EXERCISE 39   Japanese Goods

Your U.S. corporation is considering importing certain goods from Japan for sale in the corporation's nationwide chain of general merchandise stores. The corporation has narrowed its interest to three items—a decorative vase, a battery-powered electric hand drill, and a combination stereo radio and disc player—each of which is manufactured by a different Japanese firm. Because these firms historically have refused to deal with non-Japanese-owned companies, persuading them to sell their product to the corporation will be expensive and time-consuming. But they are feeling the pinch of increased competition and have begun making noises about relaxing their self-imposed prohibition against dealing with foreign merchandisers.

The U.S. corporation's management has decided that, rather than pursue all three Japanese firms simultaneously, it will concentrate its lobbying effort on one firm. Your job is to analyze the problem and identify which of the three products will give the biggest return to the corporation during the coming sales year. The corporation will then lobby that firm.

According to a research report, the vase will earn the corporation a profit of $100,000, the hand drill $200,000, and the stereo $500,000. The probability of persuading the firms that produce these products to sell to the corporation is estimated to be .9 for the vase, .5 for the drill, and .1 for the stereo. On which item should the corporation concentrate its lobbying effort? Using a utility tree, work out the problem on a sheet of paper.

**STOP** **BEFORE CONTINUING, WORK THE PROBLEM USING A UTILITY TREE.**

The solution to Exercise 39 shows the completed tree, whose perspective is the U.S. corporation's profits. Here again we could usefully dispense with the "No" outcomes.

We multiply the utilities ($100,000, $200,000, $500,000) by their respective probabilities (.9, .5, .1) to produce the expected values ($90,000, $100,000, $50,000). The drill option is the preferred choice because it offers the greatest expected value: $100,000. Does the drill's being the preferred choice pass the sanity check? Does it make sense? I think so. While the probability of the U.S. corporation's marketing the drill is 55 percent of the probability of its marketing the vase, the profit from the drill is 100 percent more than that from the vase. And although the profit from the stereo is 150 percent more than that from the drill, the probability of marketing the stereo is only 20 percent of the probability of marketing the drill.

## EXERCISE 40    Egg-Laying Hens

You are planning to raise egg-laying hens for sale to egg farmers and are analyzing which of three breeds—brown, white, or red—would be most profitable. One hundred brown hens will earn you $200 profit, a hundred white $300, a hundred red $400. Unfortunately, chicks are highly vulnerable to a current viral epidemic. The Department of Agriculture informs you that brown chicks have an 80 percent chance of surviving the virus, white chicks 50 percent, and red chicks 30 percent.

Considering the profit and the virus, which chicken is your best investment? Work the problem on a sheet of paper using a utility tree.

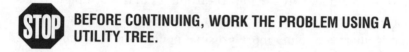 **BEFORE CONTINUING, WORK THE PROBLEM USING A UTILITY TREE.**

The solution to Exercise 40 shows the completed tree; its perspective is your profit. The brown chicks are the preferred option, but by a narrow margin. Does the brown chick option make sense? Yes, for the same kinds of profit-probability reasons we cited in the "Japanese Goods" problem.

## EXERCISE 41    Jelly Beans III

The jar still contains 90 jelly beans: 45 red, 36 yellow, 9 green. But the owner of the jar is now taking $10 bets that pay off as follows:

$100, if you pick two yellow beans and one green bean consecutively (replacing each one and stirring the beans before selecting the next one)

$90, if you pick one red, one yellow, and one green consecutively

$80, if you pick three yellows consecutively

$70, if you pick two reds and one green consecutively

Which is the best bet? Work the problem on a sheet of paper using a utility tree, but this time don't incorporate every possible scenario. We are concerned here with only four scenarios: Y-Y-G, R-Y-G, Y-Y-Y, and

R-R-G. Therefore, you may ignore all other scenarios and perform utility analysis only on these four.

 **BEFORE CONTINUING, WORK THE PROBLEM USING A UTILITY TREE.**

The solution to Exercise 41 shows the finished tree with "Your monetary profit" as the perspective. Granted, it isn't much of a tree, but it serves the purpose in any event. The yellow-yellow-yellow option is clearly the preferred bet, and it passes a sanity check.

Do you remember why the four probabilities in the completed tree don't have to add up to 1.0? Because they are not collectively exhaustive; that is, there are many more possible options such as yellow-red-green, and so on.

The utility-tree exercises we have worked thus far have involved monetary outcomes—monetary values we could add, multiply, or divide. The outcomes in the next exercise, however, are not monetary values. How can we compute expected values (probability times utility) when the utilities aren't dollars? Read on and I'll explain.

### EXERCISE 42    Securities Investment II

You are considering making a $5,000 lump-sum investment in one of the following three types of securities:

1. *Speculative high-risk stocks.* They earn more than the other two options but also are very risky; you could easily lose your investment if things don't go just right.
2. *Blue-chip medium-risk stocks.* They usually earn less than speculative stocks but are much safer.
3. *Government bonds.* They earn the smallest return but are the safest—virtually risk free.

In this hypothetical example, the value—the outcome—of the two stocks will vary according to what happens in three future scenarios: *war, peace with prosperity,* and *peace with depression.*

☐ The value of the speculative high-risk stock will increase 20 percent with the outbreak of hostilities, increase 1 percent with prosperity, and decrease 6 percent with depression.
☐ The value of the blue-chip medium-risk stock will experience a
healthy increase with either war (up 9 percent) or peace with prosperity (up 8 percent) but go nowhere (0 percent change) in a
depression.
☐ The bonds guarantee a 4 percent return regardless of the outcome.

The probability of war is .1, peace .9. If there is peace, the probability of prosperity is .4, depression .6. These probabilities apply to all
three options.

Because this problem may seem a little tricky, let me walk you
through the steps.

*Step 1:* Construct a decision/event tree for each option.

Figure 14-9 shows the set of trees.

*Step 2:* Identify the perspective of the utility analysis.

**FIGURE 14-9**

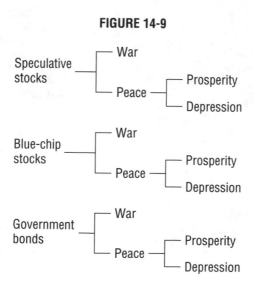

Write "Perspective: My monetary profit" above the set.

*Step 3*: Assign a utility value to each option-outcome combination—
each branch (scenario) of the tree—by asking the Utility Question:
*If we select this option, and this outcome occurs, what is the utility
from the perspective of . . . ?*

We now ask the Utility Question of each option-outcome combination (each scenario). We could, if we wished, compute the dollar earnings and losses in the value of the securities and use the resultant dollar
figures as our utility values. But since the purchase price is the same for
all, there's a simpler, more direct way. Enter adjacent to each scenario
(each branch) the percentage of increase or decrease in value that will
accrue.

Figure 14-10 shows the percentages.

Now enter an *adjective or adverb-adjective* (such as "Best," "Worst,"
"Super," "Rotten," "Very good," "Poor," "Absolutely awful") that best
characterizes our subjective judgment concerning the utility of each

**FIGURE 14-10**

**Perspective: My monetary profit**

| | Utility (%) |
|---|---|
| Speculative stocks — War | +20 |
| Speculative stocks — Peace — Prosperity | +1 |
| Speculative stocks — Peace — Depression | −6 |
| Blue-chip stocks — War | +9 |
| Blue-chip stocks — Peace — Prosperity | +8 |
| Blue-chip stocks — Peace — Depression | 0 |
| Government bonds — War | +4 |
| Government bonds — Peace — Prosperity | +4 |
| Government bonds — Peace — Depression | +4 |

percentage (each outcome) in comparison to all of the other outcomes. This is a critical feature of utility analysis. We are measuring the utility of *all nine* of the outcomes, not just the three in a single tree. Thus, we ask the Utility Question of the Speculative–War scenario: "If we invest in speculative stock and war occurs, what is the utility from the perspective of my monetary profits, that is, from a 20 percent increase in the value of the stock?" Our answer might be "Excellent," which we would enter adjacent to the end of the scenario. So go ahead and ask the Utility Question of each scenario and enter your adjectival assessments of utility. (There is no "right" utility; enter whatever your intuition indicates.)

Figure 14-11 shows my adjectival assessments of the utilities in the tree.

In determining the utilities, you discovered, I'm sure, that you quickly perceived a ranking order among them. The mind senses this order instantly. We don't have to consciously work at it. The ease with which we do it is, I'm sure, related to the mind's instinct to view things chronologically and in terms of cause and effect. In any case, the mind

**FIGURE 14-11**

**Perspective: My monetary profit**

|                        |              |            | Utility |          |
| ---------------------- | ------------ | ---------- | ------- | -------- |
|                        | War          |            | +20%    | **Super** |
| Speculative stocks     | Peace        | Prosperity | +1%     | **Bad** |
|                        |              | Depression | −6%     | **Horrible** |
|                        | War          |            | +9%     | **Very good** |
| Blue-chip stocks       | Peace        | Prosperity | +8%     | **Good** |
|                        |              | Depression | 0%      | **Very bad** |
|                        | War          |            | +4%     | **Okay** |
| Government bonds       | Peace        | Prosperity | +4%     | **Okay** |
|                        |              | Depression | +4%     | **Okay** |

is exquisitely equipped to perform this task. But let us get back to the process.

The trouble with using adjectives is that we can't multiply them by probabilities to produce expected values. Adjectives don't tell us numerically *how much* utility each scenario provides. To calculate expected value, we need somehow to quantify the adjectives. There's an easy way to do that. We simply represent utility on a scale of 0 to 100, where zero is the *worst* utility (among *all* the outcomes being considered) and 100 is the *best*. The utility numbers for all of the scenarios will lie somewhere on this spectrum of 0 to 100.

This brings up another rule regarding utility-tree analysis. There must be at least one 0 and at least one 100 in a set of trees (one *best* case and one *worst*). There can be *more* than one of each but never *less* than one of each. I say again: at least one 100 and one 0. Why this rule? Because we need to establish analytic boundaries within which to compare the relative utility of the various option-outcome combinations. Assigning at least one 0 and one 100 to the set serves the purpose of setting the lower and upper limits within which the utilities *in this particular set* will be compared.

Why put artificial boundaries on the utility judgments? Because the numbers we use to quantify utility are not real. (I'm not speaking here of those instances where we can use monetary values for utilities.) What does the 100 we assign as a utility represent? A hundred what? A *hundred units of utility*. What's a unit of utility? It's an abstraction that provides a common denominator for weighing one option-outcome combination against another. A unit of utility can't be weighed or measured by any objective standard; it's purely theoretical. Outside the set of trees, the utility we ascribe to an outcome has no meaning whatsoever. Imagine telling a business acquaintance that you are buying a particular computer because "it has a utility of 90"!

But, you may ask, if we assign a 0 to the worst utility in the set, aren't we saying that this option-outcome combination *has no utility*? Not really. We're simply saying that within this set, among these options, and considering these outcomes, this option-outcome combination has the *smallest* utility—and the smallest is zero. (There is a utility concept called "disutility" by which one assigns negative utility val-

ues from 0 to −100 to outcomes according to how *undesirable* they are.
I haven't yet found a practical use for this upside-down concept.) By the
same token, the combination with a utility of 100 has the *greatest* utility
within the set of trees. All that utility-tree analysis does, all that it can
do, is evaluate the options and outcomes incorporated *in a set of trees.*
The combinations assessed as worst and best are worst and best only in
comparison to the other combinations being considered. They are not
worst or best by some universal objective standard. The figures, then, of
0 and 100 establish the boundaries within which we measure the utility
of the outcomes in the set.

In expressing utilities we should also observe another rule of thumb
(I'm brimming over with rules): use only utility values divisible by 10
(such as 10, 40, 90, 100). There are three reasons:

1. Utility values, being subjective, are by nature imprecise. Restricting
   these values to those divisible by 10 explicitly reaffirms that impreci-
   sion. To employ more precise numbers would suggest to ourselves
   and to others that there is some objective basis for greater precision.
   But in utility analysis there is no objective basis (unless, of course,
   we are using monetary values for utilities).
2. Values in tens serve our purpose as well as more precise numbers.
3. Values in tens are especially easy to work with arithmetically.

Let us return to our trees. Convert the adjectival expressions of utility into decimal numbers from 0 to 100. These are the utility values.

Figure 14-12 shows my conversions of adjectival expressions into
decimal values from 0 to 100. As a practical matter, however, don't
use adjectives as an intermediate step to assigning utility values. I had
you do that in this exercise only as a way of teaching you the technique. In the remaining exercises, and when you perform utility
analysis on your own, go *directly* to decimal utility values. You don't
need the adjectives.

*Step 4:* Assign a probability to each outcome. Determine or estimate
   this probability by asking the Probability Question: *If this option is
   selected, what is the probability this outcome will occur?* The proba-

**FIGURE 14-12**

**Perspective: My monetary profit**
_____

|  |  |  | Utility |  |
|---|---|---|---|---|
| Speculative stocks — War |  | +20% | Super | **100** |
| — Peace — Prosperity |  | +1% | Bad | **20** |
| — Depression |  | −6% | Horrible | **0** |
| Blue-chip stocks — War |  | +9% | Very good | **80** |
| — Peace — Prosperity |  | +8% | Good | **70** |
| — Depression |  | 0% | Very bad | **10** |
| Government bonds — War |  | +4% | Okay | **40** |
| — Peace — Prosperity |  | +4% | Okay | **40** |
| — Depression |  | +4% | Okay | **40** |

bilities of all outcomes for a single option (in a single tree) must add up to 1.0.

Ordinarily, we would now ask the Probability Question in our problem, but, as the probabilities are given above, we can simply enter them at the appropriate places in the tree and calculate the probability of each scenario.

Figure 14-13 shows the probability entries.

*Step* 5: Determine the expected values by multiplying each utility by its probability and then adding the expected values for each option.

*Step* 6: Determine the ranking of the alternative options.

Figure 14-14 shows the resulting expected values and rankings. Given the probabilities of the outcomes, the government bonds are the preferred investment, blue-chip stock is second, and speculative stock third.

**FIGURE 14-13**

## Perspective: My monetary profit

| | Probabilities | | Probability of Scenario | Utility |
|---|---|---|---|---|
| **Speculative stocks** | War .1 | | .1 | 100 |
| | Peace .9 | Prosperity .4 | .36 | 20 |
| | | Depression .6 | .54 | 0 |
| **Blue-chip stocks** | War .1 | | .1 | 80 |
| | Peace .9 | Prosperity .4 | .36 | 70 |
| | | Depression .6 | .54 | 10 |
| **Government bonds** | War .1 | | .1 | 40 |
| | Peace .9 | Prosperity .4 | .36 | 40 |
| | | Depression .6 | .54 | 40 |

**FIGURE 14-14**

## Perspective: My monetary profit

| | Probabilities | | Probability of Scenario | Utility | EV | Total EV | Rank |
|---|---|---|---|---|---|---|---|
| **Speculative stocks** | War .1 | | .1 | 100 | **10.0** | | |
| | Peace .9 | Prosperity .4 | .36 | 20 | **7.2** | **17.2** | **3** |
| | | Depression .6 | .54 | 0 | **0** | | |
| **Blue-chip stocks** | War .1 | | .1 | 80 | **8.0** | | |
| | Peace .9 | Prosperity .4 | .36 | 70 | **25.2** | **38.6** | **2** |
| | | Depression .6 | .54 | 10 | **5.4** | | |
| **Government bonds** | War .1 | | .1 | 40 | **4.0** | | |
| | Peace .9 | Prosperity .4 | .36 | 40 | **14.4** | **40.0** | **1** |
| | | Depression .6 | .54 | 40 | **21.6** | | |

What if we change the probabilities? Let's say war is .5, prosperity with peace .6, and depression with peace .4. Using these new probabilities, redo the computations and determine which investment is preferred under the different circumstances.

Figure 14-15 shows the results using the new probabilities. Under these circumstances the blue-chip stocks become the preferred investment, the speculative stocks move into second place, and bonds drop to third.

*Step* 7: Perform a sanity check.

Do the results make intuitive sense? I believe they do.

## FIGURE 14-15

**Perspective: My monetary profit**

|  | Probabilities | | | Probability of Scenario | Utility | EV | Total EV | Rank |
|---|---|---|---|---|---|---|---|---|
| Speculative stocks | War .5 | | | .5 | 100 | 50.0 | | |
| | Peace .5 | Prosperity .6 | | .3 | 20 | 6.0 | 56.0 | 2 |
| | | Depression .4 | | .2 | 0 | 0 | | |
| Blue-chip stocks | War .5 | | | .5 | 80 | 40.0 | | |
| | Peace .5 | Prosperity .6 | | .3 | 70 | 21.0 | 63.0 | 1 |
| | | Depression .4 | | .2 | 10 | 2.0 | | |
| Government bonds | War .5 | | | .5 | 40 | 20.0 | | |
| | Peace .5 | Prosperity .6 | | .3 | 40 | 12.0 | 40.0 | 3 |
| | | Depression .4 | | .2 | 40 | 8.0 | | |

# Utility Versus Probability

Like all the other techniques addressed in this book, utility analysis is a method of structuring. And what does structuring do? It separates a problem into its constituent elements in an organized way that enables us to focus on each one *separately, systematically,* and *sufficiently.* The most important things that utility analysis separates are utility and probability. Why is this important? Because utility and probability are two fundamentally different subjects, each with a different focus and, most especially, a different language.

Consider the fundamental disparity between the utility and probability questions:

> *Utility:* If this option is selected and this outcome occurs, what is the utility?
>
> *Probability:* If this option is selected, what is the probability this outcome will occur?

These obviously are totally different subjects. Issues are raised and positions voiced in analyzing utility that are *not* raised or voiced in analyzing probability and vice versa. Therefore, when we mix the two together in our analysis or in discussing a problem with others, we create confusion and muddy the analytic waters.

If you're in the mood sometime for intriguing entertainment, monitor a conversation of others about politics, religion, or some other current issue and take note of how they employ utility and probability. The conversants will casually, unconsciously switch back and forth between utility and probability, frequently in a single sentence, blissfully unaware they are doing so and unaware of the consequences of mixing the two concepts. Unless we make a conscious effort to separate, that is, to structure, our discussion of utility and probability, the two inevitably become intertwined in a hopeless melange in which we lose sight of, and confuse, the underlying assumptions that drive our perceptions of what we want (utility) and what we'll get (probability). Separating utility and probability avoids these problems and, as an added bonus, provides insights into the all-powerful dynamic that exists between probability and utility, a dynamic that is otherwise obscured. The message is clear: *Always separate the analysis (including the discussion) of utility and probability.*

The relationship between the concepts of utility and probability is a familiar one to us all. From our earliest years we humans encounter it repeatedly, as when we are youngsters and yearn for a particular new toy but know our parents won't buy it for us because it's too expensive. The toy has great utility for us, but the cost makes the probability of getting it extremely low. As teens, we develop a crush on someone: if we lack self-confidence, we worry that the other person does not feel the same toward us (the affection has great utility for us, but we rate the probability low that the feeling is shared); if we are overly self-confident, we rate the probability high that the affection is mutual. As we mature and gain experience, we develop an unconscious reliance on utility and probability to inform and guide our decisions about what to do in almost every phase of life. Even so, we are seldom aware of this reliance because it is accomplished through unconscious mental shortcuts. One aim of this book is to raise awareness of utility and probability, of how dependent we are upon them in our analysis and decision making, and of how they can so easily lead our thinking astray. It's high time we learned to separate these two concepts and to use that separation to our advantage in making decisions in both our professional and private lives.

Whereas analyzing utility and probability as they relate to our own decisions is difficult, even more challenging is analyzing (forecasting) the decisions of others. When we analyze and make estimates about actions that other people, businesses, and governments will take, there is another relationship between utility and probability to which we should pay particular attention. I refer to the fact that people will work harder to achieve goals that are in their self-interest than they will for goals that are not. (That is, of course, what makes capitalism succeed and communist socialism fail.) History is replete with cases of people, businesses, and nations that by sheer determination and imagination overcame seemingly insurmountable obstacles—insurmountable probabilities—to achieve personal, institutional, or national goals, such as the athlete who overcomes a childhood muscular disability to enter the ranks of the professionals or a tiny company that competes successfully with industrial giants. The fact is, the harder people work to achieve goals that are in their self-interest, the greater is the probability of their achieving those goals.

A historic example of how ignoring this insightful maxim of human behavior can lead to miscalculation was the failure in November 1944 of the Nazi High Command to foresee Normandy as the landing site for the Allied invasion of Europe. A key item of "evidence" that misled Nazi strategists was their perception that the shallow Normandy beaches were unsuitable for use as a port through which the Allies could convey the stupendous numbers of reinforcements and supplies the invasion forces would immediately need to sustain their offensive and avoid being thrown back into the English Channel. The Nazis reasoned rightly—as did the Allies—that the invasion would require the facilities of a modern, fully equipped industrial seaport. Mainly for that reason, Adolf Hitler and key Nazi field marshals believed the invasion would come at the major French port of Calais and that landings, if any, at Normandy would be only a diversion. Indeed, one report from Nazi Intelligence actually predicted the invasion's exact landing site, day, and hour, yet Hitler reportedly disregarded the information, believing it was a deliberate deception.

What Hitler and his military advisers failed to recognize was that the Allies were so intent on (saw such great utility in) invading at Normandy that they would devise some way of overcoming its inhospitable shore, thereby increasing the probability of the invasion's success. What they did—a spectacular feat of engineering—was to build two complete prefabricated artificial harbors, each comprising a breakwater of sunken ships, an outer seawall of huge concrete boxlike structures (some the size of three-story buildings), and floating roadways and piers. Some twenty thousand workers in harbors all over Britain constructed the components in only seven months, and an armada of two hundred tugboats towed them to Normandy. The Nazis obtained photoreconnaissance of the structures under construction but did not discern their real purpose. The Allies' determination and ingenuity surprised the Nazi High Command and led directly to the invasion's success and Nazi Germany's defeat.

Utility analysis is really quite easy, once you grasp the basic principles involved. To some people it seems at first to be nothing more than "number crunching," which instinctively puts them off, making them suspicious of the validity of the results. These people feel that they aren't using their minds, that they aren't intellectually involved, which makes them ill at ease. This uneasiness is to be expected, however, since they have never before used this analytic method. Nor had I, when I first learned about utility analysis fourteen years ago. Since then, with repeated practice, I have come to place complete confidence in the technique because I understand the process and what it accomplishes.

# 15
# The
# Utility
# Matrix

A matrix offers two important advantages over a tree for performing utility analysis. First, the relative differences in utility values of outcomes are more easily perceived in a matrix than in a tree. Second, arithmetic calculations are easier to perform. This is due, in part, to the different configurations of the two structuring devices: a tree is busy, sort of sprawls out, and is sometimes unsymmetrical, while a matrix is a compact, tightly organized, symmetrical unit. Also, the focus of a utility matrix is squarely on *alternative outcomes*, while a tree portrays *whole scenarios* in which outcomes are only a part. Depicting scenarios—the strong suit of trees—tends to overshadow and divert attention from the outcomes.

Which is a better vehicle for utility analysis: a matrix or a tree? Naturally, the answer depends on the nature of the problem being analyzed and on the personal preference of the analyst. The analytic steps are the same in either case: construct a matrix or a tree, enter the options and outcomes, define the analytic perspective, assign utility values, assign probabilities, compute expected values, and determine the rankings.

Because it facilitates arithmetic operations, however, a matrix is more suitable than a tree for analyzing a problem from different per-

spectives and with different classes of outcomes. I address these complexities in the next two chapters.

For now, let me demonstrate how a utility matrix works. Figure
15-1 shows the basic elements of a utility matrix.

The analytic perspective is given in the upper left-hand corner.
Options are listed down the left. The class of outcomes is entered above
the outcome columns. Each option-outcome combination is represented by a cell. We enter in the cell the utility values and probabilities
of that combination and compute its expected value. We then add the
expected values for each option and enter the sums in the "Total EV"
column, indicating the ranking in the last column.

You can see this more clearly as I convert into a matrix the three
utility trees (Figure 15-2) we constructed for the "Japanese Goods"
problem in Chapter 14. The resulting matrix is shown in Figure 15-4.

Observe how the matrix does, indeed, focus your attention on the
outcomes, placing all the numerical data for each option-outcome
combination neatly into a single cell. I find it easier to discern patterns,
differences, and similarities with a matrix than with trees, but it's really
a matter of personal preference.

To get a feel for what makes up a utility matrix, try your hand at
converting the trees we constructed for the "Egg-Laying Hens" exercise
in Chapter 14 (see solution to Exercise 40).

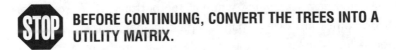
**BEFORE CONTINUING, CONVERT THE TREES INTO A
UTILITY MATRIX.**

Figure 15-5 is the utility matrix for the "Egg-Laying Hens" problem.

Now convert to a matrix the utility trees for the "Jelly Beans" problem
(Figure 15-6).

**BEFORE CONTINUING, CONVERT THE TREES INTO A
UTILITY MATRIX.**

**FIGURE 15-1**   Utility Matrix

| Perspective: | Class of Outcomes | | | Total EV | Rank |
|---|---|---|---|---|---|
| | A | B | C | | |
| Option 1 | | | | | |
| Option 2 | | | | | |
| Option 3 | | | | | |

**FIGURE 15-2**

**Perspective: U.S. corporation's profit**

| Option | (Outcome) Sell to U.S. Corporation | Utility | Probability | Expected Value | Total EV | Rank |
|---|---|---|---|---|---|---|
| Vase | Yes | $100,000 | .9 | $90,000 | $90,000 | 2 |
| | No | 0 | .1 | 0 | | |
| Drill | Yes | $200,000 | .5 | $100,000 | $100,000 | 1 |
| | No | 0 | .5 | 0 | | |
| Stereo | Yes | $500,000 | .1 | $50,000 | $50,000 | 3 |
| | No | 0 | .9 | 0 | | |

**FIGURE 15-3**

| Perspective: U.S. corporation's profit | | Outcome: Sell to U.S. corporation | | Total EV | Rank |
|---|---|---|---|---|---|
| | | Yes | No | | |
| Option | Vase | U  $100,000<br>P        .9<br>EV  $90,000 | 0<br>.1<br>0 | $90,000 | 2 |
| | Drill | $200,000<br>.5<br>$100,000 | 0<br>.5<br>0 | $100,000 | 1 |
| | Stereo | $500,000<br>.1<br>$50,000 | 0<br>.5<br>0 | $50,000 | 3 |

Figure 15-7 is the utility matrix for the "Jelly Beans" problem.

Convert the trees for the "Securities Investment" problem (Figure 15-8).

 **BEFORE CONTINUING, CONVERT THE TREES INTO A UTILITY MATRIX.**

Figure 15-9 is the utility matrix for the "Securities Investment" problem. "National political and economic situation" is the class of outcome.

# The Seven Steps of Utility-Matrix Analysis

*Step 1*: Construct a utility matrix.

*Step 2*: Identify the perspective of the utility analysis.

*Step 3*: Assign a utility value to each option-outcome combination— each cell of the matrix—by asking the Utility Question: *If we select this option, and this outcome occurs, what is the utility from the perspective of . . . ?*

*Step 4*: Assign a probability to each outcome. Determine or estimate this probability by asking the Probability Question: *If this option is selected, what is the probability this outcome will occur?* The probabilities of all outcomes for a single option must add up to 1.0.

*Step 5*: Determine the expected values by multiplying each utility by its probability and then adding the expected values for each option.

*Step 6*: Determine the ranking of the alternative options.

*Step 7*: Perform a sanity check.

Apply these seven steps in analyzing the "Weather Forecaster's Dilemma" (Exercise 15), which we encountered in Chapter 8. Here are the particulars again.

FIGURE 15-4

Perspective: My monetary profit

| Option | (Outcome) Survive Virus | Utility | Probability | Expected Value | Total EV | Rank |
|---|---|---|---|---|---|---|
| Brown | Yes | $200 | .8 | $160 | $160 | 1 |
| | No | 0 | .2 | 0 | | |
| White | Yes | $300 | .5 | $150 | $150 | 2 |
| | No | 0 | .5 | 0 | | |
| Red | Yes | $400 | .3 | $120 | $120 | 3 |
| | No | 0 | .7 | 0 | | |

FIGURE 15-5

| Perspective: My monetary profit | | Outcome: Survive virus | | Total EV | Rank |
|---|---|---|---|---|---|
| | | Yes | No | | |
| Option | Brown | U $200<br>P .8<br>EV $160 | 0<br>.2<br>0 | $160 | 1 |
| | White | $300<br>.5<br>$150 | 0<br>.5<br>0 | $150 | 2 |
| | Red | $400<br>.3<br>$120 | 0<br>.7<br>0 | $120 | 3 |

FIGURE 15-6

Perspective: My monetary profit

| (Bet) Option | Outcome | Utility | Probability | EV | Rank |
|---|---|---|---|---|---|
| Y-Y-G | Y-Y-G | $90 | .016 | $1.44 | 4 |
| R-Y-G | R-Y-G | $80 | .02 | $1.60 | 2 |
| Y-Y-Y | Y-Y-Y | $70 | .064 | $4.48 | 1 |
| R-R-G | R-R-G | $60 | .025 | $1.50 | 3 |

FIGURE 15-7

| Perspective: My monetary profit | | Outcome | | | | Total EV | Rank |
|---|---|---|---|---|---|---|---|
| | | Y-Y-G | R-Y-G | Y-Y-Y | R-R-G | | |
| Option | Y-Y-G | $ 90 .016 $1.44 | $ 0 .02 0 | $ 0 .064 0 | $ 0 .025 0 | $1.44 | 4 |
| | R-Y-G | $ 0 .016 0 | $ 80 .02 $1.60 | $ 0 .064 0 | $ 0 .025 0 | $1.60 | 2 |
| | Y-Y-Y | $ 0 .016 0 | $ 0 .02 0 | $ 70 .064 $4.48 | $ 0 .025 0 | $4.48 | 1 |
| | R-R-G | $ 0 .016 0 | $ 0 .02 0 | $ 0 .064 0 | $ 60 .025 $1.50 | $1.50 | 3 |

FIGURE 15-8

## Perspective: My monetary profit

| | Probabilities | | Probability of Scenario | Utility | EV | Total EV | Rank |
|---|---|---|---|---|---|---|---|
| Speculative stocks | War .1 | | .1 | 100 | 10.0 | | |
| | Peace .9 | Prosperity .4 | .36 | 20 | 7.2 | 17.2 | 3 |
| | | Depression .6 | .54 | 0 | 0 | | |
| Blue-chip stocks | War .1 | | .1 | 80 | 8.0 | | |
| | Peace .9 | Prosperity .4 | .36 | 70 | 25.2 | 38.6 | 2 |
| | | Depression .6 | .54 | 10 | 5.4 | | |
| Government bonds | War .1 | | .1 | 40 | 4.0 | | |
| | Peace .9 | Prosperity .4 | .36 | 40 | 14.4 | 40.0 | 1 |
| | | Depression .6 | .54 | 40 | 21.6 | | |

**FIGURE 15-9**

| Perspective: My monetary profit | | Outcome: National political and economic situation | | | Total EV | Rank |
|---|---|---|---|---|---|---|
| | | War | Prosperity | Depression | | |
| **Option** | Speculative stocks | 100 <br> .1 <br> ——— <br> 10 | 20 <br> .36 <br> ——— <br> 7.2 | 0 <br> .54 <br> ——— <br> 0 | 17.2 | 3 |
| | Blue-chip stocks | 80 <br> .1 <br> ——— <br> 8 | 70 <br> .36 <br> ——— <br> 25.2 | 10 <br> .54 <br> ——— <br> 5.4 | 38.6 | 2 |
| | Government bonds | 40 <br> .1 <br> ——— <br> 4 | 40 <br> .36 <br> ——— <br> 14.4 | 40 <br> .54 <br> ——— <br> 21.6 | 40.0 | 1 |

## EXERCISE 43   Weather Forecaster's Dilemma II

Pretend you are the weatherperson on a local TV station. There is a 1 percent chance of snow tomorrow, which is a normal midweek workday. Determine, using a utility matrix, which of two predictions — "Snow" or "Not snow" — is in your better all-around interest. Consider only two outcomes: it snows, and it doesn't snow.

**STOP** BEFORE CONTINUING, WORK THE PROBLEM USING A UTILITY MATRIX.

The solution to Exercise 43 shows my matrix.

I gave Predict snow–Snow a utility of 100, because most people work and, though they despise how snow delays their commute or hinders their errands and deliveries, they are relieved at having been given fair warning. This is, I believe, the best cell in the matrix for the forecaster because it boosts his or her credibility and enables people to be prepared for the snow, and for that they are grateful.

The worst cell is Predict not snow–Snow. I gave that cell a utility of zero. What could be worse for a weather forecaster?

I gave Predict snow–Not snow a utility of 80. People will have been prepared for snow and be relieved that there was none. Their relief will offset the forecaster's loss of credibility, unless the forecaster gets the reputation of crying "wolf."

I gave Predict not snow–Not snow a utility of 30 because, even though working people are pleased that there's no snow, it's a nonhappening.

The probabilities were given: .1 probability for snow and, logically, .9 for not snow.

I multiplied the utilities by the probabilities to calculate the expected values. I added the expected values and determined the ranking. My assessment ranks "Predict snow" as the strongly preferred option. (This analysis may explain why weather forecasters on TV and radio tend to predict snow at the very first sign. They're afraid of ending up in the lower left-hand cell.)

Try the "Weather Forecaster's Dilemma" exercise at a party some time. I guarantee the discussion of what each cell's utility should be will liven things up.

In the last exercise in this chapter, to challenge your understanding of how to perform utility analysis, I want you to analyze a problem first with utility trees and then with a matrix.

## EXERCISE 44   Airliner Hijacking II

A group of terrorists has commandeered an airliner to force release of several comrades imprisoned in a foreign capital. You are the commander of a counterterrorist unit. Your supervisor has directed you to determine whether an armed assault of the aircraft should be attempted to save the passengers and crew.

You have carefully analyzed the situation and estimate that, should a rescue be attempted, there is a .1 probability that all passengers and crew will be killed; a .8 probability that only some will be killed; a .1 probability that none will be killed; a 0 probability that, if all are killed, comrades will be released; and a .1 probability that comrades will be released if some or none of the passengers and crew are killed. You have further estimated that, if a rescue is not attempted, there is a .9 probability that comrades will be released.

Applying the seven steps of utility-tree analysis (and assigning your own utilities), determine whether a rescue attempt is advisable.

 **BEFORE CONTINUING, WORK THE PROBLEM USING UTILITY-TREE ANALYSIS.**

Part 1 of the solution to Exercise 44 shows my version of the completed utility trees.

A rescue attempt is preferred as its total expected value is nearly twice that of no rescue attempt.

Now convert these utility trees into a utility matrix.

 **BEFORE CONTINUING, CONVERT THE TREES INTO A MATRIX.**

Part 2 of the solution to Exercise 44 shows my version of the matrix.

# 16

# Advanced Utility Analysis

 Thus far we have performed utility analysis on problems that involved multiple options and multiple outcomes but only a single perspective. It is frequently advisable, even necessary, however, to assess utilities from the vantage of more than one perspective. A planning conference can serve as an example for illustrating how utility analysis copes with multiple perspectives.

## EXERCISE 45   Planning Conference

The administrative staff of a nationwide hotel chain is selecting a site for the annual winter planning conference of its top managers. The choice of site depends on the recreational activities in which attendees can engage. Three sites are being considered: New York City (theaters and restaurants), Palm Beach, Florida (swimming and sunbathing), and Stowe, Vermont (skiing). The administrative staff has just been informed that the top managers attending the conference will be accompanied by their spouses and children. As a result, the staff, in selecting the site, must now take into account the recreational preferences—*recreational utilities*—of three different groups of people: attendees, spouses, and children. In other words, the staff must view the problem of site selection from three different perspectives.

Utility analysis handles *multiple perspectives* quite easily by analyzing each perspective separately (constructing a utility matrix for each) and then merging the results to rank the options. Because the options being weighed are the same for each, *the matrices are identical in structure*. Ensuring this uniformity of structure is critical to the process. Each matrix contains the same options and outcomes, and the probabilities of the outcomes are identical. *Only the utility values will vary* because each matrix, as I said, views the problem from a distinctly different perspective (identified in the upper left-hand corner) with different self-interests in mind.

In the case of our "Planning Conference" problem, each matrix contains the same three options (New York City, Florida, Vermont). Because weather more than any other factor usually determines whether attendees at a conference are pleased with recreational activities, we will use weather as a class of outcomes and consider two outcomes: "warm-and-sunny" versus "cold-and-rainy." Construct three utility-analysis matrices, one for each perspective. Do not include a "Rank" column in the matrix. (I'll explain why momentarily.)

 **BEFORE CONTINUING, CONSTRUCT ONE MATRIX FOR EACH PERSPECTIVE.**

Figure 16-1 shows what your three matrices should look like.

The utility analysis process for multiple perspectives is exactly the same as that followed in the preceding chapters: ask the Utility Question for each option-outcome combination, assign utility values, ask the Probability Question, enter the probability values, compute the expected values, add the expected values for each option, and enter the sums in the "Total EV" column.

To expedite the exercise, I am furnishing the utility values for each of the matrices (Figure 16-2). The values were obtained by asking the Utility Question for each option-outcome, for example, "If the conference is held in New York City and the weather is warm and sunny, what is the utility from the perspective of the attendees' enjoyment?" Enter the utilities in the matrices.

**FIGURE 16-1**

| | Perspective: | Outcome | | Total EV |
| --- | --- | --- | --- | --- |
| | | Warm and sunny | Cold and rainy | |
| **Option** | New York City | | | |
| | Florida | | | |
| | Vermont | | | |

**FIGURE 16-2**

| | Utilities | |
| --- | --- | --- |
| | Warm and sunny | Cold and rainy |
| Attendees: | | |
| New York City | 100 | 80 |
| Florida | 50 | 10 |
| Vermont | 20 | 0 |
| Spouses: | | |
| New York City | 10 | 0 |
| Florida | 50 | 10 |
| Vermont | 100 | 80 |
| Children: | | |
| New York City | 10 | 0 |
| Florida | 100 | 10 |
| Vermont | 80 | 30 |

**BEFORE CONTINUING, ENTER THE UTILITY VALUES IN THE MATRICES.**

I am also furnishing the weather forecast—the probabilities for the outcomes (Figure 16-3). Enter the probabilities in the matrices and calculate the expected values, add them for each option, and enter the sums in the "Total EV" columns.

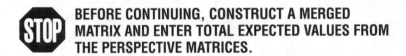

**BEFORE CONTINUING, ENTER THE PROBABILITIES AND COMPUTE TOTAL EXPECTED VALUES.**

Figure 16-4 shows the computations in each matrix.

The next step is to combine the option rankings in the three matrices. We do this by merging the expected values from each of the three matrices in a fourth, appropriately named, *merged matrix* (Figure 16-5). Construct a duplicate of this merged matrix and enter in each cell the total expected value from the perspective matrices.

**BEFORE CONTINUING, CONSTRUCT A MERGED MATRIX AND ENTER TOTAL EXPECTED VALUES FROM THE PERSPECTIVE MATRICES.**

Figure 16-6 shows the merged matrix with total expected values.

We could, of course, just add the total expected values for each option and accept the one with the greatest expected value as the preferred choice. However, this method of merging preferences would be appropriate only if the administrative staff takes the Laplace approach (meaning it doesn't have any basis to distinguish differences in the importance of the three perspectives) and values them equally.

**FIGURE 16-3**

|  | Warm and sunny | Cold and rainy |
|---|---|---|
| New York City | .3 | .7 |
| Florida | .6 | .4 |
| Vermont | .5 | .5 |

**FIGURE 16-4**

| Perspective: Attendees' enjoyment | Outcome | | Total EV |
|---|---|---|---|
| | Warm and sunny | Cold and rainy | |
| **Option** New York City | U 100<br>× P .3<br>EV 30 | 80<br>.7<br>56 | 86 |
| Florida | 50<br>.6<br>30 | 10<br>.4<br>4 | 34 |
| Vermont | 20<br>.5<br>10 | 0<br>.5<br>0 | 10 |

| Perspective: Spouses' enjoyment | Outcome | | Total EV |
|---|---|---|---|
| | Warm and sunny | Cold and rainy | |
| **Option** New York City | 10<br>.3<br>3 | 0<br>.7<br>0 | 3 |
| Florida | 50<br>.6<br>30 | 10<br>.4<br>4 | 34 |
| Vermont | 100<br>.5<br>50 | 80<br>.5<br>40 | 90 |

| Perspective: Children's enjoyment | Outcome | | Total EV |
|---|---|---|---|
| | Warm and sunny | Cold and rainy | |
| **Option** New York City | 10<br>.3<br>3 | 0<br>.7<br>0 | 3 |
| Florida | 100<br>.6<br>60 | 10<br>.4<br>4 | 64 |
| Vermont | 80<br>.5<br>40 | 30<br>.5<br>15 | 55 |

**FIGURE 16-5**

| Perspective: Merged | | Total Expected Value | | |
| --- | --- | --- | --- | --- |
| | | Attendees | Spouses | Children |
| Option | New York City | | | |
| | Florida | | | |
| | Vermont | | | |

But what if the staff considers the enjoyment of the managers to be many times more important than that of the spouses and children? In that event, we might weight the perspectives as follows: attendees .8, spouses .1, and children .1. Enter these weights at the top of the perspective columns in the merged matrix and add two columns ("Total Weighted EV" and "Rank") to your merged matrix. Now multiply the total expected values of each perspective by its weight, add the resulting

**FIGURE 16-6**

| Perspective: Merged | | Total Expected Value | | |
| --- | --- | --- | --- | --- |
| | | Attendees | Spouses | Children |
| Option | New York City | 86 | 3 | 3 |
| | Florida | 34 | 34 | 64 |
| | Vermont | 10 | 90 | 55 |

products, enter the sums in a "Total Weighted EV" column, and indicate the final rankings of the options in the "Rank" column.

 **BEFORE CONTINUING, ADD "TOTAL WEIGHTED EV" AND "RANK" COLUMNS TO THE MERGED MATRIX, COMPUTE TOTAL WEIGHTED EXPECTED VALUES, AND DETERMINE RANKINGS.**

Figure 16-7 shows what your merged matrix should now look like. With this distribution of weights, New York City is clearly the choice.

Naturally, different weightings will produce different results. Figure 16-8 shows three sample distributions of weight among the three groups. Figure 16-9 shows how the rankings of the options change when the spouses' perspective is dominant and when the children's is dominant.

This technique for utility analysis of multiple perspectives has wide application in problem-solving situations where conflicting interests render a choice among alternative courses of action difficult. Multiple-perspective utility analysis produces decisions that take equitable account of each party's interests, especially when these parties actively participate in the analysis.

**FIGURE 16-7**

| Perspective: Merged (attendees dominant) | | Total Expected Value | | | Total Weighted EV | Rank |
|---|---|---|---|---|---|---|
| | | Attendees, Weight: .8 | Spouses, Weight: .1 | Children, Weight: .1 | | |
| Option | New York City | 86<br>.8<br>‾‾‾‾<br>68.8 | 3<br>.1<br>‾‾‾<br>.3 | 3<br>.1<br>‾‾‾<br>.3 | 69.4 | 1 |
| | Florida | 34<br>.8<br>‾‾‾‾<br>27.2 | 34<br>.1<br>‾‾‾<br>3.4 | 64<br>.1<br>‾‾‾<br>6.4 | 37.0 | 2 |
| | Vermont | 10<br>.8<br>‾‾‾<br>8 | 90<br>.1<br>‾‾‾<br>9 | 55<br>.1<br>‾‾‾<br>5.5 | 22.5 | 3 |

**FIGURE 16-8**

## Weight of Influence on Final Decision

|                               | Attendees | Spouses | Children |         |
| ----------------------------- | :-------: | :-----: | :------: | ------- |
| Attendees are most important  |    .8     |   .1    |    .1    | = 1.0   |
| Spouses are most important    |    .1     |   .8    |    .1    | = 1.0   |
| Children are most important   |    .1     |   .1    |    .8    | = 1.0   |

(The sum of the weights for each distribution must, of course, equal 1.0.)

**FIGURE 16-9**

| Perspective: Merged (spouses dominant) | | Total Expected Value | | | Total Weighted EV | Rank |
| --- | --- | --- | --- | --- | --- | --- |
| | | Attendees, Weight: .1 | Spouses, Weight: .8 | Children, Weight: .1 | | |
| Option | New York City | 86 / .1 / 8.6 | 3 / .8 / 2.4 | 3 / .1 / .3 | 11.3 | 3 |
| | Florida | 34 / .1 / 3.4 | 34 / .8 / 27.2 | 64 / .1 / 6.4 | 37.0 | 2 |
| | Vermont | 10 / .1 / 1 | 90 / .8 / 72 | 55 / .1 / 5.5 | 78.5 | 1 |

| Perspective: Merged (children dominant) | | Total Expected Value | | | Total Weighted EV | Rank |
| --- | --- | --- | --- | --- | --- | --- |
| | | Attendees, Weight: .1 | Spouses, Weight: .1 | Children, Weight: .8 | | |
| Option | New York City | 86 / .1 / 8.6 | 3 / .1 / .3 | 3 / .8 / 2.4 | 11.3 | 3 |
| | Florida | 34 / .1 / 3.4 | 34 / .1 / 3.4 | 64 / .8 / 51.2 | 58.0 | 1 |
| | Vermont | 10 / .1 / 1 | 90 / .1 / 9 | 55 / .8 / 44 | 54.0 | 2 |

**FIGURE 16-10**

| Perspective | (Outcomes) | Total EV |
|---|---|---|
| (Options) | | |

# The Twelve Steps of Multiple-Perspective Utility Analysis

*Step 1:* Identify and weight the perspectives to be analyzed.

*Step 2:* Construct an identical utility matrix (Figure 16-10) for each perspective—same options, same outcomes.

Perform Steps 3 through 6 with each matrix.

*Step 3:* From each matrix's particular perspective, assign utilities from 0 to 100 to the outcome of each option-outcome combination (each cell of the matrix).

*Step 4:* Assign a probability to the outcome of each option-outcome combination (each cell).

*Step 5:* Compute expected values.

*Step 6:* Add expected values for each option and enter the totals in the "Total EV" column.

*Step 7:* Construct a single merged matrix (Figure 16-11)—the same options as in the perspective matrices.

*Step 8:* Enter opposite each option the total expected values for that option from the perspective matrices.

*Step 9:* Multiply the total expected values under each perspective by the perspective's weight.

*Step 10:* Add the resulting products (weighted expected values) for each option and enter the sums in the "Total Weighted EV" column.

**FIGURE 16-11**

| Perspective: Merged | (Perspectives) | Total Weighted EV | Rank |
|---|---|---|---|
| (Options) | | | |

*Step 11*: Rank the options. (The one with the greatest total weighted expected value is the preferred option.)

*Step 12*: Perform a sanity check.

You may wonder why we don't perform Step 9 (multiplying expected values by each perspective's weight) *before* transferring the total expected values from the utility matrices to the merged matrix. Why wait? The answer is that transferring the unweighted values to the merged matrix allows us, first, to view these values side by side, to compare and validate them and, second, to perform more easily sensitivity analysis by applying different combinations of weights to the criteria as we did in Exercise 45, the "Planning Conference."

Follow these twelve steps as you work the two problems that follow.

## EXERCISE 46  Cruise Ship Hijacking

Ruthless terrorists have hijacked a luxury cruise ship with 1,200 passengers and crew aboard. They have anchored the ship under the central span of the Golden Gate Bridge in San Francisco Bay and claim to have placed more than one ton of plastic explosives in fifty-gallon drums around the decks and below the waterline. They are threatening to blow up the ship—and the bridge with it—unless the following three demands are met:

☐  Payment of $10 million to a bank in a named Third World country
☐  Release of five named terrorists imprisoned in the United States

☐ Unfettered passage out of U.S. territory for the terrorists
☐ Amnesty from prosecution for the terrorists

If these demands are met, the terrorists promise to release the hostages unharmed.

The president of the United States has directed you, his special security adviser, to analyze the situation and recommend which of the following three options for dealing with the crisis will best serve the president's overall interests:

1. Acquiescing to all of the terrorists' demands.
2. Negotiating with the terrorists for (a) release of the hostages, (b) unfettered passage for the terrorists out of U.S. territory, and (c) amnesty for the terrorists from prosecution but *refusing* to release the imprisoned terrorists.
3. Launching a surprise paramilitary assault at night by U.S. Navy SEALs to rescue the hostages and apprehending or, if necessary, killing the terrorists.

The options are to be analyzed against the following classes of outcomes: damage to the ship and the Golden Gate Bridge combined with harm to the passengers and crew. The two factors are combined because the degree of physical damage to the ship and bridge will largely correspond in equal measure to the harm sustained by the hostages; that is, the more damage to the ship and bridge, the more harm to the passengers and crew. Engineers estimate that detonation of one ton of explosives aboard the ship would destroy the ship as well as the bridge's central span.

The probabilities of the outcomes are the same for both perspectives (Figure 16-12).

You are to analyze the problem applying utility analysis from two perspectives, weighted as follows:

1. The president's public approval rating in the United States (.7)
2. Congressional funding of the president's highly touted antiterrorism program, which will be the centerpiece of the president's forthcoming reelection campaign (.3)

Assign utilities as you see fit.

**FIGURE 16-12**

| Option | Outcome | | |
|---|---|---|---|
| | **None killed, none wounded** | **Some killed, many wounded** | **All killed** |
| | No damage to ship or bridge | Moderate damage to ship and bridge | Ship and bridge destroyed |
| Acquiesce | .99 | .01 | 0 |
| Negotiate | .1 | .6 | .3 |
| Assault | .3 | .6 | .1 |

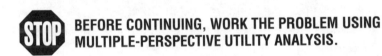

**BEFORE CONTINUING, WORK THE PROBLEM USING MULTIPLE-PERSPECTIVE UTILITY ANALYSIS.**

The solution to Exercise 46 presents my analysis of the problem. My analysis indicates that the paramilitary assault option is strongly preferred. Change the utilities, probabilities, and weights (such sensitivity analysis provides valuable practice in this and other structuring techniques—and it's fun) and see which changes most affect the ranking of the options. In this way we learn a great deal about the internal workings of a problem.

## EXERCISE 47    NBA Players' Strike

With only two weeks left in the regular season and critical games coming up that will decide which of several teams will enter the playoffs, contract negotiations between owners and players in the National Basketball Association have reached a stalemate. The players' union is deliberating whether to strike to force the owners to retreat from their insistence on a 20 percent reduction in the salary cap. The players' decision on whether to strike rests on two major factors with weights indicated in parentheses:

1. *What effect striking or not striking would have on the salary cap (.6).*

   The owners appear determined to lower the cap to offset reduced revenue from television and ticket sales.
2. *What effect striking or not striking would have on the working relationship between the players' union and the owners (.4).*

   In past years players have benefitted from the union's cordial, mutually respectful, productive working relationship with the owners. The players are therefore concerned that a strike may impact adversely on this relationship with undesirable consequences in the near and longer term. More specifically, the players fear that, if the union comes across as too conciliatory, the otherwise balanced power in the relationship could shift to the owners. On the other hand, if the union appears uncompromising and overly demanding, the owners, in reaction, could become more adamant and unyielding in their positions and again jeopardize the equilibrium.

The players' union foresees three possible outcomes: the owners' threatened *20 percent reduction* in the salary cap, a compromise *10 percent reduction,* and *no reduction.* The union anticipates that if the players strike, there is a .7 probability of a 20 percent reduction, .3 probability of 10 percent, and 0 probability of no reduction. If the players do not strike, there is a .8 probability of 20 percent, .1 probability of 10 percent, and .1 probability of no reduction.

Using multiple-perspective utility analysis—and assigning your own interpretations of the utility values—analyze the players' decision from two viewpoints (the players' monetary interests and the working relationship between the owners and the union) and determine whether or not the players should strike.

 **BEFORE CONTINUING, WORK THE PROBLEM USING MULTIPLE-PERSPECTIVE UTILITY ANALYSIS.**

Addressing the players' monetary interests perspective (see Solution to Exercise 47, Part 1), I first assigned utilities. I gave Strike–20%, the worst option-outcome combination, a utility of 0, because the players suffer the greatest monetary loss from unearned income while no games were being played and from future income because of the 20 percent reduction in the salary cap. Strike–10% received a utility of 50 because the lost future income was halved. Strike–None received an 80 because, though the cap was not reduced, the players lost money while games were not being played. Don't strike–20% got 50 because, although the cap was reduced 20 percent, the players lost no income during the remainder of the regular season and the playoffs. Don't strike–10% got 70 because the reduction in the cap was cut in half. Don't strike–None got 100; that's the best option-outcome combination. I then entered the given probabilities, computed the expected values, and entered the sums in the "Total EV" column.

I then repeated these steps in the matrix addressing the perspective of the owners' and union's working relationship (see Solution to Exercise 47, Part 2).

I gave Strike–20% zero utility because the outcome humiliated the union and shifted power overwhelmingly in the owners' favor; this was one of two worst option-outcome combinations. Strike–10% got 90 because the owners were forced to compromise, while the union showed courage and decisiveness in standing its ground; this was largely a win-win situation. Strike–None got 50 because, although there was no reduction in the salary cap, the owners were forced to back down, thereby losing face, which will come back to haunt future owner-union negotiations. Don't strike–20% (the other worst combination) got zero utility because the owners cowed the union, making the latter appear weak and ineffective, thereby enhancing the owners' sense of power and compelling the union to be more aggressive in the future. Both of these effects will work against a harmonious relationship. Don't strike–10% got 20 because it was only slightly better than Don't strike–20%. Don't strike–None, the best combination, received a utility of 100. I then entered the probabilities, computed expected values, and entered the totals in the last column.

I next constructed a merged matrix and entered the total expected values from the two perspective matrices, multiplied these values by the weights of the perspectives, added the weighted values, entered the totals in the "Total Weighted EV" column, and determined the ranking of the two options (see Solution to Exercise 47, Part 3).

This analysis indicates that the players' union should not strike.

# Multiple Classes of Outcomes

In the utility exercises thus far, no problem has involved more than one class of outcomes. Restricting the exercises to a single outcome class was, of course, intentional, as I have striven to reduce the complexity of the problems to facilitate your learning the utility analysis structuring technique. But problems involving a single class of outcomes are rare, probably limited to crises in which there is a single overriding issue such as whether one remains employed, gets married, or dies. In such crucial situations a single outcome class dominates all other factors.

In most problems there is a bevy of outcome classes that we consider when choosing among alternative courses of action. Let's look at three examples (Figure 16-13). You will note that, in problems involving multiple classes of outcomes, each class equates to a different perspective. For example, examining the medical risks of having an abortion is the same as examining the problem *from the perspective of medical risks*.

Let us examine the twelve steps for handling multiple classes of outcomes in utility analysis.

# The Twelve Steps of Utility Analysis (Multiple Classes of Outcomes)

*Step 1:* Identify the outcome classes and each one's range of outcomes and weight each class according to its importance.

*Step 2:* Construct for each class of outcomes a utility matrix (Figure 16-14) with identical perspective and options.

Perform Steps 3 through 6 with each matrix.

*Step 3:* Assign utilities from 0 to 100 to the outcome of each option-outcome combination (each cell of the matrix).

*Step 4:* Assign a probability to the outcome of each option-outcome combination (each cell).

**FIGURE 16-13**

| Option | Outcome Classes | Spectrum of Outcomes |
|---|---|---|
| Disciplining misbehaving child | Degree to which the child's behavior is corrected | None/partially/fully |
| | Degree to which the child suffers emotionally | None/some/lots |
| | Impact of the discipline on brothers and sisters | None/some/lots |
| | Impact of the discipline on relations between parents | None/some/lots |
| Reorganizing management structure in a company | Financial costs | Less/same/more |
| | Psychological impact on the labor force | Negative/neutral/positive |
| | Psychological impact on the managerial force | Negative/neutral/positive |
| | Company's public image | Worse/same/better |
| Having an abortion | Medical risks | None/some/many |
| | Moral reservations | None/some/many |
| | Postoperative short-term psychological condition | Poor/so-so/good |
| | Postoperative long-term psychological condition | Poor/so-so/good |
| | Medical insurance coverage | None/partial/full |

**FIGURE 16-14**

| Perspective | Class of Outcomes | Total EV |
|---|---|---|
| | (Outcomes) | |
| (Options) | | |

*Step* 5: Compute expected values.

*Step* 6: Add expected values for each option and enter the totals in the "Total EV" column.

*Step* 7: Construct a single merged matrix (Figure 16-15) with the same options as in the classes-of-outcomes matrices.

*Step* 8: Enter opposite each option the total expected values for that option from the classes-of-outcomes matrices.

*Step* 9: Multiply the total expected values under each class of outcomes by the class's weight.

*Step* 10: Add the resulting products (weighted expected values) for each option and enter the sums in the "Total Weighted EV" column.

*Step* 11: Rank the options. (The one with the greatest total weighted expected value is the preferred option.)

*Step* 12: Perform a sanity check.

**FIGURE 16-15**

| Perspective: Merged | Classes of Outcomes | | | Total Weighted EV | Rank |
|---|---|---|---|---|---|
| (Options) | | | | | |

One can, of course, take multiple-outcome analysis one step further by analyzing each class of outcomes from multiple perspectives, but I strongly recommend against it. Combining multiple-outcome and multiple-perspective analysis would spin the analytic web much too fine. Doing so is akin to studying subtleties—lesser factors and lesser issues. One can analyze them, but, as I said in my earlier discussion of major factors, incorporating subtleties into our analysis is a waste of time because they never play a significant role.

These steps treat classes of outcomes like perspectives. That being the case, what do we enter as the perspective in the upper left-hand corner of each matrix in Step 2? Enter whoever or whatever is the "owner" of the problem—the person or entity that weights the outcome classes and that must ultimately choose among the options. The perspective must be the same for each utility matrix.

Apply these twelve steps in the exercises that follow.

## EXERCISE 48   Campus Speech Code

You are the president of a state-funded college and are strongly opposed to the college's current policy of disciplining students and faculty for insensitive speech. In the wake of several controversial, widely publicized incidents in which both students and faculty members at the college were disciplined for insensitive speech, you are considering whether to abolish or continue the college's speech code. You are mainly concerned about three things:

1. *Whether your decision will prompt public demonstrations and other disruptions of campus activities (.2).*

   Three outcomes: no disruptions, peaceful disruptions, and violent disruptions. The probability for each outcome, if the code is abolished, is .1, .7, and .2, respectively. The probability, if the code is continued, is .8, .2, and 0, respectively.

2. *How the state legislature will react to the decision; that is, how state funding (which covers two-thirds of the college's annual budget) might be affected (.5).*

Three outcomes: less funds, same funds, more funds. The probability for each outcome, if the code is abolished is .1, .6, and .3; if continued, .3, .5, and .2.

3. *How the decision will affect student enrollment (.3).*

Three outcomes: smaller enrollment, same enrollment, greater enrollment. If the code is abolished, the probabilities are .1, .3, and .6; if continued, .3, .5, and .2.

Using utility analysis with multiple classes of outcomes, analyze the problem and determine which option is preferable. Assign utility values as you see fit.

 **BEFORE CONTINUING, WORK THE PROBLEM.**

I analyzed the problem as follows. In Step 1, I identified three classes of outcomes (campus disruption, state funding, and student enrollment) and weighted them .2, .5, and .3, respectively. In Step 2, I constructed an identical utility matrix for each outcome class (Figure 16-16), identifying the perspective in each matrix as the college president and listing the two options. I then performed Steps 3 through 6 with each matrix (Figure 16-17), assigning utilities and probabilities, computing expected values, and entering the totals in the "Total EV" columns. In Steps 7 through 11, I constructed a merged matrix (Figure 16-18),

**FIGURE 16-16**

| Perspective: College president | | Outcomes: | | | Total EV |
|---|---|---|---|---|---|
| **Option** | Abolish speech code policy | | | | |
| | Don't abolish | | | | |

**FIGURE 16-17**

| Perspective: College president | | Outcome: Campus disruption | | | Total EV |
|---|---|---|---|---|---|
| | | None | Peaceful | Violent | |
| Option | Abolish speech code policy | 100 .1 ⎯⎯ 10 | 90 .7 ⎯⎯ 63 | 10 .2 ⎯⎯ 2 | 75 |
| | Don't abolish | 30 .8 ⎯⎯ 24 | 20 .2 ⎯⎯ 4 | 0 .0 ⎯⎯ 0 | 28 |

| Perspective: College president | | Outcome: State funding | | | Total EV |
|---|---|---|---|---|---|
| | | Less | Same | More | |
| Option | Abolish speech code policy | 30 .1 ⎯⎯ 3 | 80 .6 ⎯⎯ 48 | 100 .3 ⎯⎯ 30 | 81 |
| | Don't abolish | 0 .3 ⎯⎯ 0 | 50 .5 ⎯⎯ 25 | 60 .2 ⎯⎯ 12 | 37 |

| Perspective: College president | | Outcome: Student enrollment | | | Total EV |
|---|---|---|---|---|---|
| | | Smaller | Same | Greater | |
| Option | Abolish speech code policy | 20 .1 ⎯⎯ 2 | 50 .3 ⎯⎯ 15 | 100 .6 ⎯⎯ 60 | 77 |
| | Don't abolish | 0 .3 ⎯⎯ 0 | 40 .5 ⎯⎯ 20 | 60 .2 ⎯⎯ 12 | 32 |

entered the total expected values from the three classes-of-outcomes matrices, multiplied these values by their respective class weights, entered the products in the "Total Weighted EV" column, and determined from the ranking that abolishing the campus speech code was the strongly favored option. In Step 12, I asked myself whether the results made sense intuitively, which I deemed they did.

**FIGURE 16-18**

| | | Classes of Outcome | | | | |
|---|---|---|---|---|---|---|
| Perspective: Merged | | Campus disturbances, Weight: .2 | State funding, Weight: .5 | Student enrollment, Weight: .3 | Total Weighted EV | Rank |
| Option | Abolish speech code policy | 75 .2 ―― 15 | 81 .5 ―― 40.5 | 77 .3 ―― 23.1 | 78.6 | 1 |
| | Don't abolish | 28 .2 ―― 5.6 | 37 .5 ―― 18.5 | 32 .3 ―― 9.6 | 33.7 | 2 |

# EXERCISE 49   Career Move

You are a midlevel industrial manager who has just been offered an executive position in San Francisco with a significant increase in salary and related perquisites. The problem is that you reside in a small town in Indiana and commute daily to your present job in Indianapolis. The move to San Francisco will uproot your family. Your spouse is a Ph.D. biologist with a full-time career position in a pathology laboratory five miles from your home. Your two teenage children are in the ninth and tenth grades and fully engaged in high school academics, sports, and leadership activities. They have lived their entire lives in this one town and this one home. Your spouse, who has misgivings about forfeiting hard-won opportunities for advancement in the pathology lab, has agreed nonetheless to move to San Francisco if that's what you want, the two of you having faithfully supported each other's professional ambitions throughout your marriage of eighteen years.

You determine that your decision to accept or not accept the job offer rests on three factors (three classes of outcomes) which you have weighted with their importance:

1. Career advancement potential of the new job (.4). There are three outcomes: worse than, same as, better than the potential of your current position.

2. Potential for your spouse's career advancement in San Francisco (.3). There are three outcomes: worse than, same as, better than the potential of your spouse's current position.

3. Your children's intellectual and social development through high school activities that enhance their academic standing, self-assurance, leadership skills, physical fitness, and overall maturity (.3). There are three outcomes: worse than, same as, better than the development possible where you now live.

You estimate that, if you move to San Francisco, the probabilities of your career potential will be 0 worse, 0 same, and 1.0 better; if you stay in Indiana, the probabilities will be .1 worse, .8 same, .1 better. Whether you move or not, the probabilities of your spouse's career potential and the children's development will be .1 worse, .8 same, and .1 better.

Using utility analysis with multiple classes of outcomes, analyze the problem and determine which of the two options—accepting the San Francisco job or rejecting it—is preferable. Assign utility values as you see fit.

 **BEFORE CONTINUING, WORK THE PROBLEM.**

My analysis of the problem, presented in the solution to Exercise 49, indicates that declining the job offer in San Francisco is the preferred option.

For our final multiple-classes-of-outcomes problem, let us revisit the Algona pollution case, which we looked at earlier when addressing problem restatements.

### EXERCISE 50   Algona Pollution III

The Environmental Protection Agency (EPA) has discovered volatile organic compounds (VOCs) in effluents from a processing plant of the Algona Fertilizer Company (AFC) in Algona, Iowa. These toxic waste products bypass the city of Algona but are carried into the East Fork Des Moines River, a tributary that feeds into Saylorville Lake, the principal source of water for Des Moines, a city of more than 300,000 people. The Des Moines city council, through the news media and political channels, is putting enormous public pressure on state and federal environmental agencies to shut down the Algona plant. Environmental action groups, with full media coverage, demonstrated yesterday in front of the Iowa governor's mansion demanding immediate closure of the plant. Local TV news and talk shows are beginning to focus on the issue. AFC's executive board has hired you, a private research consultant, to analyze the following three options that the Board is considering:

1. Capturing the toxic runoff in holding ponds for transport by truck and rail to nearby federally approved toxic waste dumps.

    This would cost $50,000 per month and is only a short-term solution, because these federal dumps are for emergency, not continuing, use.
2. Installing state-of-the-art chemical scrubbing and purifying equipment in the plant to remove the toxic waste before it enters the drainage system.

    This would cost $3 million and take eighteen months.
3. Redesigning the plant's chemical process to eliminate the VOCs.

    This involves basic R&D, would cost many millions, and might take years to accomplish. The executive board was recently briefed by a German firm on new experimental technology that totally eliminates the toxic by-products. The technology has been undergoing tests for the past three years in a plant similar to AFC's, but the German firm has so far not released any test results.

    Closing the plant or keeping it running without any changes in its operation are not options.

    The board wants you to rank the options from best to worst based on the following major factors (outcome classes):

1. *The degree to which the company's plan to deal with the problem will eliminate the VOCs from the plant's effluents (.5).*

There are three outcomes to be considered: none of the VOCs are removed, they are partially removed, they are totally removed. No matter which option is implemented, the probabilities of these outcomes are 0 none, .1 partial, .9 total.

2. *How the company's plan will affect next week's vote in the state legislature on a bill that would grant significant tax benefits to the state's fertilizer industry (.3).*

   There are three outcomes to be considered: the legislation is killed, it is passed with reduced tax benefits, it is passed with full tax benefits.

   The probabilities with the transport option are .6 killed, .3 reduced, .1 full. With the scrub—.1 killed, .4 reduced, .5 full. With the redesign—.1 killed, .2 reduced, .7 full.

3. *The cost to AFC of dealing with the toxic effluents (.2).*

   There is only one outcome considered. Its probability with every option is 1.0.

| Options | Cost | Period |
|---|---|---|
| 1. Transport toxic waste | $600,000/year | 1–2 years |
| 2. Scrub waste chemically | $3 million | 1.5 years |
| 3. Redesign process | Many millions of dollars | Many years |

Using utility analysis with multiple classes of outcomes, analyze the problem and determine which of the three options is preferable. Assign utility values as you see fit.

 **BEFORE CONTINUING, WORK THE PROBLEM.**

My analysis, presented in the solution to Exercise 50, indicates that AFC should install state-of-the-art chemical scrubbing and purifying equipment in the plant to remove the toxic waste before it enters the drainage system.

Part **Three**

# Where Do We Go from Here?

# 17
# Your
# Next Steps

 So there you have it. Fourteen techniques for structuring analysis:

| | |
|---|---|
| Problem Restatement | Decision/Event Tree |
| PROs-CONs-and-FIXes | Weighted Ranking |
| Divergent Thinking | Hypothesis Testing |
| Sorting | Devil's Advocacy |
| Chronologies and Time Lines | Probability Tree |
| Causal Flow Diagrams | Utility Tree |
| Matrix | Utility Matrix |

This is a veritable armory of analytic weapons (or, for the more peace-minded, a potent assortment of *analytic tools*) with which to survey, probe, dissect, diagnose, and resolve every kind of problem from the simplest to the most complex and foreboding.

I originally intended to summarize in this final chapter the many wonderful attributes of structuring analysis, but I now feel that, if you have read the book and completed the exercises as I instructed, you have already discovered these attributes. Moreover, if you have *not* read the book or completed the exercises, there is, I believe, little more I can say that will persuade you of the immense potential of structuring analysis.

Nor have I attempted to advise you which structuring technique is best suited for which type of problem. That is for you to decide, creatively and resourcefully. Whichever technique works best for you on whichever problem is the "right" application.

The best way—the only way—to learn how to use these techniques effectively is to practice applying them to a variety of problems. I therefore urge you to follow my own time-tested approach, namely, structuring the analysis of problems (events, issues, statements) reported in the news media. News reports provide an endless variety of intriguing problems on which to practice. Try your hand at it with pencil and paper. It's fun and always enlightening. You will find how the underlying complexities of a problem open up almost magically before your eyes to reveal startling insights into the nature and solutions of problems. Such is the power of structuring one's analysis.

A word of caution: We must resist at all costs being captivated by the numbers (like weights and utility values) we use in applying some of these techniques. We must constantly focus on and fully understand the analysis underlying these numbers, for they inevitably tend to take on a life of their own and to *drive*, not *reflect*, our analysis. The fact is, they are nothing more than a device, a vehicle, for achieving analytic ends that cannot be accomplished as easily or effectively any other way. We must keep this fact in mind and be ever on guard, lest we become mesmerized by the numbers and allow them to mislead our analysis.

And now a special word for educators at the secondary and higher levels. Because of your position, you have a unique opportunity—perhaps even a moral obligation—to teach students how to analyze problems. Yet, as I pointed out in the opening chapter, our educational system has historically taught people how to be *subjective advocates*, not *objective analysts*. True objectivity is, indeed, a rare commodity due principally to the way the human mind is programmed to work. As I have explained, we are instinctively subjective, marching obediently to the constant drumbeat of our own self-interest.

But subjectivity is a poor catalyst for finding the best solutions to problems, and that's where educators have a giant role to fill: teaching students how to approach problems objectively. The only sure way I know to achieve objectivity when analyzing a problem is to structure the analysis, setting up at the outset a rigorous step-by-step process to which the subconscious is forced to adhere and which ensures our complete understanding of the problem and full consideration of all reasonable alternative solutions. It is futile to instruct students, or anyone, to "be objective" without equipping them with the knowledge and the tools to do so. I fervently hope that you will integrate into your teaching the structuring techniques presented in this book.

For assistance in understanding these techniques and to obtain information either about computer software with which to implement the techniques or about attending a workshop on analytic structuring techniques, readers are invited to contact the author at the following address:

Analytic Prowess
7131 Baldwin Ridge Road
Warrenton, VA 22186

Phone: (540) 347-2870
Fax: (540) 341-0306
Internet: aprowess@ccncom.net

If you know of a tried-and-true structuring technique that is not included among the fourteen techniques in this book, please inform the author so that it might be included in future editions. Also, the author welcomes any accounts, positive or negative, of how these techniques have been used in analyzing problems. Should the author wish to make use of these accounts in future writings, he will, of course, obtain approval in advance from the submitters and protect the identities of individuals and organizations involved.

# Solutions to Exercises

## EXERCISE 6

### Part 1

- ☐ Establish separate periods (hours, days of the week, months of the year) when each of the three groups—pedestrians, bikers, and Rollerbladers—has exclusive use of the trail.
- ☐ Restrict certain sections of the trail to only one of the three groups of users.
- ☐ Rotate among the groups the times when they have exclusive use of certain sections.
- ☐ Prohibit pedestrians during weekday rush hours (allow only bikers and Rollerbladers).
- ☐ Arrest, fine, and jail tack throwers.
- ☐ Punish tack throwers by making them clean the trail daily for one month.
- ☐ Publicize the identities of tack throwers.
- ☐ Publicly recommend that users of the trail carry cameras to photograph violators of common courtesy.
- ☐ Publicize offenders' photographs with names and addresses.
- ☐ Widen the trail, fencing off lanes for each group to use.
- ☐ Construct a new asphalt-covered trail parallel to the old one and designed exclusively for bikers and Rollerbladers.

- ☐ Post guards along the trail to enforce courtesy and safety, arbitrate disagreements, and apprehend offenders.
- ☐ Post large but attractive signs publicizing the "Rules of the Trail."
- ☐ Establish a volunteers' action group that, working with the National Park Service, would study the problem, recommend corrective measures, and monitor the situation.
- ☐ Place brooms and waste cans along the trail for people to use to remove tacks.
- ☐ Install video cameras at the most contested stretches of the trail, monitor the cameras at National Park Service headquarters, and direct National Park Police to preserve order where needed.
- ☐ Use the video cameras to apprehend tack throwers.
- ☐ Establish speed limits for bikers and Rollerbladers.
- ☐ Install radar (monitored at National Park Service headquarters) along the trail to detect, identify, and apprehend speed violators.
- ☐ Prohibit Rollerbladers altogether.
- ☐ Appeal on TV and radio for common courtesy on the trail.
- ☐ Put articles into the local newspapers about incidents and appeal for common courtesy.
- ☐ Install special barriers and texturing of the asphalt at intervals on the trail to discourage Rollerblading.
- ☐ Drive motorized "tack sweepers" along the trail several times a day every day.
- ☐ Control access to the trail by fencing it and putting gates manned by National Park Police at all access points.
- ☐ Let pedestrians carry spiked wooden bats for striking offenders.
- ☐ Let pedestrians shoot offenders with paint guns.
- ☐ Have the president of the United States make a public appeal for courtesy and safety on the trail.
- ☐ Have the governor of Virginia make a public appeal for courtesy and safety on the trail.
- ☐ Post humorous signs along the trail to raise users' consciousness of the problem and appeal for their cooperation.
- ☐ Permanently restrict use of the trail at any time to only one of the three contending groups.

# Part 2
## *Rules and Regulations*
- ☐ Establish separate periods (hours, days of the week, months of the year) when each of the three groups—pedestrians, bikers, and Rollerbladers—has exclusive use of the trail.
- ☐ Restrict certain sections of the trail to only one of the three groups of users.
- ☐ Rotate among the groups the times when they have exclusive use of certain sections.
- ☐ Prohibit pedestrians during weekday rush hours (allow only bikers and Rollerbladers).
- ☐ Establish a volunteers' action group that, working with the National Park Service, would study the problem, recommend corrective measures, and monitor the situation.
- ☐ Prohibit Rollerbladers altogether.
- ☐ Establish speed limits for bikers and Rollerbladers.
- ☐ Permanently restrict use of the trail at any time to only one of the three contending groups.

## *Punish Offenders*
- ☐ Arrest, fine, and jail tack throwers.
- ☐ Punish tack throwers by making them clean the trail daily for one month.
- ☐ Publicize the identities of tack throwers.
- ☐ Publicly recommend that users of the trail carry cameras to photograph violators of common courtesy.
- ☐ Publicize offenders' photographs with names and addresses.

## *Physical Construction*
- ☐ Widen the trail, fencing off lanes for each group to use.
- ☐ Construct a new asphalt-covered trail parallel to the old one and designed exclusively for bikers and Rollerbladers.
- ☐ Install video cameras at the most contested stretches of the trail.
- ☐ Install radar (monitored at National Park Service headquarters) along the trail to detect, identify, and apprehend speed violators.

☐ Install special barriers and texturing of the asphalt at intervals on the trail to discourage Rollerblading.
☐ Control access to the trail by fencing it and putting gates manned by National Park Police at all access points.

### Enforcement
☐ Post guards along the trail to enforce courtesy and safety, arbitrate disagreements, and apprehend offenders.
☐ Install video cameras at the most contested stretches of the trail, monitor the cameras at the National Park Service headquarters, and direct National Park Police to preserve order where needed.
☐ Use the video cameras to apprehend tack throwers.
☐ Install radar (monitored at National Park Service headquarters) along the trail to detect, identify, and apprehend speed violators.

### Clean Up Tacks
☐ Place brooms and waste cans along the trail for people to use to remove tacks.
☐ Drive motorized "tack sweepers" along the trail several times a day every day.

### Promote Courtesy and Safety
☐ Post large but attractive signs publicizing the "Rules of the Trail."
☐ Appeal on TV and radio for common courtesy on the trail.
☐ Put articles into the local newspapers about incidents and appeal for common courtesy.
☐ Post humorous signs along the trail to raise users' consciousness of the problem and appeal for their cooperation.

### [Delete as Impractical]
☐ [Let pedestrians carry spiked wooden bats for striking offenders.]
☐ [Let pedestrians shoot offenders with paint guns.]
☐ [Have the president of the United States make a public appeal for courtesy and safety on the trail.]
☐ [Have the governor of Virginia make a public appeal for courtesy and safety on the trail.]

## Part 3: Program of Corrective Measures

### *Short-Term Measures*

☐ Establish a four-member citizens' advisory group, made up of a representative from each of the three competing groups and the National Park Service, that, working with the NPS, would study the problems, recommend remedial measures, and monitor the situation.

☐ Run articles in local newspapers about incidents and appeal for common courtesy.

☐ Establish certain hours and days of the week when each of the three groups—pedestrians, bikers, and Rollerbladers—has exclusive use of the trail (e.g., Monday, Wednesday, and Friday, 9:00 A.M.–12:00 P.M., bikers only; Tuesday and Thursday, 9:00 A.M.–12:00 P.M., Rollerbladers only).

☐ Prohibit pedestrian use during weekday rush hours (6:30–9:00 A.M. and 4:00–6:30 P.M.).

☐ Publicly recommend that users of the trail carry cameras to photograph violators of the periods of exclusive use.

☐ Punish offenders with fines and newspaper announcements including their names, addresses, and photographs.

### *Alternative Long-Term Measure*

☐ Widen the trail, fencing off lanes for each group's exclusive use.

## EXERCISE 9

**Part 1**

### Cause-and-Effect Table

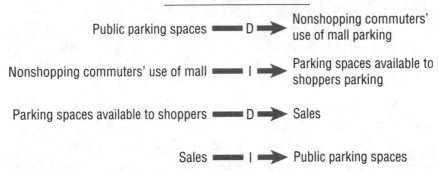

Public parking spaces ━━ D ➡ Nonshopping commuters' use of mall parking

Nonshopping commuters' use of mall ━━ I ➡ Parking spaces available to shoppers parking

Parking spaces available to shoppers ━━ D ➡ Sales

Sales ━━ I ➡ Public parking spaces

**Part 2**

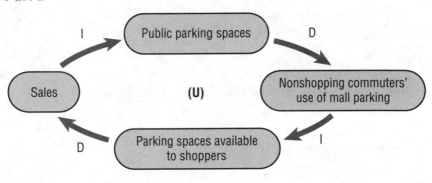

# EXERCISE 10

## Part 1

### Cause-and-Effect Table

Toxic effluents **— D ➤** Contamination of East Fork River

Contamination of East Fork River **— D ➤** Contamination of Saylorville Lake

Contamination of Saylorville Lake **— D ➤** Contamination of Des Moines city water

Contamination of city water **— D ➤** City council pressure on state and environmental agencies

Contamination of city water **— D ➤** Demonstrations by environmental action groups

City pressure on environmental agencies **— D ➤** Pressure on Algona management for corrective action

Demonstrations by action groups **— D ➤** Pressure on Algona management for corrective action

Pressure on Algona management for corrective action **— D ➤** Corrective action by Algona management

Corrective action by Algona management **— I ➤** Toxic effluents

## EXERCISE 10

**Part 2**

### CAUSAL FLOW DIAGRAM

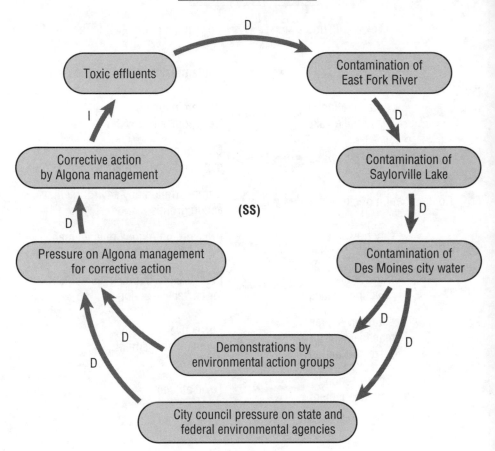

# EXERCISE 11

## Part 1

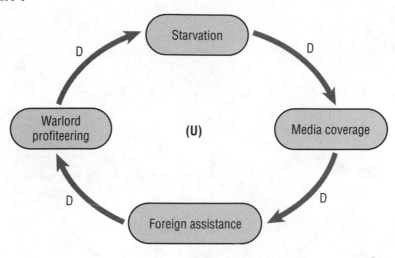

## Part 2

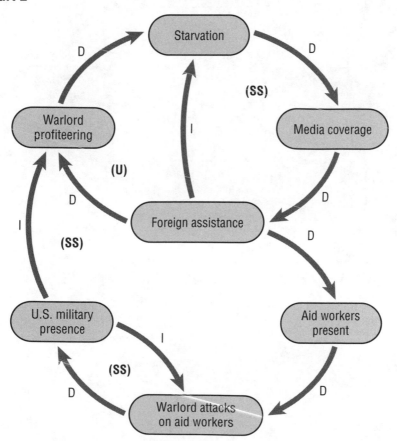

**EXERCISE 11**

**Part 3**

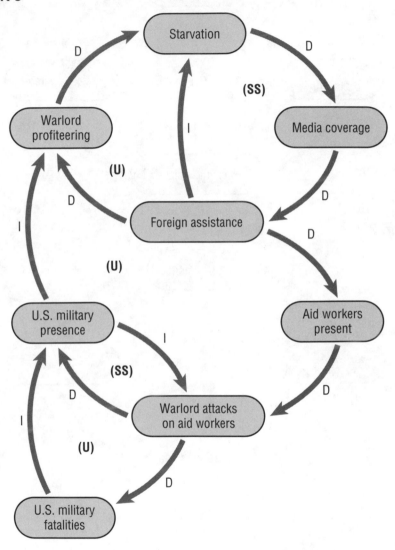

## EXERCISE 13

**Part 1**

### Symptom and Disease Matrix

|          |     | Disease |     |
|----------|-----|---------|-----|
|          |     | Yes     | No  |
| Symptom  | Yes | 37      | 33  |
|          | No  | 17      | 13  |

**Part 2**

### Symptom and Disease Matrix
### (symptom percentages)

|          |     | Disease |     |         |
|----------|-----|---------|-----|---------|
|          |     | Yes     | No  |         |
| Symptom  | Yes | 53%     | 47% | (100%)  |
|          | No  | 57%     | 43% | (100%)  |

**Part 3**

### Symptom and Disease Matrix
### (disease percentages)

|          |     | Disease |      |
|----------|-----|---------|------|
|          |     | Yes     | No   |
| Symptom  | Yes | 69%     | 72%  |
|          | No  | 31%     | 28%  |
|          |     | (100%)  | (100%) |

## EXERCISE 15

| | | Outcome | |
|---|---|---|---|
| | | **Snow** | **Not snow** |
| **Prediction** | Snow | | |
| | Not snow | | |

## EXERCISE 16

| Staff Size | Building | |
|---|---|---|
| | **Same** | **Larger** |
| Smaller | | |
| Same | | |
| Larger | | |

## EXERCISE 17

| | **Position A** | **Position B** | **Position C** |
|---|---|---|---|
| Employee 1 | | | |
| Employee 2 | | | |
| Employee 3 | | | |

# EXERCISE 18

**Part 1**

**Length of conference:**

# EXERCISE 18

**Part 2**

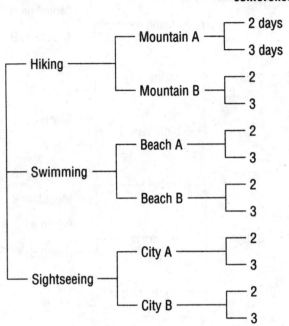

Length of
conference:

Hiking
 — Mountain A — 2 days / 3 days
 — Mountain B — 2 / 3

Swimming
 — Beach A — 2 / 3
 — Beach B — 2 / 3

Sightseeing
 — City A — 2 / 3
 — City B — 2 / 3

# EXERCISE 19

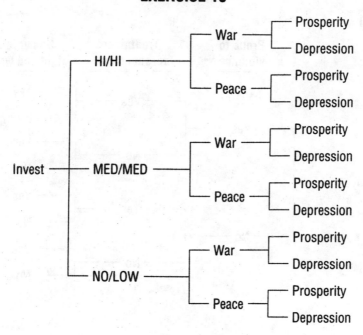

# EXERCISE 20

## Part 1

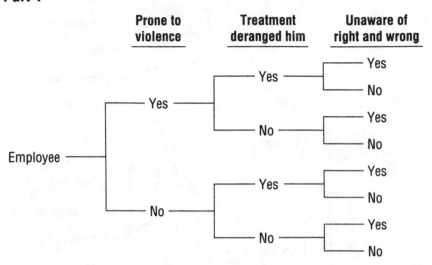

## Part 2

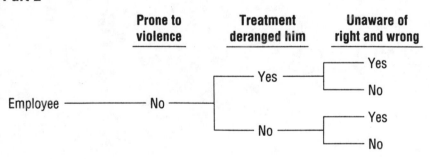

## Part 3

Employee ——————— No ——————— Yes ┬ Yes
                                    └ No

| Prone to violence | Treatment deranged him | Unaware of right and wrong |
|---|---|---|

# EXERCISE 21

**Employees'
desired degree
of participation
in management:**

**Employees'
preferred means
of bargaining
with management:**

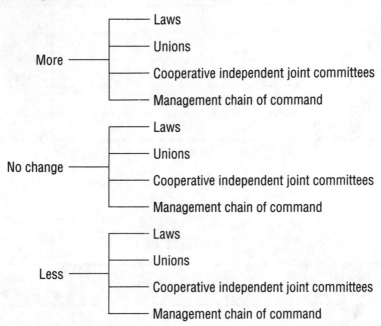

More

- Laws
- Unions
- Cooperative independent joint committees
- Management chain of command

No change

- Laws
- Unions
- Cooperative independent joint committees
- Management chain of command

Less

- Laws
- Unions
- Cooperative independent joint committees
- Management chain of command

## EXERCISE 25

| Items to Be Ranked | Criteria | | | |
|---|---|---|---|---|
| | Price, Weight: | Food, Weight: | Service, Weight: | Atmosphere Weight: |
| Restaurant | | | | |
| Restaurant | | | | |
| Restaurant | | | | |
| Restaurant | | | | |
| Restaurant | | | | |

## EXERCISE 26

| Items to Be Ranked | (Criteria/Weights) | | | Total Points | Final Ranking |
|---|---|---|---|---|---|
| Ross Perot | | | | | |
| Donald Trump | | | | | |
| Lee Iacocca | | | | | |
| Bill Gates | | | | | |
| Michael Eisner | | | | | |

**EXERCISE 36**

| Outcome of<br>Test Launch | Production<br>in Two Months | Probability of<br>Meeting Deadline |
|---|---|---|
| | Yes  .1 | .2 × .1 = .02 |
| Failure   .2 | No  .9 | .2 × .9 = .18 |
| Flight success<br>Technical failure  .6 | Yes  .4 | .6 × .4 = .24 |
| | No  .6 | .6 × .6 = .36 |
| Success  .2 | Yes  .9 | .2 × .9 = .18 |
| | No  .1 | .2 × .1 = .02 |

Karati test launch

1.00

**EXERCISE 37**

| Probability of<br>Rescue Attempt | Probability Passengers<br>and Crew Will Be Killed<br>During Rescue Attempt | Probability<br>Comrades Will<br>Be Released | Probability<br>of Scenario |
|---|---|---|---|
| | All    .1 | Yes  0 | — |
| | | No  1.0 | .090 |
| Yes   .9 | Some   .8 | Yes  .1 | .072 |
| | | No  .9 | .648 |
| | None   .1 | Yes  .1 | .009 |
| | | No  .9 | .081 |
| No   .1 | | Yes  .9 | .090 |
| | | No  .1 | .010 |

Total Probability:   1.000

# EXERCISE 38

## Part 1

### Phone Probability Tree

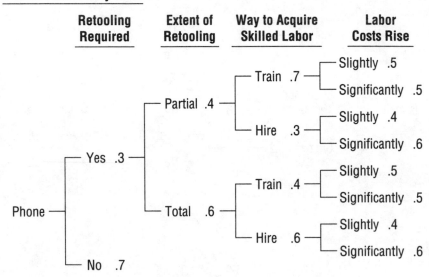

### Antenna Probability Tree

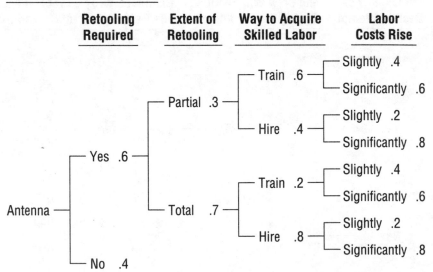

# Part 2

| | Phone (%) | Antenna (%) |
|---|:---:|:---:|
| 1. Assembly line totally retooled? | 18 | 42 |
| 2. Current employees retrained? | 16 | 19 |
| 3. New employees hired? | 14 | 41 |
| 4. Labor costs rise slightly? | 14 | 16 |
| 5. Labor costs rise significantly? | 16 | 44 |

**1. Assembly line totally retooled?**

Phone:     $.3 \times .6 = .18$
Antenna:   $.6 \times .7 = .42$

**2. Current employees retrained?**

Phone:
$$.3 \times .4 \times .7 = .084$$
$$+ .3 \times .6 \times .4 = \underline{.072}$$
$$.156$$

Antenna:
$$.6 \times .3 \times .6 = .108$$
$$+ .6 \times .7 \times .2 = \underline{.084}$$
$$.192$$

**3. New employees hired?**

Phone:
$$.3 \times .4 \times .3 = .036$$
$$+ .3 \times .6 \times .6 = \underline{.108}$$
$$.144$$

Antenna:
$$.6 \times .3 \times .4 = .072$$
$$+ .6 \times .7 \times .8 = \underline{.336}$$
$$.408$$

**4. Labor costs rise slightly?**

Phone:
$$.3 \times .4 \times .7 \times .5 = .0420$$
$$.3 \times .4 \times .3 \times .4 = .0144$$
$$.3 \times .6 \times .4 \times .5 = .0360$$
$$+ .3 \times .6 \times .6 \times .4 = \underline{.0432}$$
$$.1356$$

Antenna:
$$.6 \times .3 \times .6 \times .4 = .0432$$
$$.6 \times .3 \times .4 \times .2 = .0144$$
$$.6 \times .7 \times .2 \times .4 = .0336$$
$$+ .6 \times .7 \times .8 \times .2 = \underline{.0672}$$
$$.1584$$

**5. Labor costs rise significantly?**

Phone:
$$.3 \times .4 \times .7 \times .5 = .0420$$
$$.3 \times .4 \times .3 \times .6 = .0216$$
$$.3 \times .6 \times .4 \times .5 = .0360$$
$$+ .3 \times .6 \times .6 \times .6 = \underline{.0648}$$
$$.1644$$

Antenna:
$$.6 \times .3 \times .6 \times .6 = .0648$$
$$.6 \times .3 \times .4 \times .8 = .0576$$
$$.6 \times .7 \times .2 \times .6 = .0504$$
$$+ .6 \times .7 \times .8 \times .8 = \underline{.2688}$$
$$.4416$$

# EXERCISE 39

**Perspective: U.S. corporation's profit**

| Option | (Outcome) Sell to U.S. Corporation | Utility | Probability | Expected Value | Total EV | Rank |
|---|---|---|---|---|---|---|
| Vase | Yes | $100,000 | .9 | $90,000 | $90,000 | 2 |
|  | No | 0 | .1 | 0 |  |  |
| Drill | Yes | $200,000 | .5 | $100,000 | $100,000 | 1 |
|  | No | 0 | .5 | 0 |  |  |
| Stereo | Yes | $500,000 | .1 | $50,000 | $50,000 | 3 |
|  | No | 0 | .9 | 0 |  |  |

# EXERCISE 40

**Perspective: My monetary profit**

| Option | (Outcome) Survive Virus | Utility | Probability | Expected Value | Total EV | Rank |
|---|---|---|---|---|---|---|
| Brown | Yes | $200 | .8 | $160 | $160 | 1 |
|  | No | 0 | .2 | 0 |  |  |
| White | Yes | $300 | .5 | $150 | $150 | 2 |
|  | No | 0 | .5 | 0 |  |  |
| Red | Yes | $400 | .3 | $120 | $120 | 3 |
|  | No | 0 | .7 | 0 |  |  |

## EXERCISE 41

**Perspective: My monetary profit**

| (Bet) Option | Outcome | Utility | Probability | EV | Rank |
|---|---|---|---|---|---|
| Y-Y-G | Y-Y-G | $90 | .016 | $1.44 | 4 |
| R-Y-G | R-Y-G | $80 | .02 | $1.60 | 2 |
| Y-Y-Y | Y-Y-Y | $70 | .064 | $4.48 | 1 |
| R-R-G | R-R-G | $60 | .025 | $1.50 | 3 |

## EXERCISE 43

| Perspective: Weather forecaster's reputation | | Outcome | | Total EV | Rank |
|---|---|---|---|---|---|
| | | **Snow** | **Not snow** | | |
| **Option** | Predict snow | U 100<br>P .1<br>EV 10 | 80<br>.9<br>72 | 82 | 1 |
| | Predict not snow | U 0<br>P .1<br>EV 0 | 30<br>.9<br>27 | 27 | 2 |

# EXERCISE 44

## Part 1

**Perspective: Commander of counterterrorist unit**

| Rescue Attempt | Probability Passengers and Crew Killed During Rescue | | Probability Comrades Released | | Probability of Scenario | Utility | EV | Total EV |
|---|---|---|---|---|---|---|---|---|
| Yes | All | .1 | Yes | 0 | 0 | 0 | 0 | |
| | | | No | 1.0 | .1 | 10 | 1.0 | |
| | Some | .8 | Yes | .1 | .08 | 20 | 1.6 | |
| | | | No | .9 | .72 | 30 | 21.6 | 34.0 |
| | None | .1 | Yes | .1 | .01 | 80 | .8 | |
| | | | No | .9 | .09 | 100 | 9.0 | |
| No | None | 1.0 | Yes | .9 | .9 | 10 | 9.0 | |
| | | | No | .1 | .1 | 90 | 9.0 | 18.0 |

## Part 2

| Perspective: Commander of counterterrorist unit | | Outcome | | | | | | Total EV | Rank |
|---|---|---|---|---|---|---|---|---|---|
| | | Passengers and crew killed during rescue/ comrades released | | | | | | | |
| | | All | | Some | | None | | | |
| | | Yes | No | Yes | No | Yes | No | | |
| Option | Attempt rescue | 0 / 0 / 0 | 10 / .1 / 1.0 | 20 / .08 / 1.6 | 30 / .72 / 21.6 | 80 / .01 / .8 | 100 / .09 / 9.0 | 34 | 1 |
| | Do not attempt rescue | — | — | — | — | 10 / .9 / 9.0 | 90 / .1 / 9.0 | 18 | 2 |

# EXERCISE 46

## Part 1

| | Outcome | | | |
|---|---|---|---|---|
| **Perspective:** President's public approval rating | **None killed, none wounded** No damage to ship or bridge | **Some killed, many wounded** Moderate damage to ship and bridge | **All killed** Ship and bridge destroyed | **Total EV** |
| **Acquiesce to all of the demands** | 10 .99 9.9 | 0 .01 0 | 0 0 0 | 9.9 |
| **Negotiate but refuse to release prisoners** | 90 .1 9 | 10 .6 6 | 0 .3 0 | 15 |
| **Paramilitary assault** | 100 .3 30 | 10 .6 6 | 0 .1 0 | 36 |

## EXERCISE 46

### Part 2

| | | Outcome | | | |
|---|---|---|---|---|---|
| **Perspective:** Congressional funding of the antiterrorism program | | **None killed, none wounded, no damage to ship or bridge** | **Some killed, many wounded, moderate damage to ship and bridge** | **All killed, ship and bridge destroyed** | **Total EV** |
| Option | Acquiesce to all of the demands | 20<br>.99<br>19.8 | 10<br>.01<br>.1 | 0<br>0<br>0 | 19.9 |
| Option | Negotiate but refuse to release prisoners | 80<br>.1<br>8 | 40<br>.6<br>24 | 10<br>.3<br>3 | 35 |
| Option | Paramilitary assault | 100<br>.3<br>30 | 50<br>.6<br>30 | 20<br>.1<br>2 | 62 |

# EXERCISE 46

## Part 3

| Perspective: Merged | | President's public approval rating: .7 | Congressional funding of antiterrorism program: .3 | Total Weighted EV | Rank |
|---|---|---|---|---|---|
| Option | Acquiesce to all of the demands | 9.9<br>.7<br>‾‾‾‾<br>6.93 | 19.9<br>.3<br>‾‾‾‾<br>5.97 | 12.9 | 3 |
| | Negotiate but refuse to release prisoners | 15.0<br>.7<br>‾‾‾‾<br>10.5 | 35.0<br>.3<br>‾‾‾‾<br>10.5 | 21.0 | 2 |
| | Paramilitary assault | 36.0<br>.7<br>‾‾‾‾<br>25.2 | 62.0<br>.3<br>‾‾‾‾<br>18.6 | 43.8 | 1 |

# EXERCISE 47

## Part 1

| Perspective: Players' salaries | | Reduction in the Salary Cap | | | Total EV |
|---|---|---|---|---|---|
| | | 20% | 10% | None | |
| Option | Strike | 0<br>.7<br>‾‾<br>0 | 50<br>.3<br>‾‾<br>15 | 80<br>0<br>‾‾<br>0 | 15 |
| | Don't strike | 50<br>.8<br>‾‾<br>40 | 70<br>.1<br>‾‾<br>7 | 100<br>.1<br>‾‾<br>10 | 57 |

## EXERCISE 47

**Part 2**

| Perspective: Owner-union relationship | | Reduction in the Salary Cap | | | Total EV |
|---|---|---|---|---|---|
| | | **20%** | **10%** | **None** | |
| Option | Strike | 0<br>.7<br>―――<br>0 | 90<br>.3<br>―――<br>27 | 50<br>0<br>―――<br>0 | 27 |
| | Don't strike | 0<br>.8<br>―――<br>0 | 20<br>.1<br>―――<br>2 | 100<br>.1<br>―――<br>10 | 12 |

**Part 3**

| Perspective: Merged | | Perspective | | Total Weighted EV | Rank |
|---|---|---|---|---|---|
| | | Players' salaries: .6 | Owner-union relationship: .4 | | |
| Option | Strike | 15<br>.6<br>―――<br>9 | 27<br>.4<br>―――<br>10.8 | 19.8 | 2 |
| | Don't strike | 57<br>.6<br>―――<br>34.2 | 12<br>.4<br>―――<br>4.8 | 39.0 | 1 |

# EXERCISE 49

| Perspective: Your happiness | | Outcome: Your career | | | Total EV |
|---|---|---|---|---|---|
| | | Worse | Same | Better | |
| **Option** | Accept the position | U  0<br>P  0<br>EV  0 | 10<br>0<br>0 | 90<br>1.0<br>90 | 90 |
| | Do not accept the position | 10<br>.1<br>1 | 80<br>.8<br>64 | 100<br>.1<br>10 | 75 |

| Perspective: Your happiness | | Outcome: Spouse's career | | | Total EV |
|---|---|---|---|---|---|
| | | Worse | Same | Better | |
| **Option** | Accept the position | 0<br>.1<br>0 | 10<br>.8<br>8 | 90<br>.1<br>9 | 17 |
| | Do not accept the position | 10<br>.1<br>1 | 80<br>.8<br>64 | 100<br>.1<br>10 | 75 |

| Perspective: Your happiness | | Outcome: Children's development | | | Total EV |
|---|---|---|---|---|---|
| | | Worse | Same | Better | |
| **Option** | Accept the position | 0<br>.1<br>0 | 10<br>.8<br>8 | 90<br>.1<br>9 | 17 |
| | Do not accept the position | 10<br>.1<br>1 | 80<br>.8<br>64 | 100<br>.1<br>10 | 75 |

| Perspective: Merged | | Class of Outcome | | | Total Weighted EV | Rank |
|---|---|---|---|---|---|---|
| | | Your career: .4 | Spouse's career: .3 | Children's development: .3 | | |
| **Option** | Accept the position | 90<br>.4<br>36 | 17<br>.3<br>5.1 | 17<br>.3<br>5.1 | 46.2 | 2 |
| | Do not accept the position | 75<br>.4<br>30 | 75<br>.3<br>22.5 | 75<br>.3<br>22.5 | 75.0 | 1 |

# EXERCISE 50

## Part 1

| Perspective: AFC | | Outcome: Eliminate VOCs | | | Total EV |
|---|---|---|---|---|---|
| | | None | Partial | Total | |
| Option | Transport | 0<br>.0<br>0 | 10<br>.1<br>1 | 30<br>.9<br>27 | 28 |
| | Scrub | 0<br>.0<br>0 | 10<br>.1<br>1 | 90<br>.9<br>81 | 82 |
| | Redesign | 0<br>.0<br>0 | 10<br>.1<br>1 | 100<br>.9<br>90 | 91 |

## Part 2

| Perspective: AFC | | Outcome: Legislation | | | Total EV |
|---|---|---|---|---|---|
| | | Killed | Passed with reduced benefits | Passed with full tax benefits | |
| Option | Transport | 0<br>.6<br>0 | 30<br>.3<br>9 | 50<br>.1<br>5 | 14 |
| | Scrub | 0<br>.1<br>0 | 70<br>.4<br>28 | 90<br>.5<br>45 | 73 |
| | Redesign | 0<br>.1<br>0 | 80<br>.2<br>16 | 100<br>.7<br>70 | 86 |

# EXERCISE 50

## Part 3

| Perspective: AFC | | Outcome: Cost to AFC | Total EV |
|---|---|---|---|
| Option | Transport | 100 $\frac{1.0}{100}$ | 100 |
| | Scrub | 50 $\frac{1.0}{50}$ | 50 |
| | Redesign | 0 $\frac{1.0}{0}$ | 0 |

## Part 4

| Perspective: Merged | | Class of Outcomes | | | Total Weighted EV | Rank |
|---|---|---|---|---|---|---|
| | | Eliminate VOCs: .5 | Legislation: .3 | Cost to AFC: .2 | | |
| Option | Transport | 28 $\frac{.5}{14}$ | 14 $\frac{.3}{4.2}$ | 100 $\frac{.2}{20}$ | 38.2 | 3 |
| | Scrub | 82 $\frac{.5}{41}$ | 73 $\frac{.3}{21.9}$ | 50 $\frac{.2}{10}$ | 72.9 | 1 |
| | Redesign | 91 $\frac{.5}{45.5}$ | 86 $\frac{.3}{25.8}$ | 0 $\frac{.2}{0}$ | 71.3 | 2 |

# For Further Reading

Andriole, Stephen J. *Handbook of Decision Support Systems*. Blue Ridge Summit, PA: Professional and Reference Books, 1989.

Concerned with the design of applied decision-support systems in industry and the federal government.

Describes (pages 63–78) multiattribute-utility analysis and software (DecisionMap, Expert Choice, and Arborist), probability trees, influence diagraming (but only as it relates to probability analysis), and decision trees.

Explains Bayes' Theorem in simple clear language with examples.

Balachandran, Savrojini. *Decision Making: An Information Sourcebook*. Phoenix: Oryx, 1987.

Comprehensive bibliography through 1987 on decision analysis.

Baron, Jonathan. *Thinking and Deciding*, 2nd ed. Cambridge, MA: Cambridge University Press, 1988.

An informative undergraduate text on thinking processes and decision making. Stresses the importance of considering alternative hypotheses and ensuring they are consistent with the evidence. Elucidates and gives a brief history of expected-value theory.

Bolles, Edmund. *A Second Way of Knowing: The Riddle of Human Perception*. New York: Prentice-Hall, 1991.

A thought-provoking work on the question of whether objective external reality exists or is purely in our minds: "We don't know how perception works and we haven't a clue how it might work." Discussion supports the idea that humans instinctively focus mentally. Quotation by psychologist Max Wertheimer (1910)—"Isolate the elements, discover their laws, then reassemble them and the problem is solved"—captures the divergent-convergent cycle of analysis.

Brown, Rex V. "Do Managers Find Decision Theory Useful?" *Harvard Business Review*, May/June 1990: 78–89.

Discusses a survey of large companies concerning decision-tree analysis. Considers the impact of decision-tree analysis on the companies.

Campbell, Jeremy. *The Improbable Machine: What the Upheavals in Artificial Intelligence Research Reveal About How the Mind Really Works.* New York: Simon and Schuster, 1989.

Enlightening comparisons between the human mind and the computer (artificial intelligence). Addresses human illogic, bias, and schemas (mind-sets) and the human penchant to seek explanations and to view the world in terms of cause-and-effect patterns.

Daniel, Wayne W. *Decision Trees for Management Decision Making: An Annotated Bibliography.* Vance Bibliographies, Public Administration Series, June 1979.

Selected bibliography on decision trees.

De Bono, Edward. *New Think: The Use of Lateral Thinking in the Generation of New Ideas.* New York: Basic Books, 1968.

A treatise on creative decision making. Recommends "lateral thinking" as a way of generating alternative ways of seeing the pattern of a problem before seeking its solution; another way of restating the problem.

Fishburn, Peter C. *The Foundations of Expected Utility.* Boston: D. Reidel, 1982.

A technical, understandable explanation of expected-utility theory.

Page 1: In the early eighteenth century mathematicians Daniel Bernoulli and Gabriel Cramer (Bernoulli, 1738) proposed that risky monetary options be evaluated not by their expected return but rather by the expectation of the utilities of their returns. Other thinkers developed this idea in the centuries that followed, but it was Leonard J. Savage's classic work on the foundation of statistics (Savage, 1954) that presented the first complete axiomatization of subjective expected utility, in which the notion of personal or subjective probability is integrated with expected utility.

Gilovich, Thomas. *How We Know What Isn't So: The Fallibility of Human Reason in Everyday Life.* New York: The Free Press, 1991.

A seminal exposition—and the principal foundation of Chapter 1—of the ways in which human reasoning and decision making go awry and why.

Herbert, Theordore T., and Ralph W. Estes. "The Role of the Devil's Advocate in the Executive Decision Process." *Business Quarterly* (Canada), Summer 1981: 56–63.

Discusses the use of devil's advocacy for formalized dissent.

Hicks, Michael J. *Problem Solving for Business and Management.* New York: Chapman & Hall, 1991.

An outstanding treatise for those seeking a deeper understanding of problem-solving strategies. Addresses among other things problem restatement, brainstorming, the synectics process, divergent thinking, group process, and satisficing.

Hunt, Morton. *The Universe Within.* New York: Simon & Schuster, 1982.

Another fundamental source of material for Chapter 1. Consolidates and summarizes what cognitive science had learned as of 1982 about how the mind works. Discusses basic mental traits, logical and analogical reasoning, "mental messing around," the self-correcting mind, pattern recognition, bias, hypothesis testing, and creativity.

Laplace, Marquis de. *Philosophical Essay on Probability* (translation of 1825 text). New York: Springer-Verlag, 1995.

Laplace's classic work on probability.

Pages 3–4: ". . . if nothing leads us to believe that one of them [possible outcomes] will happen rather than the others . . . it is impossible to say anything with certainty about their occurrence."

Machina, Mark J. "Decision-Making in the Presence of Risk," *Science*, May 1, 1987: 537–543.

An insightful discussion of expected-utility and non-expected-utility models.

Magee, John F. "Decision Trees for Decision-Making." *Harvard Business Review*, July/August 1964: 126–138.

Explains the role of decision trees in identifying choices, risks, objectives, monetary gains, and information needs for investment decisions.

Margolis, Howard. *Patterns, Thinking, and Cognition.* Chicago: University of Chicago Press, 1987.

A lively treatise on the central role that pattern recognition (patterning) plays in analysis and decision making. Discusses false patterns: illusions.

McCormick, John. "The Wisdom of Solomon," *Newsweek*, August 17, 1987: 62–63.

Informative article that highlights significant flaws in the way humans inherently make decisions.

McKim, Robert H. *Thinking Visually.* Belmont, Calif.: Lifetime Learning Publications, 1980.

An engaging book on the importance of visual thinking (drawing, sketching, diagramming, etc.) to effective problem solving. Argues that the limits of language constrain verbal (nonvisual) thinking. Relates patterning to

Gestalt theory (page 9): "A Gestalt is a directly perceived grouping of elements." Indirectly endorses (page 67) the value of restating a problem at the outset: "The pattern, or Gestalt, that you perceive in a problem strongly influences the way you attempt to solve that problem."

Mockler, Robert J. *Computer Software to Support Strategic Management Decision Making.* New York: Macmillan, 1992.

Reviews a wide range of computer software that supports decision making at all levels of strategic management within a company. Software particularly relevant to *The Thinker's Toolkit:*

| | |
|---|---|
| Decision Pad | weighted ranking |
| Decision Aide II | weighted ranking |
| BestChoice3 | paired ranking/weighted ranking |
| Arborist | decision tree |
| Supertree | decision tree |
| Expert Choice | paired ranking/weighted ranking/decision tree |

Neustadt, Richard, and Ernest May. *Thinking in Time.* New York: The Free Press, 1986.

A paramount work on the critical role that knowledge of history can play in informing sound and effective decisions. Although the book is aimed at public office holders as well as those who assist, report on, study, or try to influence them and uses U.S. federal government decision making to exemplify techniques for learning and applying history (chronologies, time lines, and "placement"), the lessons are applicable to analysis of any type of problem.

Nisbett, Richard, and Lee Ross. *Human Inference: Strategies and Shortcomings of Social Judgment.* Englewood Cliffs, N.J.: Prentice-Hall, 1980.

An informative study on the fallibility of human thinking: how humans are intuitively both brilliant and bungling when trying to solve problems. Addresses bias and the vividness criterion (effect).

Nutt, Paul C. *Making Tough Decisions.* San Francisco: Jossey-Bass, 1989.

An insightful discussion of the human decision-making process, different kinds of faulty reasoning, how to manage a decision-making group to overcome these faults, and how our cognitive makeup, interpreted through Myers-Briggs Temperament Indicators, creates preferences for how we approach problem solving. Presents a form of weighted ranking, describes how to use a decision tree, especially for sensitivity analysis, and briefly addresses the role of vivid information (the vividness effect).

Ornstein, Robert. *The Psychology of Consciousness*. San Francisco: W. H. Free-
man, 1972.

A scholarly, comprehensive treatise on human consciousness. On the
autocracy of the human mind, the author quotes a colleague (page 4): "I'll
see it when I believe it."

Ornstein, Robert. *The Evolution of Consciousness: Of Darwin, Freud, and Cra-
nial Fire—The Origins of the Way We Think*. New York: Prentice-Hall,
1991.

An absorbing, provocative discourse on the evolution of the human mind,
which the author describes as adaptive, not rational. He contends that our
"self"—our conscious mind—plays a very small role in the mind's operations: very few of our decisions get shunted up to consciousness; only
those that need a top-level decision about alternatives. He says most of our
mental reactions are automatic—stored in fixed routines. We know only
what is *on* our mind, rarely what is *in* our mind. Discusses mental shortcuts, schemas (mind-sets), biases, the vividness effect, and the mind's treatment of alternatives.

Restak, Richard, M.D. *The Brain Has a Mind of Its Own: Insights from a Practicing Neurologist*. New York: Harmony, 1991.

A compilation of essays by the author about the brain and its functions.
One essay of the same title relates to the question of who's in charge, the
conscious or unconscious mind. Decidedly arguing in favor of the latter,
the author cites experiments demonstrating unequivocally that a measur-
able burst of electricity in the brain occurs about a third of a second *before*
the "owner" of the brain is aware that he or she has decided to act. This
evidence flies in the face of common wisdom that we humans, at the
moment we make a decision, are acting freely, selecting at will from an
infinity of choices.

Rivett, Patrick. *The Craft of Decision Making*. Chichester, West Sussex,
England: John Wiley and Sons, 1994.

Another insightful study of decision making. Addresses the fallibility of
human reasoning, logic versus common sense, and the perils of following
one's intuition.

Robinson, Roxana. *Georgia O'Keeffe: A Life*. New York: Harper & Row, 1989.
Biography.

Winson, David L. *Group Power: How to Develop, Lead, and Help Groups
Achieve Goals*. Englewood Cliffs, N.J.: Prentice-Hall, 1982.
Summarizes small-group dynamics and leadership skills.

Wisniewski, Mike. *Quantitative Methods for Decision Makers*. London: Pitman, 1994.

An illuminating, clearly written introduction for MBA students to the general principles of quantitative (mathematical and statistical) techniques for decision making. Includes a simplified explanation of probability (mutually exclusive and conditionally dependent), decision making under uncertainty, and decision trees.

# Notes

Notes that refer to a book that is included in the "For Further Reading" list are referenced here in their shortened form only.

### Chapter 1

9    "... mental messing around": Hunt, p. 136.

12    "As Lawrence Shainberg": *Memories of Amnesia* (Lathan, 1988), quoted in Bolles, p. 60.

15    "People all over": Walter Lord, *Day of Infamy* (Bantam, 1958), p. 72.

17    "Humans are pattern-seeking": Stephen Jay Gould, "The Panda's Thumb of Technology," *Natural History*, January 1987, p. 14.

22    "Most human beings": Hunt, p. 128.

23    "Compelling research": Campbell, p. 14.

23    "Despite the uncertainties": Hunt, p. 145.

25    "Natural [plausible] reasoning": Hunt, pp. 137–138.

28    "Sixty percent of": William Raspberry, "Judgment, Black and White," *The Washington Post*, July 8, 1994, p. A23.

28    "It can obscure": Donna Britt, "For O.J., They Can't Cross Color Line," *The Washington Post*, June 24, 1994, p. D1.

28    "Indeed, the lines": Peter Cary, "Death at Sea," *U.S. News & World Report*, April 23, 1990, p. 30.

30    "To live, it": Gilovich, pp. 22–23.

31    "We expect *everything*": Bolles, p. 103.

34    "We shift attention": Bolles, p. 37.

39 "Robert Abelson": Robert P. Abelson, "Beliefs are like possessions." *Journal for the Theory of Social Behaviour*, 16, 1986, pp. 222–250.

39 "Georgia was suddenly": Bolles, p. 121.

39 "That day, she": Bolles, p. 121.

## Chapter 5

72 "BIKE TRAIL": Steve Bates, "Bike Trail Turns into Mean Street," *The Washington Post*, May 15, 1994, p. A1.

## Chapter 6

79 "A Navaho was": Steve Sternberg, "Tracking a Mysterious Killer Virus in the Southwest," *The Washington Post*, June 14, 1994, p. 10 (Health section).

80 "A time-line is": Neustadt and May, p. 106.

82 "Implicitly: vicarious experience": Neustadt and May, p. 232.

## Chapter 8

106 "Symptom and Disease": Hunt, p. 185.

## Chapter 9

121 "Groping Toward a Way": Frank Swoboda, "Groping Toward a Way to Share the Reins," *The Washington Post*, December 11, 1994, p. H10.

## Chapter 11

163 "Illustrative of the problems": Thomas W. Lippman, "A Researcher's Dream Find on U.S. POWs Turns into a Nightmare," *The Washington Post*, April 25, 1993, p. A4.

177 "An epic struggle": Larry Van Dyne, "Hit the Road, Mick," *The Washingtonian*, January 1995, p. 60.

177 "I'm shocked by": Van Dyne, p. 122.

178 "But it was": Van Dyne, p. 114.

187 "Exercise 28": Based on Carolyn Weaver, "The Chilling Case of Nurse 14," *Regardie's*, May 1988, pp. 92–100, 138–144.

187 "Jane Bolding was": Ibid., p. 5 (Contents).

191 "Exercise 29": Based on the following articles:

Cary, Peter, "Death at Sea," *U.S. News & World Report*, April 23, 1990, pp. 20–30.

Associated Press, "Ex-*Iowa* Officer Reprimanded," *The Washington Post*, October 29, 1989, p. A7.

Editorial, "More Doubts About the *Iowa*," *The Washington Post*, October 29, 1989, p. B6.

Tyler, Patrick, and Molly Moore, "U.S.S. *Iowa* Captain Calls Blast Deliberate," *The Washington Post*, December 12, 1989, p. A7.

Associated Press, "Prober Admits Error in U.S.S. *Iowa* Report," *The Washington Post*, December 13, 1989, p. A18.

Reuters, "Sailor Charges Navy Coverup in U.S.S. *Iowa* Probe," *The Washington Post*, December 14, 1989, p. A22.

Reuters, "*Iowa* Blast Was Deliberate," *The Washington Post*, December 22, 1989, p. A13.

Moore, Molly, "Navy's U.S.S. *Iowa* Probe Called Flawed," *The Washington Post*, March 3, 1990, p. A14.

Page, D.W., "Sailors Mourned a Year After Blast," *The Washington Post*, April 20, 1990, p. B7.

Associated Press, "Skipper Faults U.S.S. *Iowa* Blast Probe," *The Washington Post*, May 5, 1990, p. A5.

Rowe, James L. Jr., "Sister Says Hartwig Is Vindicated," *The Washington Post*, May 26, 1990, p. A3.

Tyler, Patrick, "Scientists Dispute U.S.S. *Iowa* Finding," *The Washington Post*, May 26, 1990, p. A3.

## Chapter 12

202 "I want to play": Tom Clancy, *The Sum of All Fears* (Berkley edition, August 1992), p. 453.

204 "Exercise 30": Based on John Mintz, "U.S., Contractors in Dogfight Over MiG Modernization," *The Washington Post*, June 14, 1994, p. D1.

## Chapter 13

207 "Most of the concepts": Hunt, p. 184.

207 "People do not": Campbell, p. 238.

208 "Judging by our": Neustadt and May, p. 152.

210 "The U.S. Fire": Jessica Gaynor, Ph.D., and Daniel Stern, Ph.D., "Juvenile Firesetters: Part II: Effective Intervention," *Firehouse*, October 1993, p. 52.

212 "I don't think": Warren Tute, John Costello, and Terry Hughes, *D-Day* (London: Pan, 1974), p. 175.

## Chapter 14

232 "Events are all": Neustadt and May, p. 181.

233 "something is better": Neustadt and May, pp. 185–186.

# Index